The Origins of Indigenism

The Origins
of Indigenism

HUMAN RIGHTS AND
THE POLITICS OF IDENTITY

RONALD NIEZEN

UNIVERSITY OF CALIFORNIA PRESS
Berkeley   Los Angeles   London

University of California Press
Berkeley and Los Angeles, California

University of California Press, Ltd.
London, England

© 2003 by
The Regents of the University of California

Library of Congress Cataloging-in-Publication Data

Niezen, Ronald.
   The origins of indigenism : human rights and the politics of identity /
Ronald Niezen.
      p.   cm.
   Includes bibliographical references and index.
   ISBN 0-520-23554-1 (cloth : alk. paper)—ISBN 0-520-23556-8 (pbk. : alk.
paper)
      1. Indigenous peoples—Politics and government.   2. Indigenous
peoples—Civil rights.   3. Indigenous peoples—Ethnic identity.
4. Human rights.   5. Ethnicity—Political aspects.   I. Title.

GN380.N54   2002
306'.08—dc21   2002008938

Manufactured in the United States of America

10   09   08   07   06   05   04

10   9   8   7   6   5   4   3   2

To Erik and Alexander

Toleration is historically the product of the
realization of the irreconcilability of equally
dogmatic faiths, and the practical improbability
of complete victory of one over the other.

ISAIAH BERLIN
The Originality of Machiavelli

Contents

Preface

This book began as an article in *Comparative Studies in Society and History* (Niezen 2000a) with the title "Recognizing Indigenism: Canadian Unity and the International Movement of Indigenous Peoples." Much of the material from this article is reproduced here in various places (which I indicate in footnotes and for which I gratefully acknowledge the permission of *CSSH*), but the opportunity to expand it into a book has allowed me to put more historical emphasis on the global nature of the indigenous peoples' movement and to pay greater attention to such issues as cultural relativism, collective versus individual rights, and the legal/political implications of indigenous peoples' claims of self-determination. I have also more fully developed an approach to indigenous identity that emphasizes its recent origin and the creative uses to which it has been put. The study of indigenous identity is, in a sense, an ideal way to approach the formation of new categories of thought, social formation, and the human sense of self—ideal because the term itself is relatively new, actively used for only the past few decades, yet it invokes people's sense of permanence and their ability to survive and stay close to their cultures and home-lands despite almost insurmountable odds. With this paradox as its start-ing point, indigenous identity reveals itself to be a quintessentially mod-ern phenomenon. The international movement of indigenous peoples carries the central paradoxes of identity into the realms of international law, above all the development of human rights standards, and the less concrete debates surrounding multiculturalism and the limits of social tolerance in liberal states. This is a different starting point from that of the article, and this by itself provided a good reason for writing this book.

Those who attend international meetings on the rights of indigenous peoples are sometimes told that these peoples include some three hun-dred million members of at least four thousand distinct cultures. Whether or not we accept this estimate as accurate, the number of groups that can be identified as "indigenous" is considerable, and writing on the topic immediately poses an ethnographic challenge. Clearly it would be impos-sible to describe much more than, in general terms, the range of variation encompassed by the term "indigenous peoples" or those who currently claim indigenous identity. But the topic also calls for specific examples and case studies, and I have tried to provide these from my own research material and experience with self-identifying indigenous peoples. In fol-lowing the new influences of international indigenous politics to their destinations and points of origin in indigenous communities, I have lim-ited myself mainly to the Cree villages of northern Canada, where I have lived for more than three years, including two years (from 1998 to 2000) with my wife and two sons in Cross Lake, Manitoba.

My relationship with the eastern James Bay Crees began in the late 1980s, when I was hired as a researcher for the Cree Board of Health and Social Services of James Bay. For more than ten years I maintained this connection whenever possible with trips to northern Québec. The James Bay Crees also introduced me to international politics. I first traveled to a U.N. meeting (the 1994 meeting of the Working Group on Indigenous Populations) as an observer delegate with the Grand Council of the Crees. Since then I have attended the 1996 meeting on the draft U.N. Declaration on the Rights of Indigenous Peoples, the World Health Organization's first International Consultation on the Health of Indigenous Peoples in

1999, and a meeting on the (then) proposed U.N. Permanent Forum on Indigenous Issues in February 2000.

It was neither the community-based research nor the international meetings that encouraged me to develop the topic of the international movement of indigenous peoples into a book project; rather, it was the juxtaposition of the two. One moment, for example, I would be coping with daily life in a reservation village (much of which involved witnessing the failure of others to cope) in a community that had fallen (or been pushed) into the routines of hopelessness and dependency, manifested in alcohol abuse, family violence, and suicide. Then, after a day or so of travel, I would suddenly and miraculously be in the vaulted rooms and corridors of the Palais des Nations in Geneva, discussing and hearing about indigenous issues. This stark change in perspective, easily dismissed as yet another by-product of modernity, was for me an experience worth reflecting on more thoroughly.

From living in and visiting isolated northern reserve communities in Canada, I began to realize the extent to which the international movement of indigenous peoples was influencing local political behavior. Information about human rights and about the struggles of other indigenous communities circulated within a small network of the politically active in the form of photocopied newspaper clippings and stories printed from the Internet. Some community leaders came to see themselves as leading a cause for justice directly analogous to (and without distinguishing among) a variety of liberation movements, including the American civil rights movement and resistance to South African apartheid.

I had originally thought that the Grand Council of the Crees and its constituents in the communities of northern Québec would furnish most of the material for this book concerning the local perspective, the ways that human rights activism and networks with other indigenous peoples influence, and are influenced by, local views about rights, justice, self-governance, and the state; but I had other research experience that also found a place in the writing of this book, experience that did not at first occur to me as being significant. My work on Islamic reform in West Africa, the product of my doctoral work in social anthropology at Cambridge University in the mid-1980s, had faded a little from view and didn't seem relevant to my new focus on international indigenous human rights activism, but after meeting West African delegates at several U.N. meetings I began to look again at the situation I had encountered in Mali, especially the circumstances surrounding drought, forced settlement, and the subsequent so-called nomad rebellion. I was shown by the West African delegates to international meetings that the crisis (best described as an environmental cataclysm accompanied by an extension of state domination) I had witnessed more than a decade before was directly relevant to their subsequently formed identities as indigenous peoples and their efforts to develop human rights standards appropriate to their concerns.

The research I undertook in the Cree community of Cross Lake, Manitoba, on the other hand, did not begin as a major source of information for this book because I was initially too close to the material to see its relevance. The Cross Lake leadership was so closely focused on its grievances with Manitoba Hydro and the governments of Canada and Manitoba that it had little energy or inclination to pursue the wider, long-range goals, mostly concerned with self-determination, that are a major part of the indigenous human rights agenda; and while I was living there my attention was to some extent drawn in the same direction. The background to my fieldwork in Cross Lake is in some ways an illustration of the networks between indigenous groups and their development of new forms of resistance that I write about here. Having been introduced to Cross Lake's leadership through our mutual connections with the Grand Council of the Crees, I was first invited to visit the community and then invited to stay for two years (after I was assured that my curriculum vitae had been distributed and discussed in an open community meeting) to act as an observer, witness, advocate, author—roles that were pretty much informally developed as needs became felt, reached the point of crisis, and then gradually faded into the background to be replaced by other urgencies. The Cross Lake Crees seemed to take readily to my status as observer, as a connection to a dominant society from which many felt excluded, and as a source of communication between aboriginal and state governments that had in many ways failed. I was witness to the environmental abuses of hydroelectric development: slumping shorelines, inundated woodland, submerged islands, floating debris, the loss of fish, animals, medicines, and livelihood. I was also witness to things that might be considered largely the results of political failure: stalemated negotiations and clearly flourishing manifestations of the ills of unemployment (or lack of meaningful occupation in the subsistence economy) and welfare dependency: addictions, crime, family violence, suicide, and child neglect. I was invited to the meetings with government intended to alleviate the environmental conditions and distress in the community and to observe the community's own lawmaking process, developed as a way to gain control over local governance and assert the community's will to redress its grievances. In the midst of all this, the influence of the international movement of indigenous peoples was not in the foreground, but it eventually drew my attention in ways that should be apparent in the pages of this book.

My intention has been, not to write a series of case studies based upon field research, but rather to use the information I have gleaned from community-based research to illustrate global phenomena. Instead of beginning with the accumulation of case material in an attempt to build toward general observations, I move back and forth between global phenomena and local illustrations of their effects. In the case of indigenous peoples attending international meetings, I am able to see global patterns in specific behavior or utterances, and in such instances the tight focus of ethnography actually lends itself directly to wider observations. What I am striving for is a better understanding of a worldwide phenomenon, the international movement of indigenous peoples, which I illustrate with examples drawn mainly from Canada, partially from Africa, and of course partially from international meetings.

The renewal or adoption of indigenous identity, as I intend to show, is manifested in cultural and political reforms at a variety of levels: in strengthening community loyalties; challenging state notions of citizenship, national culture, and individual rights; and, internationally, striving not only for equality within states—antidiscrimination with respect to participation in such things as higher education and the workforce—but also for a greater measure of self-determination, recognition of indigenous peoples' status as distinct societies with rights of self-governance and control of land and resources that derive, in turn, from their status as original peoples. The studies that concentrate on indigenous-state relations (e.g., Perry 1996; Ramos 1998; Warren 1998) cannot do full justice to the ways indigenous identities are globalizing, organizing in and through international networks and seeking redress and recognition of rights to self-determination in international forums. International law and the human rights movement in particular are important for another reason: as the source and place of nurturance of the concept of "indigenous peoples," giving rise to a new global identity—or a new way of formulating traditional identities based on notions of loyalty to family and community, ancestral wisdom, permanent homelands, and cultural durability—and, in the process, opening up new strategies of resistance to the centralizing tendencies of states.

Turku/Åbo
May 16, 2001

Acknowledgments

There is a sense in which all authors owe a lifetime of debt for their creative work, but there are tacit limits to the thanks they can acceptably convey in writing. It is considered gauche, for example, to reach back to one's infancy to thank family members and grade school teachers. In this case, however, I am making direct use of material acquired over a span of twenty years, and I feel the corresponding obligation to acknowledge support for this project in a way that almost runs up against the limits of propriety.

My doctoral research in Mali from June 1984 to April 1985 was funded through a Grant-in-Aid from the Wenner-Gren Foundation for Anthropological Research, an IODE War Memorial Scholarship, the Wyse Fund of Trinity College, Cambridge, St. John's College, and the Richards Fund of Cambridge University's Department of Social Anthropology. My African research benefited greatly from the support and interest of Jean-Loup Amselle, Khadidia Bocoum, Lewis Brenner, Fanny Colonna, Tiebélé Dramé, Jack Goody (through a prefieldwork year of supervision), Martin

xviii   ACKNOWLEDGMENTS

Hinds, Claude Meillassoux, Donal Cruise O'Brien, and Jean-Louis Triaud.
Ernest Gellner was judicious in his guidance as a dissertation supervisor
and was a continuing source of inspiration (though I did not always agree
with him); he is greatly missed. The most important contribution to this
project was made by the people of Mali, especially those from the desert
and villages, whom I cannot mention by name.

The work I undertook in northern Canada was supported by a Milton
Fund Research Grant from the Harvard Medical School, a Clark Fund
Research Grant, the Cree Board of Health and Social Services of James
Bay, the Nishnawbe-Aski Nation, Pimicikamak Cree Nation, and the Assembly of First Nations. The Grand Council of the Crees provided me
with observer status and an indispensable entrée to a variety of international meetings (mentioned in the preface), for which I am especially
grateful. The Sami Council made a similar contribution to my attendance
at a 2001 meeting of the Arctic Council in Rovaniemi, Finland, and the Pimicikamak Cree Nation invited me to attend several meetings on Northern Flood Agreement implementation in Winnipeg and Cross Lake. The
Department of History at the University of Winnipeg provided me with
a professional home from 1998 to 2000 while I conducted research in
Cross Lake. As was my experience in Africa, the people from the villages
made the most significant contribution to my understanding of northern
Canada.

In researching documentary sources, I was assisted by the staff of the
Bibliothèque Nationale in Paris; the League of Nations Archives and the
Documentation Centre on Indigenous Peoples (doCip) in Geneva; Cross
Lake First Nation Band Office in Cross Lake, Manitoba; and the Human
Rights Library at Åbo Akademi University in Turku/Åbo, Finland.

My thinking on the topics covered by this book was greatly stimulated
by teaching a course, Anthropological Approaches to the Rights of Indigenous Peoples, offered jointly in the Turku Law School and the Institute for Human Rights at Åbo Akademi University in the spring of 2001.
My background in human rights issues also benefited by presenting
some of the material for this book more intensively in seminars that I
conducted at the University of Oulu and the Norwegian Institute of Human Rights at the University of Oslo. My understanding of Nordic in-

digenous issues was also filled out by the information and hospitality I received at the Sami Parliament in Inari, Finland.

I have in recent years come to owe a great deal to the information and ideas provided by friends and colleagues working in a wide range of fields, among them Jennifer Brown, Jean-Luc Chodkiewitz, Asbjørn Eide, Stener Ekern, Robert Epstein, Colin Gillespie, Robert Harris, Arthur Kleinman, David Maybury-Lewis, Ted Moses, Romeo Saganash, Galit Sarfaty, and Ann Stewart. Comments on the manuscript were provided at various stages by Barbro Bankson, John Hall, Charles Lindholm, Martin Scheinin, and three anonymous reviewers for the University of California Press (two of whom collaborated on one review). I did not, of course, pursue every suggestion or agree with every idea placed before me, and I am solely responsible for the contents of this book.

Last, I would like to thank my seventh-grade teacher, Mr. Howe, for his suggestion, which I rebelled against, that I attend vocational school.

1 A New Global Phenomenon?

Anthropology is known for its tendency to focus on social microcosms, and the microcosm that I as an anthropologist have chosen to study is the world. Twenty or more years ago this would have made little sense. The bounded, preferably isolated, community would have been virtually the only option, the only way to establish one's credentials, to do respectable "fieldwork." Today, the broader goal of my work can be understood by most with an interest in social research as somehow reflecting the phenomenon of global "shrinking," associated with such things as the increasing mobility of people and the relatively instantaneous spread of information, ideas, and diseases.

I

One product of globalization is a revolt against the forces of cultural uniformity and against the appropriation of indigenous peoples' sovereignty by states.[1] Its main premise is that by removing such people from their land, educating their children in state schools, eliminating their languages, and usurping their own systems of justice and conflict resolution, states are imposing a gray uniformity on all of humanity, stifling and suppressing the creative cultural energies of those who are most knowledgeable and prescient about the forces of nature. "Those who would destroy their way of life," states a report from the United Nations' International NGO Conference on Discrimination against Indigenous Populations in the Americas, "would first have us believe that this task is already accomplished. We now have proof to the contrary, and we have received, with gratitude, the message of harmony and respect for all life brought to us by an ancient people whose culture may still yet be allowed to make a worthy contribution to the world community of nations" (United Nations 1977: 21). One of the revealing things about this passage is its use of the singular to describe the numerous indigenous participants in a conference organized around the theme of discrimination against indigenous populations in the Americas. These delegations are somehow seen as speaking with one voice, representing a unified way of life defending itself against the destructive forces of modernity. The clearest expression of human diversity can thus be found in a category now widely referred to as "indigenous peoples"; yet the very creation of this category involves a common origin, is predicated upon global sameness of experience, and is expressed through the mechanisms of law and bureaucracy, the culprits most commonly associated with the steady gains of cultural uniformity. This in itself raises questions of a global nature. Under conditions not only of rapid travel, communication, and access to information but also of internationalized nationalism and the global advent of identical pressures of resource extraction upon subsistence-based communities and peoples, how are cultural differences being defended? And how does that defense in itself influence the way cultures and identities are reformulated?

A search of the term "indigenous" in book titles from twenty or more years ago might reveal only a scattering of botanical works on indigenous plants. Similarly, scholarly journal articles, popular magazines, and newspapers made very few references to the term as a category of human society. But from the 1980s onward, it has attained an ever-widening circulation, to the point where it is no longer a specialized legal term but is recognized by a lay audience. The interesting thing about the relative newness of this concept is that it refers to a primordial identity, to people with primary attachments to land and culture, "traditional" people with lasting connections to ways of life that have survived "from time immemorial." That this innovation should be so widely accepted is a startling achievement.

It is rare that circumstances in world history are favorable to the creation of a new kind of global political entity. Nationalism and the nation-state were novelties in the nineteenth century, at least so the mainstream of political thought now tells us, but their connection with modernity was concealed by nationalist identifications with natural ties, permanent homelands, archaic cultures, and timeless bonds of common history.[2] Indigenism is a similar global movement that has gained momentum over the last few decades largely out of the notice of observers, pundits, and theorists of international events. This movement, it is true, is smaller in scale, more fragile, and less turbulent than the nationalist upheavals of the past two centuries, but it nevertheless has the potential to influence the way states manage their affairs and even to reconfigure the usual alignments of nationalism and state sovereignty.

The terms "ethnicity" and "ethnic group" went through a similar vogue starting in the 1960s, working their way into a profuse literature and culminating in a more recent coinage, "ethnonationalism." But these are analytical concepts, not terms of identity. A proud Serbian might refer to him- or herself as a Serb, not as an "ethnic Serb" or an "ethnic person." The term "indigenous," however, has been taken a step further. It is not only a legal category and an analytical concept but also an expression of identity, a badge worn with pride, revealing something significant and personal about its wearer's collective attachments.

Cultural differences have thus defiantly entered the public sphere. They have been internationally politicized. Indigenous leaders from Asia, northern Europe, Africa, the Americas, and the South Pacific (including

Australia, New Zealand, and the Pacific Islands) meet regularly in groups ranging in size from a dozen to several hundred to discuss the development of human rights standards for indigenous peoples. In this context the ambition to study the world can be realized, for in meeting rooms, usually in Europe, differences are being defended and changes wrought that do have global origins and implications. Indigenous internationalism is both a product of social convergence and an agent of it.

The United Nations is well known as an unfathomable bureaucracy and, frighteningly, also as the arbiter of the world's important and usually bloody contests, but it is less recognized as a locus for village politics and for struggles between states and marginalized communities. In this new venture, in its regular meetings between indigenous and state representatives, it has created an original institutional space constituting a distinct social world.

The emerging identity and legal term "indigenous peoples" is embodied in those who sit together at indigenous conferences and working group meetings. The term was included in the International Labour Organization (ILO) Convention (No. 107) Concerning the Protection and Integration of Indigenous and Other Tribal and Semi-Tribal Populations in Independent Countries (1957) and the accompanying ILO Recommendation (No. 104) of the same year, at a time when scholars still commonly referred to the subjects of their investigations as "primitives."[3] Yet members of the "indigenous populations" being referred to had little input into the convention (see chapter 3 below), and few, if any, had developed a self-referential "indigenous" identity. Today the term is both a fragile legal concept and the indefinite, unachievable sum of the historical and personal experiences of those gathered in a room who share, at the very least, the notion that they have all been oppressed in similar ways for similar motives by similar state and corporate entities.

The United Nations has thus become a new focal point of "indigenism," a term I use to describe the international movement that aspires to promote and protect the rights of the world's "first peoples."[4] These are the estimated three hundred million people from four thousand distinct societies, strongly attached to regions that were recently, and in a few instances still are, the world's last "wild" places.[5] They are those who share the claim to have survived on their lands through the upheavals of colonialism and corporate exploitation. Their unbroken ancestry is not seen as protecting them from the deleterious impacts of industrial and state ambitions. Their territories are imposed upon by extractive industries; their beliefs and rituals are imposed upon by those who would convert them (or selfishly acquire their knowledge); and their independence is imposed upon by states striving for political and territorial control. They are those people whose position in the modern world is the least tenable. They are especially vulnerable to warfare, genocide, dispossession, disease, and famine.

Indigenous peoples, like some ethnic groups, derive much of their identity from histories of state-sponsored genocide, forced settlement, relocation, political marginalization, and various formal attempts at cultural destruction. Indigenous peoples and ethnic groups alike can have primary attachments to land, and similar attachments derived from primordial use and occupancy of land—though perhaps with less spiritual resonance—can even be found in some groups commonly referred to as "ethnic." How, then, can we usefully distinguish ethnic groups and indigenous peoples?

David Maybury-Lewis (1997) partially resolves this problem by outlining a continuum ranging from "indigenous/tribal peoples to indigenous (but not tribal) peoples, to peoples stigmatized as tribal, to people considered ethnic minorities, to people considered ethnic nationalities, though they coexist in a single state" (55). He concludes that "there are no distinctions that enable us to place societies unambiguously within these categories" (55). But a continuum of social organization does not do justice to the recent complexities of the international movement of indigenous peoples. The growing national and international influence of indigenous governments and nongovernmental organizations, combined with the concerns of some state representatives over the potential for indigenous chauvinism and secessionist politics, has reshuffled the order of things and provided grounds for a more direct comparison of ethnic nationalism and indigenism. I will develop this comparison more fully in chapter 6, but it is necessary to begin here by summarizing some of the features that make indigenism a distinct phenomenon.

INDIGENISM AND ETHNONATIONALISM

Assertions of distinct collective identities and claims to rights give every indication of increasing in salience. The growth of reinvigorated identity as a source of group membership and the pursuit of distinct rights to protect identity boundaries have increased almost exponentially during the past several decades. Paradoxically, bonds that are seen by community members as inherent, timeless, and indissoluble have been reformulated and given new political standing only very recently. The "We the Peoples" of the U.N. Charter was formulated in the years immediately after World War II, when it was still possible to argue, however misguidedly, that only natural boundaries separated distinct cultures.[6] Islands, deserts, forests, and mountains created unique lifestyles and identities, much like the ecological niches of flora and fauna. Today it is much easier to see that other forces are at work in the reformulation of identities and that some of the strongest claims of difference are made by the marginalized and deracinated, by those who would otherwise be absorbed, eliminated, and forgotten by dominant societies. Cultural identities are stimulated by their denial, and the social landscape has far overtaken geography and ecology as the most important source of human differences.[7]

Today we are witness to the fact that cultural and political barriers between human societies are in some ways being solidified by the breakdown of other barriers, mainly those that have to do with travel, communication, and access to information. As many anthropologists have recently pointed out, cultures are often impermanent, complex, "creolized," hybrid, and contested.[8] Culture is a verb, not a noun, a process, not a thing in itself. But an outcome of cultural overlapping and contestation—one that is not as frequently recognized as the impermanence that goes with it—is a process of sharpening boundaries, drawing identities more firmly, making unequivocal the division between those who belong and those who do not. Paradoxically, the solidifying of cultural boundaries is predicated upon the malleability of cultures—on the ability, especially by those with power, to reshape cultural properties and attachments, sometimes to make them fit more comfortably with political interests.

This is not to trivialize the importance of renewed identities for those who are attached to them. Recovering the past is usually seen as a matter of great importance for future survival. It requires a sense of urgency—distinct societies are easily overwhelmed by the forces of state centralization and large-scale projects resulting in loss of livelihood—and at the same time a delicate approach to piecing together constituent elements of culture that can be understood only as an intricate whole, sometimes barely visible through its internal complexities, tensions, and differences. The question "Who are we?" is thus being answered by empirically strengthening the "we" as an ethnic or indigenous entity.

The term "ethnicity" is sometimes used in a general way to refer to such reconstituting of collective identities, but the amount of power and the political goals, choices, and surrounding contexts of ethnic groups vary tremendously, making it nearly impossible to build globally applicable analytical models or sometimes even to get a handle on events as they happen. Not all ethnic groups or other minorities want to secede from states, and not all are violent (despite the imprint of the Balkans on our consciousness). Some are quietly dominated by states; others are the beneficiaries of federalism, consociation, regional autonomy, or other power-sharing arrangements.[9] But where some of the most important analytical differences can be drawn is among those societies whose leaders voice unappeased discontent and unfulfilled yearnings for self-determination and whose ambitions at some level involve a rejection of the multicultural projects proposed by states and international organizations.

There are two categories of societies or "peoples" whose claims to self-determination can pose challenges to the constitutional uniformity of states and raise the issue—some might say the specter—of the politics of difference in international organizations. Ethnic groups are already familiar from a vast literature that began in the 1960s with questions surrounding the sources of ethnic differentiation in contexts of mobility and cultural interaction, a literature that has been kept alive by more recent concerns over the origins of nationalism, strident ethnonationalism, and interethnic conflict. Another type of claimant to self-determination, indigenous peoples, has made a more recent appearance on the international scene, with political objectives and strategies that differ in important ways from those of other minorities. The differences between these two kinds of collective entity are sometimes overlooked, despite their relevance for the development of strategies against intolerance.

"Ethnonationalism" is the term sometimes given to those people who have defined their collective identities with clear cultural and linguistic contours and who express their goals of autonomy from the state with the greatest conviction and zeal, sometimes with hatreds spilling over into violence. In Canada, Québec sovereigntists have expressed their goal of an independent French-speaking nation-state mostly through the orderly, though occasionally disputed, mechanisms of referenda,[10] the most recent in 1995 being defeated by the smallest possible margin, with the Parti Québecois since then promising to continue a strategy of orderly independence seeking.[11] In other regions ethnonationalism is more turbulent. Stanley Tambiah, in his book *Leveling Crowds* (1996), has argued convincingly that ethnonationalist violence in India is a form of routine instability, often coordinated, or at least strategically manipulated, by those who stand to benefit from social and political cleavages. Ethnic groups often identify themselves in opposition to rival ethnicities, with rival claims to statehood. Some of the worst abuses of human rights in the past fifty years have occurred where these rival identities overlap and where there is no longer any overarching state power to keep their hostilities in check. In Africa, particularly Rwanda and the Congo, for example, the world has witnessed to its horror some of the most lethal genocidal violence since the Holocaust, the outcome of ethnically inspired hatred. Such events overshadow more numerous conflicts in other parts of the world in which political claims based upon cultural distinctiveness and occupancy of territories are frustrated, leading to revolt or to violent repression by states, or sparking unrest from rival groups. Even within the category "ethnonationalism," therefore, there is great variety and an absence of predictability. What we do find very often, however, is that ethnonationalists' expressed political aspirations take the form of an independent nation-state, occasionally a nation-state purified or "cleansed" of its rival minorities. At some level, therefore, they have signed on to the notion of equality as a goal of liberation; except that to them equality within an existing state is neither the best guarantee of collective security nor the best way to express their collective being. Equality can truly be realized only through the highest form of recognized difference: statehood.

Many of the patterns commonly recognized in the identity formations of ethnic nationalisms—above all the development of a historiography through which the ethnic group sees itself as a unique community, the infusion of collective identity with exclusivist moral imperatives, and the use of identity to consolidate and pursue political goals—are shared with indigenous identity. Indigenism, however, is not a particularized identity but a global one that acts almost the same way as ethnic particularism. It sets social groups and networks apart from others in a global "we-they" dichotomy. It identifies a boundary of membership and experience that can be crossed only by birth or hard-won international recognition. It links local, primordial sentiments to a universal category.

The origins of indigenism (discussed more fully in chapter 2) are much more clear than were the coalescing of nationalism in the eighteenth- and nineteenth-century expansion of European states, the contagion effects of decolonization, and the contests of rival ethnonationalisms. The indigenous peoples' movement has arisen out of the shared experiences of marginalized groups facing the negative impacts of resource extraction and economic modernization and, as Benedict Kingsbury (1998) sagely notes, the social convergence and homogenization that these ambitions tend to bring about (42). Indigenous identity has also grown largely out of the institutions of successful nationalisms themselves; the international legislative bodies of states—the United Nations and its satellite agencies—have provided the conceptual origins and practical focus of indigenous identity. With little public awareness, and with the obvious terminology ("indigenism") little used up to this point, an international movement has led to the creation of an important new "ism."

One of the distinguishing marks of this movement is the extent to which, unlike ethnonationalism, it is grounded in international networks. In Asia, for example, transnational networks of indigenous organizations are new sources of ideas, identity, legitimacy, and money for groups and communities that were once thoroughly marginalized (Barnes, Gray, and Kingsbury 1995: chs. 1–4). Similar transnational networks are built into indigenous organizations themselves, such as the Inuit Circumpolar

Conference, the International Indian Treaty Council, and the World Council of Indigenous Peoples. Indigenous organizations defending local attachments to land and simple subsistence technologies make use of electronic media and technologies of communication and transportation to establish and maintain international connections.[12]

Ethnic groups, by contrast, tend to see their experiences of oppression and marginalization as uniquely their own and their suffering as a source of inspiration that cannot be shared with those who do not belong. Politically active members of ethnic groups may be aware of others who experience a similar fate, sometimes at the hands of the same oppressor-state, but there is almost always at least a hint, if not a full measure, of in-group exclusiveness that discourages solidarity with "outsiders." The claim to statehood pursued by many ethnic groups, more than anything else, has a dampening effect on interethnic sociability. If any such claim is as good as the next, what value is there in independence? More to the point, if too many claims are made, what happens to any one group's chances of success? Ethnic groups are like auditioners for a drama on the world's stage, unwilling to reveal too much of themselves to their rivals in their competition for the cast list.

Indigenous peoples have more collective goals and work more cooperatively to achieve them. The mere fact that indigenous leaders gather in international meetings to share experiences and pursue collective strategies suggests a greater degree of global interaction. There are, of course, groups and regional blocs that tend to go their own way, making consistent strategy frustratingly elusive (and at least one indigenous representative at U.N. meetings is so out of sync with the indigenous caucus that he is sometimes privately accused of espionage and political sabotage on behalf of states), but the general climate in which indigenous delegations function is one of shared experience and intensive collaboration.

Indigenous history is "invented" in different ways than are the narratives of large ethnic groups or nation-states. It is developed largely in response to oppression, usually at the hands of the state. This makes indigenous historical identity, like that of many ethnonationalisms, in large measure a counterpoint to state domination, based largely upon victimization. But, much more than ethnonationalism, indigenous identity both struggles against and is implicated with popular stereotyping—usurpation by the spiritual eclecticism of the New Age movement and other sources of popular romanticism. Many of the ecological, spiritual, and egalitarian ideals associated with indigenous identity have thus been distorted by pseudosympathizers. Rousseau's portrayal of humans emerging from a state of nature as robust, guileless, and quintessentially democratic was an early form of third-party representation that has become more potent as those weakened by policies of cultural annexation have sought to reconstitute themselves. [13] There is, in popular imaginings of the inherently ecological Indian or egalitarian hunter, an element of fertile nostalgia, a longing for things that cannot be found in conditions of modernity. Indigenous leaders must struggle against a temptation to take both libels and outrageous flattery as the truth about themselves and their peoples.

One of these externally imagined, then internalized, identities is the very notion of an international underclass or "underethnicity" known as "indigenous peoples." It is a category of human society first invented through human rights reforms, then adapted, internalized, personalized, and collectively transformed by "indigenous peoples" themselves, with conviction and occasionally strident passion.

GRIEVANCE, RIGHTS, AND IDENTITY

If some of the most cherished aspects of indigenous identity (including the term itself) come from quarters that have little or nothing to do with indigenous people or societies, where does the near-global attachment to this identity come from? A radically constructivist approach to identity, besides offering insult to those with cherished assumptions about ageless traditions, tends to be dismissive of such important questions as the circumstances under which a new identity gains acceptance, who benefits from its acceptance, who opposes it, and why some accept or oppose it. It is important to recognize that indigenous identity is invoked by a minority of educated leaders in any given society, by an intelligentsia. It is part of a shifting continuum or *bricolage* of identities ranging from the individual actor to the family, clan, tribal group, language group, village, region, province, nation, and, not least of all, international affiliation. Under what circumstances is indigenous identity invoked or added on to other markers, and by whom?

The revival of indigenous identities has taken place largely through the medium of writing and is occasionally expressed in the formal style and logic of law. Whatever incompatibilities we might suppose to exist between written and oral cultures, the permanence and protections of written resolutions have great appeal among those faced with instability, impermanence, and, ultimately, isolated defeat. Indigenous revival cannot be understood without reference to the technology, power, and legitimacy of states. Renewed tradition confers a shared identity and sense of community on those faced with racial segregation and the stigmas associated with identification as an underclass of the underprivileged. At some point in the colonization of indigenous nations, a tremendous disparity between the technology and organizational powers of dominant and dominated peoples makes itself felt. It is astonishing, under the circumstances, how readily indigenous peoples have tended to borrow and adapt useful features of majority societies with little or no apparent disruption. But when social and technological powers are associated with direct assaults on indigenous identity and esteem through the inherently contradictory vehicles of racism and assimilation, indigenous societies become infected with cultural malaise—a widespread sense of wounded pride, violated honor, and lack of self-esteem.

In response to the tremendous pressures and opportunities inherent in this major social transition, many groups have reformulated and codified what they could of the accumulated traditional memory. Cumulatively, many small efforts of this kind have produced a global cultural revolution, little noticed by outside observers because of the relative insignificance of its components. These traditional orthodoxies are not uncontested, even in their communities of origin, but they have one attraction that sets them apart from all rivals, whether Christianity and other scriptural religions, state-sponsored nationalism, or liberal human rights universalism: reinvigorated traditional values and worldviews are identified as indigenous, as having always existed. They confer pride of ownership (and to some extent authorship) on their adherents. They belong to no other. They are permanent and inalienable. Through the new written and visual media that transcend the memories, and even the temporal presence, of elders, traditional ideas and values have acquired the imprimatur of orthodoxy.

But it is a special kind of orthodoxy. Notwithstanding a few widely prevailing notions of indigenous peoples' innate environmental wisdom, what really sets this cultural movement apart is its absence of centralized dogma. Its main ideas coalesce within a large number of micronationalisms and micro-orthodoxies, each a discrete movement oriented toward small communities or regions but at the same time communicated to other, like-minded indigenous nations by networks of news exchange through telephone, fax, and e-mail communication and international meetings. Indigenism involves reinvigoration of the comfort and color of local traditions with the safety-in-numbers effect of a global movement.

In the absence of a uniform creed, membership is usually determined by birth. Outsiders of various kinds can be given nominal or provisional membership, but at the international level, to belong—to unquestionably participate as an indigenous person—one has to represent an indigenous nation, preferably as an elected leader, at the very least as a citizen. And within the indigenous nation itself it is mostly blood and place of parentage that determine who belongs and who does not.

Such observations, however, still do not tell us what truly inspires the movement or whence it originates. The varied, sometimes discordant, voices of indigenous leaders at international gatherings are consistent at some points, consistent in ways that provide clues as to the origins of their identity and its appeal (the theme of chapter 3). Stories from the victims of dictatorships—of such horrors as secret massacres, forced relocations, imprisonment without trial, and torture—find resonance with indigenous delegates from democratic states who have had merely to contend with imposed megaproject development, dispossession, broken treaties, loss of subsistence, and the imposition of tormented idleness. A patriotic citizen can, in defense of hearth and homeland, often endure hardship, even torture, with a sense of purpose. A common experience of those who identify themselves as indigenous, however, is a sense of illegitimate, meaningless, and dishonorable suffering.

The collective suffering that transposes onto identity is usually multigenerational.[14] It can be separated by the space of decades, perhaps even centuries, from the immediate horrors of dispossession and death, kept alive by stories or written histories, to be recalled later, like the rekindling of smoldering ashes.

Only in recent years has such experience found an outlet in the standard-setting activities of international organizations, channeled into the work of achieving higher state standards of justice and accountability. The ambitious goals of indigenous peoples' initiatives are no less than the global improvement of health and prevention of repression and political violence among the approximately three hundred million people categorized as "indigenous."

International organizations are at their slowest and most frustratingly cumbersome, however, when pursuing ambitious goals that do not necessarily correspond with government perceptions of state interests. This seems especially true when one is closely involved, representing an organization or constituency that expects to see results—and when these results are continually transforming into promises that seem to recede ever further into the future.

At the same time, however, the unity of indigenous people as a social category, above all as compatriots in suffering, occasionally receives independent confirmation by high-ranking international officials. Measures for the protection and promotion of indigenous cultures were supported in an April 2000 meeting of the U.N. Commission on Human Rights by Alfredo Sfeir-Younis of the World Bank, who stated that institutional ignorance of indigenous cultures is "like burning the library before reading the books" (United Nations 2000d: 2). And Mary Robinson (2000), U.N. High Commissioner for Human Rights, addressing a February 2000 Working Group on the Permanent Forum for Indigenous People, conceded that "indigenous peoples are . . . one of the most excluded and marginalized groups in society" (5). Her encouragement of the establishment of a new and unprecedented forum for indigenous peoples at a high level in the U.N. system is a further indication of the momentum that is building to eliminate the "scourge of racism" in the relationships of many states with their indigenous inhabitants.

Indigenous peoples are increasingly viewed as canaries in the iron cage of modernity. There is nothing equivocal, metaphorical, or too terribly mysterious about the demise of an indigenous society when it occurs. Sociohistorical autopsies reveal consistent patterns of conquest, genocide, ethnocide, and political marginalization. Indigenism is an identity, like that which unifies survivors of the Holocaust, grounded in evidence, testimony, and collective memory.

FORMS OF RESISTANCE

The international movement of indigenous peoples also acts very differently from patterns of resistance in politically marginal communities described in the anthropological literature. For example, indigenous lobbying and political mobilization is a far cry from the "ordinary" forms of resistance by powerless groups examined in James Scott's widely cited *Weapons of the Weak* (1985)—the "food dragging, dissimulation, false compliance, pilfering, feigned ignorance, slander, arson, sabotage, and so forth [which] . . . require little or no coordination or planning[;] . . . represent a form of individual self-help; and . . . typically avoid any direct symbolic confrontation with authority or with elite norms" (29). These actions are premised upon people lacking formal organization and have little in common with the presentations of indigenous delegates to conferences and closed sessions of international political forums.

More public attention is paid to violent insurrections—and the usually more violent suppression of them by governments. Such events as the Zapatista Rebellion in Chiapas, Mexico (Collier 1994; Harvey 1998), the indigenous uprising and its ruthless suppression in the western high plateau of Guatemala in 1980 (Burgos-Debray 1984), the 1973 siege at Wounded Knee, South Dakota (Matthiessen 1983: ch. 3), and the Mohawk standoff against the Sureté de Québec and the Canadian Armed Forces at Oka (York and Pindera 1991) are among the most dramatic expressions of frustration at broken government treaties and promises, destruction of lands without compensation, and political marginalization. Armed resistance is a dubious strategy for reform, leading more often than not to violent repression by the state rather than to the desired concessions. The international indigenous peoples' movement addresses many of the same issues that lie behind rebellions and insurrections, but without violence or even illegal forms of protest. Instead, indigenous representatives are taking their complaints to international forums, striving to be involved at the highest level possible in international politics. The international movement of indigenous peoples is an emerging form of political resistance.

For those indigenous spokespeople who initiated the process of international lobbying, this was an especially daring strategy. It represented a new use of the international bodies of states to overcome the domestic abuses of states themselves, while pursuing development and recognition of international standards concerning the rights of indigenous peoples. The development of an international movement of indigenous peoples in recent decades reflects a changing alignment of political advocacy and shows some indigenous leaders to be, despite their limited power and resources, among the most effective political strategists on the contemporary national and international scenes. Underestimating the abilities of indigenous leaders and organizations to maneuver through complex international forums would result in a number of missed opportunities, the most significant of which would be to reconsider the place of indigenous leadership internationally, nationally, and locally and to speculate on the potential for an effective international movement of indigenous peoples to reconfigure state powers and alter, however slightly, the influence of state-sponsored nationalism.

EQUALITY AND LIBERATION

If post-Enlightenment Western thought sees toleration "not as a utilitarian expedient to avoid destructive strife, but as an intrinsic value" (Berlin 1998: 581), how did it come to pass that indigenous peoples have been so badly treated, so little tolerated? One possibility that stands out is that the implications of the categories "indigenous," "native," "aboriginal," and "First Nation" lie outside the accepted norms of nation-states and the traditions of liberal democracy. An end to discrimination, but on special terms; a desire to participate in the state, while defying restraints imposed by the state—the actions and objectives of indigenous peoples are often seen as contradictory, above all as contradicting the goals of state sovereignty and constitutional uniformity. The paradoxes of indigenous rights in some ways also run contrary to the realized aims of the civil rights movement and the antiracism of decolonization. Distinct indigenous rights go beyond rights based upon individual equality. Assimilation and extinguishment of collective rights thus continue to find powerful exponents.

As a liberation movement, indigenism thus stands apart from the twentieth century's most exalted freedom struggles: decolonization, antiapartheid, and civil rights. Each of these predecessors was in some way fixed upon a goal of equality. Mahatma Gandhi turned to archaic village-based simplicity and asceticism as an answer to the challenges of modernity, but his demand for independence ultimately became transformed into a mass movement of predominantly Hindu nationalism that embraced rapid industrialization. Free of British rule, postcolonial India, like most subsequent postcolonial states, sought national and industrial development as a new source of identity, power, and dignity. Decolonization held out the promise of membership in the community of nations, the possibility for each new state of attaining a stature in some ways equal to that of the former colonizing power.

The antiapartheid and the civil rights movements both sought to erase the racial barriers to equality within states. Liberation meant breaking down the racially discriminatory obstacles to education, work, mobility, and power. Freedom from the yoke of segregation meant the participation of all races in a shared social world. All were to have the same access to the ordinary pleasures and extraordinary opportunities provided by a just constitution. The great achievement of these movements was to make similar investments in defending human dignity at lunch counters, at drinking fountains, and in political offices.

Indigenous peoples are not engaged in a liberation struggle that aspires primarily or exclusively toward nationalist or racial equality. "Assimilation" and "cultural genocide" are terms commonly used by indigenous leaders to describe the kind of censorious "equality" that was often (and in many cases continues to be) imposed on them by religious organizations and states. Their principal goal is rather the recognition of distinct collective rights (the implications of which are discussed further in chapter 4). For most indigenous peoples, liberation means an honorable relationship with states in which their rights to land are affirmed and compensation for their losses and suffering is honorably provided. Liberation means the ability to exercise self-determination, to develop culturally distinct forms of education, spirituality, economic development, justice, and governance. The most common goals of indigenous peoples are not so much individual-oriented racial equality and liberation within a national framework as the affirmation of their collective rights, recognition of their sovereignty, and emancipation through the exercise of power.

WHO ARE THE "INDIGENOUS"?

The controversy surrounding the international movement of indigenous peoples includes not just struggles over land, resources, recognition, and sovereignty but also, perhaps as a prelude to all other contests, the complex, delicate issue of defining the term "indigenous."[15] This is becoming all the more pertinent as the term is increasingly associated with new rights and benefits (especially political power) and as the peoples claiming indigenous status emerge with greater frequency and insistence from Africa and Asia—in other words, from hemispheres that differ from the Americas in terms of the complexities of historical settlement, colonialism, and, above all, the development of various authoritarian state systems that resulted from national liberation of former European colonies in the mid- to late twentieth century. How do people from within these diverse social and historical contexts fit into a widening rubric of "indigenous peoples"?

Indigenous delegates to international meetings have often expressed the idea that a precise, legal definition of the term "indigenous" would impose standards or conditions for participation in human rights processes that would be prejudicial to their interests. For one thing, such a definition would be controlled by the very state powers that they see as the principal source of their exploitation, marginalization, and suffering. What is more, Member States of the United Nations do not follow a formal definition of the nation or the state, so a double standard would be applied to indigenous peoples if the terms that are key to their benefits of belonging were interpreted too inflexibly.

The lack of a rigorous definition of the term "indigenous" also presents a challenge to scholarly analysis. But this state of affairs is in some ways preferable: a rigorous definition, one that in effect tried to close the intellectual borders where they were still porous, would be premature and, ultimately, futile. Debates over the problem of definition are actually more interesting than any definition in and of itself. With this as our starting point, we find that there are multiple approaches to the term "indigenous," each with its own political origins and implications. The ambiguity of the term is perhaps its most significant feature.

"Indigenous peoples" have been provisionally defined in three basic ways: legally/analytically (the "other" definition), practically/strategically (the self-definition), and collectively (the global in-group definition). The analytical approach seeks to isolate those distinctive phenomena among the original inhabitants of given territories that coalesce into a global category. The exercise is frustrating because of the historical and social diversity of those who identify themselves as "indigenous." The question of definition thus has the inherent effect of pitting analysis against identity; there will inevitably be a group, seeing itself as indigenous, that is excluded from the scholarly definition, its pride assaulted, its honor tarnished, and, more to the point, its access to redress obstructed.

There are nevertheless some areas of general consensus among formal attempts at definition. The most commonly recognized features of indigenous peoples are descent from original inhabitants of a region prior to the arrival of settlers who have since become the dominant population; maintenance of cultural differences, distinct from a dominant population; and political marginality resulting in poverty, limited access to services, and absence of protections against unwanted "development." These features can be found in a seminal 1987 U.N. report by José Martínez Cobo:

Indigenous communities, peoples and nations are those which, having a historical continuity with pre-invasion and pre-colonial societies that developed on their territories, consider themselves distinct from other sectors of the societies now prevailing in those territories, or parts of them. They form at present nondominant sectors of society and are determined to preserve, develop and transmit to future generations their ancestral territories and their ethnic identity, as the basis of their continued existence as peoples, in accordance with their own cultural patterns, social institutions and legal systems. (48)

Comprehensive and durable as Martínez Cobo's definition is, it does not apply unfailingly to all situations in which people claim indigenous status and protections. It does not fit comfortably, for example, with those areas of mainland Southeast Asia in which there have been complex patterns of displacement and movements of peoples across national boundaries.[16] Some analytical approaches to defining indigenous peoples have attempted to take such complexities into account, principally by noting the possibility that indigenous peoples might not currently occupy their ancestral territories. According to James Anaya (1996), communities and nations are considered indigenous because they have deeper attachments to the lands in which they live (or ancestral lands from which they were removed) than the more powerful sectors of society that have either settled on those same lands or benefited in other ways from their resources (3). The legal approach to indigenous peoples has also developed the presupposition of their coexistence with another ethnic group, dominant either within a present-day state or within the area traditionally inhabited by the indigenous people. "There must be another ethnic group and a power relationship involved before the descendants of the original inhabitants are understood as indigenous in the legal meaning of the term" (Scheinin 2000: 161).[17]

Martínez Cobo's working definition has also been contested by some states. India, for example, has rejected its self-definitional aspect (included in the words "consider themselves") and has pressed for what I would call a "gatekeeper definition," one used to determine who can and cannot have access to U.N. meetings and the possibility they provide, however remote, of restorative justice. India has presented the view that it represents nearly one billion indigenous people (the entire population of the burgeoning nation) and that there is no need for others to present claims of indigenous ancestry that rival those of the state. This approach received support from Miguel Alfonso Martínez's (1999) study of indigenous peoples and treaties for the United Nations: "[I]n post-colonial Africa and Asia autochthonous groups/minorities/ethnic groups/peoples who seek to exercise rights presumed to be or actually infringed by the existing autochthonous authorities in the States in which they live cannot . . . claim for themselves, unilaterally and exclusively, the 'indigenous' status in the United Nations context" (para. 88).

Such reasoning runs squarely into the claims of indigenous peoples themselves, and not just those from Africa or Asia, who argue that only they, as self-determining people, can determine who they are, regardless of what the state may wish of them.[18] It matters little to those who are marginalized whether their oppressor has itself undergone a history of colonialism and passage from freedom into statehood. No one group has a monopoly on the promulgation of stigma and discrimination. It is like the intergenerational nature of family violence: the abused learn to practice abuse with greater refinement.

The disjuncture between analysis and identity has led to the implementation of a practical definition of "indigenous peoples." To avoid such thorny issues as those raised by Alfonso Martínez's report, the Working Group on Indigenous Populations has, since its inception in 1982, maintained an open-door policy toward participation in its annual two-week-long gathering of indigenous peoples and organizations. One might expect this to be a source of mystification like an Oriental paradox—the definition of no definition, the color of the wind. But the real paradox is that it works: indigenous delegates come to the meetings with little insecurity about their own status as "indigenous," and few open doubts about the claims of others.

A notable exception occurred in the 1999 Working Group meeting when a representative of the Rehoboth Baster Community entered himself on the speakers' list and read a prepared statement outlining the Rehoboth's grievances with the government of Namibia.[19] The Rehoboth Basters are descendants of indigenous Khoi and Afrikaans settlers who claim that, with Namibia's independence in 1990, they were deprived of their traditional form of self-government; had their communal land expropriated, thus losing their means of subsistence based upon cattle raising; and were denied use of their mother tongue in administration, justice, education, and public life.[20] To most other indigenous delegates, however, the Rehoboth represent a dominant white community whose claim to African homelands is spurious and who represent a backlash against Namibian independence. As the Rehoboth delegate spoke, hundreds of indigenous delegates silently left the room, then resumed their seats when he had finished. The chairperson of the meeting, Dr. Erica-Irene Daes, responded to this human tide of protest by remarking how odd it was that the call of nature should affect so many at the same time.

This brings us to the third definition of indigenous peoples, one informally developed and acted upon by indigenous delegates themselves.[21] This definition has never been made explicit or committed to writing. It begins with the fact that the leaders of indigenous communities and organizations are always careful to distinguish their identity and experience from those of states. Indigenous peoples are not mere extensions of state policy, so it will not do simply to refer to the "aboriginal peoples of Canada," the "Indians of the United States," the "indigenous peoples of Brazil," and so on. For indigenous representatives, the impulse to seek a wider identity is often regional, sometimes community based, and occasionally individual. It seems to begin with a sense of regional solidarity with those who share similar ways of life and histories of colonial and state domination that then grows into the realization that others around the world share the same experience.

There is thus a global aspect to indigenous identity, rarely expressed overtly, that functions as the basis for bringing people together in international meetings. It is close to a practical implementation of Martínez Cobo's definition, without any of the impediments or rancor of a formal system of membership. There is, nevertheless, a clear awareness among indigenous delegates of who represents an indigenous people or organization and who does not. Entering an indigenous caucus meeting as an observer has some of the same feel to it as being a scarcely tolerated visitor in a remote village. There is little overt unfriendliness, but at the same time there is a palpable sense of bonds uniting others that a mere observer can never fully share.

What is the basis of that connection? A glance around the room shows a striking variety, seemingly the entire range of human appearance and costume (including tattoos and decorative scarification). Within this variety there is an attachment that all participants share to some form of subsistence economy, to a territory or homeland that predates the arrival of settlers and surveyors, to a spiritual system that predates the arrival of missionaries, and to a language that expresses everything that is important and distinct about their place in the universe. Most importantly, they share the destruction and loss of these things. Their cultural markers gain self-conscious significance the more they are diminished by outside forces. They also share the corresponding commitment to find stability and restorative justice—even if it means using the very tools of literacy and law that, in other hands, are responsible for their oppression.

What many seek to achieve, whether realistically or not, is a correction of the historical deficit, an opportunity to present their own experience alongside the exclusionary and incomplete accounts of the founding of states, or what Prasenjit Duara (1995) describes as "the false unity of a self-same, national subject evolving through time" (4). Historical narrowness is inseparable from repression. Possessing, with the blinding clarity of a revealed truth, an original founding story that includes all the mistakes, betrayals, and bloodshed of nations built upon the lives of others is felt to be a first step toward liberation.

THE VIEW FROM AFAR

It is tempting to romanticize the efforts of indigenous leaders at the United Nations and to overestimate their impact on world affairs. The language of participants in the process of human rights standard setting provides us with a reality check and a reminder that significant obstacles remain to be overcome before a new order of relations between indigenous peoples and the state can be said to have truly arrived. International meetings of indigenous leaders are junctures of histories, longings, and potentialities. Each person in attendance brings an inheritance of oppression in some ways held in common with others; each has (sometimes extravagant) expectations of the world community's power to bring about change; and each must come to terms with a reality in which the work of human rights is slow, halting, and often ineffectual. As a whole, Member States of the United Nations do not seem to have been as responsive to efforts to define and protect the rights of indigenous peoples as they have been to other human rights initiatives. "The International Year of the World's Indigenous People," Erica-Irene Daes (1993) commented after the 1993 U.N. dedication, "is about to become the poorest and smallest event of its kind in the history of the United Nations" (v). She went on to remark: "It continues to be a matter of great disappointment to indigenous peoples, and to me, that some Member States cannot yet agree to include them in the family of nations. In an age which has overcome racism, racial discrimination and colonialism in so many fields, there are Member States that still perpetuate a myth as old as the European Colonization of the Americas: that indigenous peoples are legally unequal to other peoples" (v). In 1994, in the forty-eighth session of the U.N. General Assembly, an International Decade of the World's Indigenous People was proclaimed, intended as a springboard for the promotion of a Declaration on the Rights of Indigenous Peoples, the establishment of a permanent forum for indigenous peoples, and pursuit of the issues of indigenous peoples and development (General Assembly Resolution 48/163). Yet for representatives such as Ted Moses (1997), ambassador of the Grand Council of the Crees, the progress of the decade on the important goals it was intended to achieve was negligible and disappointing: "The International Decade of the World's Indigenous Peoples appears to be an orphan within the U.N. system. It is barely recognized or acknowledged by the United Nations and appears not to affect the work of the United Nations" (1).

Why, given the glacial progress of indigenous interests at the United Nations, do so many organizations and peoples send delegates to meetings? The exhaustion of domestic (intrastate) remedies for redressing grievances is a starting point for seeking justice elsewhere. And despite the slow pace of change within the U.N. system, there is the faint possibility that an international agency just might act with urgency and effectiveness. Like many social movements, the gatherings of indigenous leaders at the United Nations are driven by the prospect of sudden and dramatic change to their conditions of life. There are no signs of apocalyptic or revolutionary fervor at these meetings, but they nevertheless provide mundane venues for the expression of extravagant hope.

It is relatively easy to understand the persistence of indigenous peoples in the face of disappointment; similarly, the reasons for the apparently active disinterest of states lie fairly close to the surface. International recognition of the rights of indigenous peoples includes recognition of a wide range of safeguards and rights, including control over valuable natural resources and, as some state representatives see it, the potential for acquisition of a level of international representation and acceptance of international principles of self-governance that raise the alarming specter of breakaway indigenous states. This concern, whether justified or not, has been an obstacle to virtually every significant initiative to recognize and secure indigenous rights in the U.N. system.

Taking a longer view, however, puts things in a different light. Consideration of less than a century of world politics makes it possible to see that the international movement of indigenous peoples has introduced extraordinary changes, especially during the past several decades and especially in the so-called developed countries. Although indigenous identity tends to be reinforced by the devices of timelessness and permanence, the term itself and the political climate in which it took root are products of the latter half of the twentieth century.

Now that this chapter has presented the case that indigenism is a significantly distinct global phenomenon, at least not to be confused with ethnonationalism or a civil rights form of struggle for equality, the obvious next step is to determine its antecedents: how, when, and for what motives it came into being. I make a foray into these questions in chapters 2 and 3. In chapter 2 my main objective is to illustrate the way indigenous sovereignty was responded to differently by the international organizations of states at the beginning and at the end of the twentieth century. This contrast of the two responses includes discussion not only of what motivated indigenous activism in the League of Nations and later the United Nations but also of how these forums have responded differently to indigenous appeals for recognition of their sovereignty, control of their territory, and preservation of their cultural distinctiveness. The change in responses to indigenism over the twentieth century and a summary of the global changes that have produced it highlight the recent emergence of new forms and exercises of indigenous internationalism.

Chapter 3 approaches the historical questions with a more ethnographic comparison between the experiences of marginalization, oppression, and claims of special rights by one indigenous society in Canada and another in West Africa.[22] These two cases allow me to discuss some of the various ways distinct societies or peoples claiming indigenous identity are marginalized and diminished by states, dominant ethnic groups, and multinational corporations. Although I do not attempt to present the complete tool kit of oppression employed against distinct societies, the strategies I have encountered—and those that seem to most clearly stimulate grievance and identity politics—range from ethnocidal policies (such as, for example, language- and culture-effacing state education) to the perpetration of ethnic cleansing (such as, for example, forced relocation, massacres, and extrajudicial executions). The Canada/ Africa comparison also reveals something of the history of the indigenous peoples' movement itself, for it was through an extension of participation in international consultations and standard-setting exercises to self-identifying indigenous peoples from Africa and Asia in the 1990s that the indigenous peoples' movement became more fully global.

There is a common belief, sometimes quite literally an article of faith, that the opportunities for restorative justice through human rights instruments and procedures hold the key for distinct societies to find peace, prosperity, empowerment, and fulfillment of a need for cultural expression. But such hopes cannot be acted upon without in some ways simultaneously being diminished. In particular, the area of overlap between two issues (which I discuss in chapter 4) that are usually discussed separately—cultural relativism versus ethical universalism and collective versus individual rights—presents significant dilemmas for those whose goals are indigenous cultural preservation and self-determination. Starkly put, affirmation of collective rights is being sought through legal channels grounded in liberal individualism. Oral cultures are being defended by the mechanisms of bureaucracy and law—formal, written rules and procedures. To what extent, under these circumstances, is the defense of distinct culture self-defeating? Human rights universalism also highlights the dilemmas present for those who study indigenous societies. Relativism in anthropology is especially challenged by the transitions taking place in every distinct society—the advent of new elites, new uses of technology, and new sources of power, but also new avenues of discrimination by states and by distinct societies claiming rights of self-determination. Yet many anthropologists are understandably resistant to universals, with the discipline as a whole grounded largely in the notion that standards of judgment should come from within societies and that the imposition of values or ethical norms from outside leads to ethnocentric intolerance. This lends itself easily to a rejection of human rights universals or a concern with the variegated cultural meaning of group behavior that has the effect of diminishing the effectiveness of universals. On the other hand, those who seek universals, who perceive abuses within tradition or witness needless misery resulting from the transitions of modernity, sometimes do so intuitively and risk acting upon the subjective standards of ethnocentric reflex, or they interpret human rights in a way that unintentionally strengthens the hand of states, usually by overlooking the legitimate boundaries of self-determination by distinct societies. Is there a way to profit from human rights universalism, to apply an ethical system based ideally upon culture-transcending consensus and knowledge, without compromising distinct cultural identity or shoring up illegitimate elites?

One of the ways that internationally active indigenous leaders are seeking to apply human rights to their own interests is to prioritize recognition by states and international organizations of indigenous self-determination. In chapter 5, I discuss the implications of this strategy for the development of human rights standards specific to indigenous peoples and some of the ways the assertion of self-determination influences indigenous-state relations. The pursuit of self-determination, while clearly a resistance strategy in its own right, has led to the development and use of other forms of resistance by peoples and minorities on the margins of nation-states. The development of local laws and other exercises of inherent legal authority are taking place in some indigenous communities and organizations and are possible in others, largely encouraged by recognition of the wide implications of indigenous self-determination. Another recent use of the human rights system is as a focal point of embarrassment—the "politics of shame," or use of the electronic and print media, political lobbying, and public relations campaigns to communicate the neglect and abuses of states and corporations to wide audiences of citizens and consumers. This tactic has been effectively applied by indigenous organizations to encourage government recognition of indigenous peoples' distinct claims to self-determination and of the need to provide subsidized, semiautonomous regional administrations. It is the only real leverage possible in a human rights system that, aside from several criminal tribunals pursuing war crimes and acts of genocide, for the most part is lacking in meaningful sanctions against states or those in control of state power.

Chapter 6 considers other political implications of indigenous peoples' assertions of self-determination and use of the symbols of statehood. Are indigenous claims of "nationhood" and self-determination, as some state representatives assert, likely to lead to new possibilities for indigenous secessions from states and thus the violent instability that we now associate with the separatist demands of some ethnic groups? Even if indigenous peoples pose no such threat, are their claims to distinct status within nation-states something that can be productively affirmed and acted upon by state governments, or do they go too far beyond liberal expectations of equality and protection of individual rights? Do indigenous peoples represent a form of civil society that can fruitfully resist the centralizing and homogenizing tendencies of states, or should there be more international concern over new possibilities of human rights abuses by increasingly powerful indigenous political entities? And are indigenous demands for recognition part of a more general decline in the identities of nation-states and their ability to remain (or become) cohesive?

Such questions, however, cannot be addressed, or even meaningfully posed, until other things are in place, including some consideration of when, why, and how the international movement of indigenous peoples began.

2 The Origins of the International Movement of Indigenous Peoples

It can be argued that relations between indigenous peoples and colonial powers have always been international, since the signing of treaties included a tacit or explicit acknowledgment that the original inhabitants of a territory were "nations," to be dealt with through existing mechanisms of international negotiation, conquest, and secession of land and sovereignty through treaties. Only as the balance of power shifted in favor of immigrant peoples with a growing settler population, increased military power, and the decimation of indigenous populations through diseases of European origin was the status of indigenous peoples as nations reappraised and legally diluted. Thus, in one form or another, indigenous peoples came to be seen as minority groups inevitably to be assimilated in the dominant society or marginalized by colonial strategies of displacement and "improvement" in the use of their territories.

This view of indigenous peoples was a major impediment to their ability to find redress of grievances against states that had failed to honor treaties and were intent on acquiring land and resources even in violation of their own laws and agreements. The self-evident futility of appealing to the courts and legislatures of the national governments committing such violations did not in itself lead to an internationalization of indigenous politics. There was a lack of awareness among indigenous groups of the widespread, almost global nature of the crises they faced, a situation that changed significantly only through an expansion of indigenous organizations and networks of communication between them in the 1960s and 1970s. Until the mid-twentieth century there was also an absence of international forums to which such grievances could be addressed. The existence of the British Empire did create an opportunity for redress through appeal to the monarch in London; and, in fact, such initiatives were taken by Canadian Indians and the New Zealand Maori beginning in the mid-nineteenth century. Although these efforts did not lead to anything more than a polite hearing, as Minde (1996) points out, "they are nevertheless illustrative of the indigenous peoples' belief that they were not subject to the ultimate authority of the governments in their nation-states, but rather that the pattern of international relations—nation to nation—continued" (229).

The willingness and capacity of an international community of nation-states to take the first steps toward accommodating indigenous peoples' belief in their own nationhood, however, have developed relatively recently, mainly in parallel with the post–World War II elaboration of universal human rights. In this chapter I intend to consider a fragment or analytical sample of the history that involves the elaboration of "indigenous peoples" as an international legal concept and the participation of these peoples in the U.N. system. The particular case I begin with, an abortive appeal by a Six Nations representative to the League of Nations, serves to highlight the changes in the international community's approach to the rights of indigenous peoples that have taken place in the post–World War II human rights era.

DESKAHEH AT THE LEAGUE OF NATIONS, 1922 – 1924

The establishment of the League of Nations after World War I, with President Wilson's promise of self-determination for nations and the rights of minorities to protection, was the first real opportunity for international consideration of the rights of indigenous peoples.[1] The ability of the League's Member States to deny unrepresented peoples access to the forum, however, was a major stumbling block that prevented effective indigenous lobbying at the international level. The most significant illustration of this limitation can be found in the pioneering international lobbying effort of Levi General Deskaheh, chief of the Younger Bear Clan of the Cayuga Nation and spokesman of the Six Nations of the Grand River Land near Brantford, Ontario. From 1923 to 1924, Deskaheh led an abortive but historically significant effort in Geneva to obtain a hearing at the League of Nations concerning a dispute with Canada over tribal self-government.

In September 1923, Deskaheh arrived in Geneva, set up lodging in the Hôtel des Familles, and, with the assistance of a lawyer representing the Six Nations, George P. Docker, proceeded to establish contacts with officials of the League of Nations. The grievance he sought to resolve was common to aboriginal peoples in Canada: the political turmoil and loss of sovereignty resulting from tribal governance under the Indian Act (see Canada 1981).

The Indian Act, first passed in 1876 and amended numerous times since (it is today still in effect), brought into existence a pattern of deputized "self-government" in the form of band councils, elected and functioning under the rules of the act. It was long guided by the notion, common among legislators and Indian agents, that Indian government, functioning within carefully defined limits, could have the benefit of "civilizing" the Indians while protecting them from the encroachment of settlers. Its objective was perhaps most succinctly expressed by Deputy Superintendent-General Duncan Campbell Scott in 1920: "Our object is to continue until there is not a single Indian in Canada that has not been absorbed into the body politic and there is no Indian question, and no Indian Department" (Leslie and Haguire 1978: 115). At the same time, the act was designed to destabilize or eliminate traditional governments less inclined to cooperate with federal initiatives, especially in the controversies surrounding land transfers and surrenders. The Indian Act of 1876, in a comparatively benign beginning, provided a voluntary opportunity for bands to elect chiefs and councils with powers to frame regulations in the administration of public health, control of "intemperance and profligacy," prevention of trespass by cattle, maintenance of roads, bridges, and fences, construction of public buildings, and the location and register of reserve lands. These powers were extended in subsequent amendments to the act to include other, mostly trivial, local matters, such as the "repression of noxious weeds." Through many of the early versions of the Indian Act, there was an implicit tension between the desire to assimilate Indians into Canadian society through the provision of limited, "municipal" responsibilities and powers and an opposing concern about the extent of aboriginal autonomy and defiance exercised through their own leadership. The federal government's answer to Indian reluctance to do its bidding was to add to the powers of the governor-in-council, a federal official responsible for Indian matters across the nation. An 1880 amendment to the act made it possible for the Department of Indian Affairs to impose an elected council on an Indian community, without regard for the existence of thriving "traditional" governments. This had the predictable effect of dividing reserve politics between state-supported elected councils and traditional forms of leadership with spiritually sanctioned authority.

By the time of Deskaheh's campaign, the Six Nations had thus come to be divided between "modernists," who supported Canada's demands that a tribal government be replaced by an elected body, and "traditionalists" from the Council of Hereditary Chiefs, represented by Deskaheh, who opposed formal integration with Canada and stepped up the demand for full self-government. As Deskaheh (1923) expressed it: "The constituent members of the State of the Six Nations of the Iroquois, that is to say, the Mohawk, the Oneida, the Onondaga, the Cayuga, the Seneca and the Tuscarora, now are and have been for many centuries, organized and self-governing peoples, respectively, within the domains of their own, and united in the oldest League of Nations, the League of the Iroquois, for the maintenance of mutual peace" (1–2). Colonel Andrew Thompson (1923), a commissioner sent to the Six Nations reserves in 1923 (probably in response to the international lobbying of the Six Nations Indians), reported to the Canadian government on the strength of the Indians' commitment to self-determination: "The separatist party, if I may so describe it, is exceptionally strong in the Council of Chiefs, in fact it is completely dominant there. Its members maintain . . . that not being British subjects they are not bound by Canadian law, and that, in consequence, the Indian Act does not apply to the Six Nations Indians" (13).

The Six Nations had already, by the time Thompson was writing, been actively resisting the activities of the Royal Canadian Mounted Police, whose presence on the reserve, according to a 1923 statement by the Department of Indian Affairs, "has been for the purpose of suppressing illicit distilling and maintaining law and order generally" (Canada 1923: 14). In his petition to the League of Nations entitled *The Red Man's Appeal to Justice,* Deskaheh (1923) understood an escalation of the police presence to constitute an "act of war upon the Six Nations," intended to "destroy all de jure government of the Six Nations and of the constituent members thereof, and to fasten Canadian authority over all the Six Nations domain and to subjugate the Six Nations peoples, and these wrongful acts have resulted in a situation now constituting a menace to international peace" (6). In an earlier, unsuccessful petition to the League of Nations that he hoped would be conveyed through the Queen of the Netherlands, Deskaheh (1922) made perhaps his strongest argument for the recognition of his people's rights of self-government: "The Six Nations are ready to accept for the purpose of this dispute, if invited, the obligation of membership in the League of Nations upon such just conditions as the Council may prescribe, having due regard to our slender resources" (4). Deskaheh's claim to represent a sovereign state was in part based upon the Haldimand Treaty of 1784, in which King George III conveyed the Grand River Land on the Canadian side of Lake Erie to those Iroquois who had fought on the side of the British during the American Revolution (Rostkowski 1995: 1). The British monarch's act of compensating the Iroquois for the territory they lost to the United States in the war was for Deskaheh a strong affirmation of his people's sovereign status. And, as a sovereign entity, the Six Nations were justified in seeking to be heard at the League of Nations. Although the Six Nations did not expressly seek membership in the League, they saw it as potentially necessary for the international recognition of their claims.

The response by the Canadian government was, predictably, dismissive: "The Six Nations are not now, and have not been for 'many centuries' a recognized or self-governing people but are . . . subjects of the British Crown residing within the Dominion of Canada" (Canada 1923: 4).

Not everyone shared the Canadian government's view. When, in the summer of 1923, Deskaheh traveled to Geneva as head of a small delegation intending to present the grievances of the Six Nations before the Assembly of the League of Nations, the arrival of "real Indians" caused a minor sensation and almost instantly raised Deskaheh's status to that of a local celebrity. The Six Nations delegation conducted informal public lectures and circulated *The Red Man's Appeal to Justice* among League of Nations delegates. Deskaheh also attracted favorable attention from humanitarian societies, such as the Bureau International pour la Défense des Indigènes (Rostkowski 1995: 2). Yet the president of the council, Hjalmar Branting, was reluctant to promote Deskaheh's cause. According to League delegate Captain Walters: "Mr. Branting thinks it would be on the one hand rather inopportune for the Swedish government to ask for the case to be examined; on the other hand he thinks it rather hard if the poor Indian cannot even be heard" (League of Nations 1924). This expression of a moral dilemma in fact shows that Deskaheh's campaign was highly effective. The League, as a matter of policy, was not receptive to claims of sovereignty that conflicted with the interests of states: "The Assembly, while recognizing the fundamental right of minorities to be protected by the League of Nations against oppression, insists on the duty which is incumbent upon persons belonging to minorities of race, religion or language to cooperate as citizens loyal to the nation to which they now belong" (Ottlik n.d.: 438).[2] That Deskaheh garnered as much support as he did, in spite of the League's prerequisite of "good citizenship" and its hostility to rival claims of sovereignty, is surprising. But the League's negative response to his effort could have been predicted. According to one independent lobbyist, "The representative of the world's first League of Peace received no welcome from the world's newest" (League of Nations 1924).

Meanwhile, Herbert Ames (1923), a Canadian representative at the League of Nations, wrote to Prime Minister William Lyon Mackenzie King in December 1923, alerting him to the activities of the Six Nations delegation: "During the Assembly [of the League of Nations] a picturesque delegation of Iroquois Indians, with their chief, Deskehah [sic], were here in Geneva addressing meetings and interviewing delegates. They aroused a certain amount of sympathy among people who heard their side only. Since the Assembly, I understand that they have been following up this initiative by visiting several European countries. . . . I think that really it will be necessary to pay some attention to this lest our apparent indifference be misinterpreted and thus our excellent reputation over here suffer somewhat" (3).

Whether or not Mackenzie King acted upon this advice, the fact that such nations as Estonia, the Netherlands, Ireland, Panama, Japan, and Persia gave the Six Nations their support was a cause of embarrassment to both the Canadian and British governments. The United States, though not directly implicated in the controversy and not a member of the League, was not receptive to this self-government initiative because the Six Nations straddled the U.S.-Canadian border: if successful, their case would have implications for the Iroquois on both sides of the border.

In September 1924, a letter signed by representatives from Ireland, Estonia, Panama, and Persia requested that the president of the Council of the League of Nations, Hjalmar Branting, give "a small nation the opportunity at least to be heard" (League of Nations 1924).[3] But England, in a position of strength after its victory in World War I, succeeded in removing the issue from the agenda, arguing that it was an internal concern of the British Empire, and of Canada in particular. Nevertheless, by the fall of 1924 such strong sympathies had been aroused by states in support of the Six Nations, and above all by Deskaheh's local celebrity, that the mayor of Geneva convened a meeting of friendly states at the City Hall, where Deskaheh was finally able to deliver his address, albeit to an impromptu forum devoid of any other authority than the power of publicity.

On November 27, 1924, an official letter from Canada informed Deskaheh that, following an election held among the Cayuga the previous October, a new tribal council had replaced the hereditary body he represented. In effect, he had lost his power and his mandate to lobby on
behalf of the Six Nations. Dispirited by what he called the "cruel indifference" to his efforts to get a fair hearing, and with his health failing, Deskaheh left Geneva before the end of 1924 (Rostkowski 1995: 3). He died
in the United States several months later. With his death, the Six Nations'
effort to get a hearing at the League of Nations came to an end. Lacking
the leadership and funds for a long-term international campaign, they
did not pursue their lobbying effort further.

INTERNATIONAL LABOUR ORGANIZATION INITIATIVES, 1921–1989

At roughly the same time (starting in 1921) the other major international
forum created after World War I, the International Labour Organization
(ILO), initiated an involvement with concerns surrounding "native workers." The ILO has a checkered history in this field. Of the major international organizations the ILO has consistently been the first to get involved in "native" or "indigenous" issues. But this pioneering spirit has
with equal consistency been offset by the inevitably disappointing results
of early efforts.

In the case of the ILO's native workers initiatives in the 1920s, the promotion of compassionate treatment of workers seems to have been entirely subsumed within the interests of colonial powers. The ILO exercised its jurisdiction over native labor, for example, with ILO Legislative
Ordinance No. 52 of November 7, 1924, conferring upon colonial "Residents" of Burundi the "power to compel natives to perform work in connection with plantations and other undertakings carried on for profit"
(League of Nations 1929: 1). The supposedly compassionate goal of this
ordinance was to moderate the extreme punishments meted out in the
course of forced labor: "Any native who fails to perform work in connection which he is required to perform . . . or who is guilty of negligence in

the performance thereof, shall be punished by not more than seven days' penal servitude and a fine of 200 francs, or by one or other of these penalties" (2). The term "indigenous" does not yet appear in the statutes or correspondence of the ILO, but Ordinance No. 52 still reveals the prevailing orientation of an international body at a time when so-called natives were neither sovereign unto themselves nor nationals of colonizing states but were legally considered "wards." The brutal treatment of laborers was responded to, not as a violation of rights, freedom, or human dignity, but as unsound and unproductive colonial practice.

One of the peculiarities of organized politics is its blind ability to constitutionally affirm the equality of all people while the application of justice condones discrimination, even slavery. And it can take years, perhaps centuries, of nonrevolutionary struggle before the high principles of a founding document match with any consistency the lived reality of the people to whom it is meant to apply—if indeed this ever happens. The Universal Declaration of Human Rights, ratified in 1948, applied these aspirations for human equality and dignity to all nations and peoples and initiated an international nonrevolutionary struggle, sometimes referred to as the human rights movement, to translate its aspirations into reality.

We should therefore not be surprised that the first efforts to apply new human rights standards to what became known as "indigenous peoples" fell short of the postwar aspirations of the Universal Declaration. In the 1950s the ILO undertook humanitarian efforts consistent with the view of indigenous peoples as liminal societies, somewhere between savagery and modernity, impoverished and destined for extinction. A 1946 study on indigenous populations laments that "the aboriginal groups in many regions stagnate in conditions of economic destitution and pronounced cultural and technical backwardness, which severely limit their productive and consumptive conditions. This is due to the primitive conditions in which they are obliged to earn their living, to the lack of educational stimuli and opportunities and to the almost complete absence, in some areas, of welfare services and measures for social and labour protection" (cited in Tennant 1994: 14). Another ILO study released in 1952 is progressively entitled "Indigenous Peoples" but is nevertheless premised upon the inevitability of the assimilation or destruction of this category of human society. It concludes, for example, that "owing to the inferior economic, social and cultural conditions of large groups of 'Indigenous' persons, special action must be taken, on a transitional basis, in favour of such groups" (ILO 1953: 8).[4] One can safely assume that the implicit "transition" alluded to in this passage was consistent with the goal of social and cultural assimilation prevalent at the time. This, in fact, is made explicit in the legal document that resulted from the ILO's first studies and consultations on those people now being referred to as "indigenous." Article 2.1 of the ILO Convention No. 107 of 1957 assigns to governments the primary responsibility "for developing co-ordinated and systematic action for the protection of the populations concerned and their progressive integration into the life of their respective countries," with the main objective (stated in Article 2.3) being "the fostering of individual dignity, and the advancement of individual usefulness and initiative." The first piece of international legislation to specifically address indigenous peoples thus reflects the prevailing political and philanthropic attitudes of the time, in which assimilation of "backward" societies into a nation-state was seen as the first necessary step for the prosperity and liberation of their individual members.

The controversies attendant upon breaking new ground also followed the ILO in its efforts to redress the assimilationist orientation of ILO Convention No. 107 with the ILO Convention (No. 169) Concerning Indigenous and Tribal Peoples in Independent Countries (1989). The divergence of views in the development of Convention No. 169 surrounded the issue of self-determination. For three years, delegates to meetings on the revised convention engaged in an apparently arcane debate on whether to replace "populations" in Convention No. 107 with "peoples" in the new instrument (Swepston 1990: 228). State governments strongly resisted use of the word "peoples" in Convention No. 169 to identify its indigenous beneficiaries because use of the terms is associated with self-determination, which, in turn, is associated in international law with a right of independent statehood (Anaya 1996: 48). In the view of those in the ILO overseeing the development of Convention No. 169, the outcome of this debate had implications for the success of the entire project. Lee

Swepston (1990), who participated in the drafting of Convention No. 169 as the ILO's Human Rights Coordinator, understood the issue as follows: "[H]ow far could a revised Convention go in attempting to protect the rights of these peoples before crossing an invisible line that would make it unratifiable once adopted" (223). The eventual compromise, which has since satisfied few, is inclusion of the word "peoples" in the convention, but with a disqualifying clause in Article 1.3: "The use of the term 'peoples' in this Convention shall not be construed as having any implications as regards the rights which may attach to the term under international law."

There are also limitations to the initiation of a complaint procedure by an indigenous people or organization under Convention No. 169, since indigenous peoples' organizations do not have the right to file complaints on their own. A tripartite structure in which ILO representation is built around an exclusive balance of state, corporate, and labor interests makes it difficult for such a complaint to find an entry point. In Latin America there are indigenous trade unions that have submitted complaints on their own (none of which have yet resulted in a decision), and Mexico in particular has strengthened the convention with a constitution that gives it precedence over domestic law, a unique situation that gave activists leverage to block a dam project in Nahuatl territories (Brysk 2000: 126). The fact remains, however, that the ILO complaint procedures have not yet been opened up to wide use, at least not through official, legal pathways. This can be attributed to the lack of direct indigenous representation in the corporatist tripartite structure of the ILO, to the fact that the convention is relatively new (and not widely ratified by states), and to the preference that the ILO exhibits for "less contentious and less formal means of securing compliance with ILO conventions" (Anaya 1996: 162).

ILO Convention No. 169 has generally not met the expectations of indigenous peoples or organizations, despite their support of and lobbying for state ratification, which has included circulation of petitions in the annual meetings of the Working Group on Indigenous Populations. Clearly, the ILO could not have been expected to meet all the needs in international law for promotion of indigenous rights and protection of indigenous peoples; the charter of the organization, which generously interprets labor issues, still does not have the necessary scope. But ILO Convention No. 169 is seen by many indigenous leaders as having missed an opportunity to do much more. Their disappointment arises from both its absence of strong wording (especially with regard to self-determination) and the apparent inaccessibility and ineffectiveness of the ILO's complaint procedures. The focus of their efforts to secure indigenous rights has therefore shifted more fully to the parent body of the United Nations, in particular to the U.N. Commission on Human Rights.

INDIGENOUS PEOPLES IN THE UNITED NATIONS

The League of Nations gradually collapsed in the late 1930s with the advent of the Second World War. After World War II, when the League was replaced with the United Nations, more favorable conditions eventually emerged for the international recognition of the rights of indigenous peoples. Four aspects of the postwar era contributed to a new climate in international politics that encouraged the promotion of indigenous rights.

First, the struggle against fascism contributed to a greater receptiveness at the international level to measures for the protection of minorities with standards intended to resist racism and discrimination. One of the most important lessons of World War II was that states could not always be relied upon to protect their own citizens, that states could even pass laws to promote domestic policies of genocide. Strident nationalism could be directly contrary not only to world peace but to the survival of races and peoples within states. The result of this new will to promote and safeguard human rights was the adoption of the Universal Declaration of Human Rights in 1948. In 1966, two more detailed human rights instruments were adopted by the United Nations, the International Covenant on Economic, Social and Cultural Rights and the International Covenant on Civil and Political Rights [ICCPR] (entering into force in 1976, when they were ratified by the requisite thirty-five states). Together, these three instruments (together with the 1966 Optional Protocol to the ICCPR, which engage state signatories in reporting and complaint procedures) make up what is now known as the International Bill of Human

Rights. Although the United Nations in the postwar era still remained (and remains) susceptible to the agendas of powerful states, its charter and early adoption of human rights instruments—aspects of the response to Nazism—changed the reach of international law to the point where it became, as David Held (1995) puts it, "less concerned with the freedom or liberty of states and ever more with the general welfare of all those in the global system who are able to make their voices count" (84).

Second, the dismantling of European colonies raised global awareness of political hegemony and the myriad forms of cultural suppression that had seemed a natural part of the "civilizing" process in earlier generations. If European states could not be trusted to safeguard human life and dignity, colonial governments could be trusted even less. The pursuit of human rights protections at the United Nations was in part an epiphenomenon of the immediate postcolonial experience. The principle of "self-determination," despite its inconsistent application by the League of Nations and its use by Hitler to reunify the German "nation," became the guiding imperative of decolonization. In Article 2 of the U.N. General Assembly's 1960 Declaration on the Granting of Independence to Colonial Countries and Peoples, self-determination is for the first time raised to the status of a "right": "All peoples have the right to self-determination; by virtue of that right they freely determine their political status and freely pursue their economic, social and cultural development." The process of decolonization therefore provided more than a climate of liberation that carried over into a broad human rights agenda; it also produced specific changes to international law that could be used to justify the pursuit of self-determination for indigenous peoples.

Third, assimilation policies that used formal education as a means of eliminating tribal cultures and integrating indigenous peoples into mainstream societies had, by the mid-twentieth century, clearly failed in their goal of eliminating all vestiges of attachment to tradition, while unintentionally contributing to intertribal identity, broader political unity, and the training of educated leaders. There is tremendous irony in the fact that the assimilation efforts of boarding schools and the urban relocation programs of such countries as the United States, Canada, Australia, and even India led to the formation of native support groups and organizations that eventually coalesced in international lobbying efforts. Among the many impacts of the Civil Rights Movement centered in the United States in the 1960s was the organization of "pan-Indian," or what we might more broadly call "pan-indigenous," groups. These coalesced into lobbying groups capable of sending leaders to international forums, while raising international awareness of human rights violations occurring even within the major democracies.

Finally, the rise of an indigenous "middle class" as an epiphenomenon of assimilation policies would have had little effect if indigenous leaders had continued to be institutionally marginalized, working within compliant or controlled tribal governments or, at the opposite end of the spectrum, radicalized but often suppressible protest groups. The postwar era has, however, seen the florescence of another kind of entity almost tailor-made for international indigenous politics. In recent decades nongovernmental organizations (NGOs) have increased in numbers almost exponentially, and even the term, originating from the technical language of diplomacy, is gaining wide currency in academic and popular discourse. NGOs are defined by Peter Willetts (1996: 3–4) more in terms of what they *cannot* be than what they actually are. They cannot be commercial organizations with a profit-making aim. They cannot be openly engaged in violence or advocate violence as a political tactic. They cannot be systematically engaged in the overthrow or replacement of existing governments represented in the United Nations. They cannot be fundamentally opposed to the goals and activities of the international organizations that recognize them.[5] What this leaves us with is an astonishing range of organizations, from the widely known (such as Greenpeace and Amnesty International) to the positively obscure (such as the International Federation of Bee Keepers' Associations and the International Federation of International Furniture Removers). NGOs thus now constitute an international civil society consisting of socially and politically active voluntary associations, loosely regulated by states and international state organizations.

The first NGOs were founded in the nineteenth century, beginning with the World Alliance of YMCAs in 1855 and the International Committee of the Red Cross in 1859 (Seary 1996: 15). Why did these organizations arise when they did? The short answer is that the phenomena today seen as the organizational and technological foundations of "globalization"—the creation of international political blocs and alliances and improvements to the efficiency of transportation and communication—have their origins in the historically significant innovations of the nineteenth century.[6] NGOs, as catalysts for social improvement, also develop rapidly in conditions of war and insecurity. Some fifty organizations sprang up in the years during and immediately after World War I (Seary 1996: 16). However, the number of international NGOs remained relatively low until the post–World War II era. There were approximately one thousand formally constituted NGOs and joint NGO-government organizations in the 1950s, two thousand by the early 1970s, five thousand in the early 1990s, and fifteen thousand by the year 2000.[7] The Office of the U.N. High Commission on Human Rights lists 441 indigenous peoples' organizations in a February 2000 compilation (United Nations 2000c). What is perhaps more impressive than the rapid growth in numbers of indigenous NGOs is the fact that they have grown in what was once infertile territory. Nations hostile to dissent have had to accept NGOs, including NGOs representing indigenous interests, as a given part of the political scene. Nevertheless, there is no denying that civil liberties encourage civic organizations in all their myriad forms. In the post–World War II era, political repression relaxed its grip on enough indigenous groups for them to create international alliances and function in international forums. An indigenous delegate once confided to me that he missed the days before the dismantling of the Berlin Wall, when the strategically minded could play the Soviet bloc off against the Western bloc in efforts to further indigenous interests. But the fall of dictatorships through largely peaceful transitions in many parts of the world is not realistically to be regretted. One cannot be effective in international politics while being faced with concern about torture and execution at home.[8] It is difficult to imagine, for example, the thirty-six current indigenous organizations listed by the United Nations for the Russian Federation flourishing under pre-1989 political circumstances (United Nations 2000c). At the very least, functioning in exile or underground is more difficult (not to mention dangerous) than under constitutional protections and tends to narrow the goals of dissent. International NGOs have a visibility and flexibility that makes them more effective instruments of political dissent than domestic organizations or political actors. Where once a dichotomy between domestic and international politics was bridged only by statesmen and diplomats, NGOs have created a place for public involvement in international politics. Although lacking the economic clout of other international actors such as transnational corporations or governmental organizations, they have the decided advantages of self-reliance and ready access to voluntarism. Their influence is indirect, achieved not so much through the exercise of power as through lobbying those who possess it. Like any kind of political organization, NGOs can present symptoms of what Inoguchi, Newman, and Keane (1998) euphemistically refer to as "democratic deficit" (14), but the more general contribution of these organizations has been a striking development of participatory values in international affairs. NGOs might well represent "an emerging international civil society that imparts values which transcend the traditional agenda of state-centric international politics" (14). Whether or not this proves to be the case, the opportunities afforded by the participation of NGOs in international organizations have been central to the growing strength of the international movement of indigenous peoples.

The first significant opportunity for the international representation of indigenous peoples occurred when the United Nations declared the years from 1973 to 1982 the Decade for Action to Combat Racism and Racial Discrimination. This was accompanied by the establishment, under the Special NGO Committee on Human Rights, of a Sub-Committee on Racism, Racial Discrimination, Apartheid and Decolonization, which had as its principal task the organization of a series of NGO conferences on racism and racial discrimination. This series included the 1977 International NGO Conference on Discrimination against Indigenous Populations in the Americas, held at the Palais des Nations in Geneva. It assembled representatives from more than fifty international NGOs, spokespeople for sixty indigenous nations and peoples (not including those who were prevented by their state governments from attending or who "disappeared" before the meeting) from fifteen countries. Also attending were members of U.N. agencies such as the Commission on Human Rights, the Commission on the Status of Women, and UNESCO, as well as observers from forty member nations of the United Nations. The International Indian Treaty Council, which earlier in the year had been granted NGO consultative status to the Economic and Social Council of the United Nations, organized the Native American Delegation (International Indian Treaty Council 1977: 1). The conference brought out first-hand information on the conditions faced by indigenous peoples, mainly resulting from their relations with states, and recommended actions that would help combat discrimination against them. As Edith Ballantyne (1977), chairwoman of the conference, observed, it also represented an even more significant development: "the emerging ability of the indigenous peoples, in a number of regions, to organize themselves, to make their situation known and to state their needs and aspirations through their own spokesmen to the national and international communities" (i). Indigenous peoples' organizations, NGOs representing the interests of indigenous constituencies, had by this time entered the international scene, lobbying and consulting without organizational intermediaries, and in most cases without the intervention of states. The charitable uni-lateral efforts of the ILO had by this time been replaced by another pro-cess, one that clearly involved indigenous leaders but had not yet coa-lesced into anything that could be called a global movement.

In 1981, another international NGO conference at the United Nations in Geneva, this time addressing the issues surrounding indigenous peo-ples and land, established the presence of indigenous peoples at the United Nations more firmly and globally and revealed even more clearly than the first meeting the extent of suffering resulting from the appropri-ation of indigenous lands by states and transnational corporations. This was reflected in the strong wording of a report by the Legal Commission summarizing the findings of the meeting: "The dispossession of indige-nous people from their lands and policies of forced assimilation have led to . . . untold social misery. Restoration of indigenous land base and agrarian reforms which would transfer the ownership of the land back into the hands of indigenous peoples without a requirement of either purchase or taxation are crucial" (United Nations 1981: 15).

The U.N. Economic and Social Council followed up this conference

with the creation in 1982 of the Working Group on Indigenous Populations. This soon became the largest U.N. forum dealing with human
rights issues, with participation in annual meetings growing from some
thirty people in its first sessions in 1982 to over eight hundred in 2001. Indigenous delegations span the continents, with speakers representing
not only the widely known indigenous groups of North and South
America, Australia, and New Zealand but also less well-known groups,
such as the Sami of Finland, Norway, and Sweden, the Ainu of Japan, the
Tuareg of West Africa, and a growing number of previously unrecognized groups emerging from the suppression of both peoples and information in the former Soviet Union. Every year, indigenous speakers at
this one- or two-week forum report on conditions faced by the people
they represent, often making reference to states' violations of treaties and
existing international standards of human rights and fundamental freedoms. The forum also gives states, NGOs, and indigenous peoples' organizations the opportunity to present positions on developments taking place within the United Nations. Translation services and, in recent
years, written summaries of each speaker's statements made available
the following day allow for the widest possible distribution of views and
information. The presence of an international press corps often means
that statements are also made public "at home" through local and national media, giving speakers a high-profile opportunity to engage in the
"politics of embarrassment." Equally important, however, are the activities outside the main room, in the hallways, foyers, and cafeterias of the
Palais des Nations, where indigenous delegates meet among themselves,
where documents and comments are exchanged with equal informality,
and where, reinforcing formal statements of the conference, the repeated
confirmation of common experience gives added credence to indigenous
identity.

    The annual two-week meetings of the Working Group, more than any
other kind of gathering in the United Nations or any other forum, are responsible for the coalescing of an international indigenous identity. The
instrumental act of bringing people together under a common rubric—
"indigenous"—encouraged the development of a global "imagined community" brought together as much by their visible markers of cultural

uniqueness and their oral presentations of common grievances as by the literature they produced and distributed. Mick Dodson (1998), participating in meetings of indigenous peoples in his capacity as Aboriginal and Torres Strait Islander Social Justice Commissioner, recalls:

> My first session at the UN Working Group on Indigenous Populations was a moment of tremendous insight and recognition. I was sitting in a room, 12,000 miles away from home, but if I'd closed my eyes I could just about have been in Maningrida or Dommadgee or Finders Island. The people wore different clothes, spoke in different languages or with different accents, and their homes had different names. But the stories and the sufferings were the same. We were all part of a world community of Indigenous peoples spanning the planet; experiencing the same problems and struggling against the same alienation, marginalisation and sense of powerlessness. We had gathered there united by our shared frustration with the dominant systems in our own countries and their consistent failure to deliver justice. We were all looking for, and demanding, justice from a higher authority. (18–19)

The various elements that constitute this kind of epiphany cannot be separated. Visible markers of racial and cultural distinctiveness and common experiences of victimization come together in the realization that the victimization and suffering of all indigenous peoples are a product of their distinctiveness. Indigenous peoples are collectively oppressed because they are unique, and as indigenous peoples they face this situation together, on a global scale.

Recent events in the indigenous peoples' movement have implications for the structure and ethical orientation of the United Nations itself. Several international meetings bringing together indigenous NGOs and government representatives have taken place in recent years on the establishment of a permanent forum for indigenous peoples at the United Nations, following a recommendation within the 1993 Vienna Declaration and Programme of Action, approved by the World Conference on Human Rights. Workshops on the issue were held at Copenhagen in 1995, Santiago, Chile, in 1997, and Geneva in 1999 and 2000. Some state participants, especially at the first two of these meetings, disputed the proposal of a permanent forum, questioning whether the United Nations could af-

ford to create another body in times of fiscal constraint and whether a forum for indigenous peoples can be considered a genuine priority.

Support for the permanent forum, however, rapidly grew to the point
where, at an intersessional ad hoc Working Group meeting in Geneva in
February 1999, the objections were muted and the chairman-rapporteur,
Richard van Rijssen, was able to report that "no governmental delegation
had expressed formal opposition to the establishment of a permanent forum for indigenous peoples within the United Nations system" (United
Nations 1999: 8).

In a February 2000 meeting in Geneva on proposals for a permanent
forum for indigenous peoples, the unanimity among states that such a forum should be established had been maintained. Surprisingly, consensus
had also been reached on a significant membership issue, with the states
agreeing to a structure in which indigenous representatives would be
on an equal footing with states and have the same voting powers. Once
the forum itself appeared as a fait accompli, the battle shifted to the all-
important conditions in which it would operate: its mandate, rules of operation, the methods to be used to appoint a core group of indigenous
representatives, and—the issue that typically aroused some of the most
heated passion—the name to be given the forum. The Economic and Social Council formally approved establishment of the forum in December
2000, under the title "Permanent United Nations Forum on Indigenous
Issues" (thus avoiding the controversial word "peoples," as I discuss in
chapter 5).

It often happens that the focal points of political controversy divert attention away from the most significant manifestations of change; and in
this case the drawn-out decision making of the United Nations does not
tell us everything there is to know about the international recognition of
indigenous peoples as a category of people with distinct rights and needs
of protection. As international awareness of the existence of a category
of people called "indigenous" with claims of distinct rights has grown,
largely due to human rights initiatives, there has been a corresponding
increase in the number of legal, political, and scientific ventures that invite the participation of indigenous peoples' organizations.

In 1997 the Pan American Health Organization (PAHO, a regional office of the World Health Organization), for example, initiated the Health of Indigenous Peoples Initiative, aimed in part at encouraging nations of the Americas to "detect and monitor [health indicator and health service] inequities based upon ethnicity" (PAHO 1997). The Organization of American States (OAS) is currently pursuing a human rights–oriented hemispheric initiative, a proposed American Declaration on the Rights of Indigenous Peoples (OAS 2001b). In an April 2001 press release, OAS Secretary-General César Garviria expressed the view that "the status and rights of indigenous peoples deserve to be incorporated into the hemispheric agenda, alongside such other issues as poverty eradication and socio-economic inequality; strengthening and consolidation of democracy; and full respect for human rights" (OAS 2001a).

The Arctic has become another focus of regional concerns and interests, especially since the Soviet breakup facilitated circumpolar cooperation. A 2001 conference celebrating the tenth anniversary of the Arctic Council held in Rovaniemi, Finland, for example, included speakers from the Sami Council, the Inuit Circumpolar Conference, and the Russian Association of Indigenous Peoples of the North. Aqqaluk Lynge, president of the Inuit Circumpolar Conference, recalled that during the early years of Arctic Council (at its inception in 1991 called the Arctic Environmental Protection Strategy) governments were not particularly receptive to the participation of indigenous organizations: "In 1991, we were not invited to meetings. In 1993, we were thrown out of the senior Arctic officials' meeting because our points of view were considered irrelevant" (Lynge 2001: 2). Yet the very survival of indigenous peoples living in the Arctic was (and remains) clearly at stake, with issues on the council's agenda such as the effects of global warming and the long-range movement and concentration of persistent organic pollutants, heavy metals, and radionuclides in the Arctic environment, all of which have important health implications for those living close to the land. Indigenous peoples' organizations were eventually seated at the decision-making table, resulting in a useful combination of scientific and traditional knowledge about changes taking place in the fragile Arctic environment.

Such concern with indigenous rights and issues is also finding its way onto the agendas of academic associations (perhaps the surest sign that indigenous issues have hit the mainstream), as reflected in the agendas of the American Anthropological Association and the World Archaeological Congress, which have developed concerns with the human rights of indigenous peoples, the repatriation of artifacts and human remains, and in general the involvement of "local voices" from "subordinate societies" in the scientific study of humankind.

Although human rights standard setting and organizational restructuring may be slow in some areas and paralyzed by controversy in others, there are many smaller loci of recognition that are cumulatively solidifying the conceptual categories, identities, and decision-making strategies being promoted by those communities and societies calling themselves, and now widely known as, indigenous peoples.

THEN AND NOW

The differences between the results of Deskaheh's petitions to the League of Nations and the increasing momentum of the international movement of indigenous peoples at the United Nations illustrate some of the changes in the powers of statehood, the goals of international politics, and the pervasiveness of identity politics that took place in the course of the twentieth century. One of the interesting aspects of Deskaheh's campaign in Geneva is its similarities with much more recent indigenous lobbying efforts. He made appeals to public sympathy via the media (the most effective in the 1920s being newsreels), an effort to lobby individual state delegates using a printed summary of his people's grievances, use of lawyers as advisors (some indigenous representatives today hold law degrees themselves), and use of the legal logic of statehood to oppose the sovereigntist encroachments of a state. His lack of success was not from flaws of character or want of innovation, persistence, or strength of argument. The formal rejection by the international community of Deskaheh's pleas and petitions occurred at a time when international law was oriented almost exclusively toward the regulation of relations between states. The League of Nations was inherently unfriendly to his efforts, giving states wide latitude in their response to "domestic" matters. "Human rights" had not yet developed to the point of becoming a concern of the international community of states; the term itself had not even gained currency.

Since World War II much more attention has been given to the problems of peace and security within states. Among the many important consequences of this shift in orientation has been the growing recognition of indigenous people as bona fide "peoples" requiring the protections and benefits of international law. In a broadening of the human rights agenda, the first international NGO conferences at the United Nations involving indigenous organizations started mainly with participants from the Americas but soon coalesced into growing international networks and a new global form of political identity: "indigenous peoples."

These new indigenous entities do not fit into existing social categories. They are nations, yet they do not pursue statehood. The suffering of their constituents is expressed neither in the comparatively ineffectual gestures of "ordinary" resistance nor, so far, in more overt, politically dangerous rebellions. They seem to have taken some states by surprise, as though entering a landlord's house and sitting themselves down to dinner; and their status at the United Nations is at a turning point, for they have come too far to be turned away completely, and they are pressing for greater formal recognition and permanence.

The efforts made by Deskaheh in the early 1920s to assert the Six Nations' rights of self-determination at the League of Nations reveal that many of the basic ingredients of the indigenous peoples' movement have been in existence for longer than might be assumed: the awareness by an aboriginal people of their right to sovereignty, the sense of grievance over state efforts to usurp and control that sovereignty, the perception that an international community and governing body have the potential to provide redress, the mobilization of activists, lawyers, and sympathizers—these were all present when Deskaheh traveled to Geneva to try to make his case before the League of Nations.

The failure of Deskaheh's efforts, on the other hand, shows that the indigenous peoples' movement and the cultural identities it has produced are of more recent origin. The most important changes that have taken place in the interim are twofold. First, the international organizations of states have developed a body of human rights instruments and a program of standard setting that is less hostile to the rights of those, besides states, sometimes referred to (and more often referring to themselves) as "peoples." Second, indigenous peoples have organized and situated themselves in international networks in such a way that their lobbying efforts are more visible and coordinated, less reliant on the good will of one or several states, and thus less vulnerable to obstruction and veto.

The observation that indigenism is a recent phenomenon, emerging at a time when the forces of cultural change are stronger than ever, adds in some ways to its significance. Distinct rights, gingerly offered, have been hungrily taken. The needs for reassertion and protection of distinct identities, redress of grievances, and forms of self-determination separate from states have been more impelling than anyone, possibly including indigenous people themselves, could have expected. The international movement of indigenous peoples is thus more than an offshoot of the human rights movement, more than a nascent expression of globalization, more even than the sum total of efforts to protect distinct indigenous cultures. It derives much of its energy from a wide audience, a nonindigenous public, and is therefore also an expression of popular misgivings about the impacts of technology and the pace of life, and the corresponding eclectic search for spiritual expression, in modern society.

3 Sources of Global Identity

The very logic of the early colonial encounter, with European ambitions to settle and "improve" territory occupied by people very different from themselves, entailed the possibility of several courses of action, each with catastrophic implications. Those who were inconveniently present were sometimes conquered and put to the sword (the "ethnic cleansing" option). At other times, original inhabitants were bought out, negotiated with, and offered benevolence, protection, and enlightenment as they were shown the value of "civilization" (the "ethnocidal" option). The latter approach to what was sometimes referred to in the Americas as the "Indian question," though occasionally well intentioned, has nevertheless proven to be a potent source of institutional abuse, wounded pride, collective suffering, and cultural nostalgia.

The term "ethnic cleansing," although coined as a macabre euphemism by perpetrators of mass killing in the Balkans, is in some ways a more apt term than "genocide" for the physical destruction of a people arising from the logic of conquest. Under the circumstances of competition over resources and territory, a subject people is often imbued with some of the same qualities as inconvenient features of the landscape; and like trees in an area wanted for pasture, a solution to their presence is sometimes violent depopulation. The differences embodied by an indigenous people, not just their rival presence but their rival culture, can at times place them outside the category of "human" in the mind-set of a conquering people. They become a phenomenon that defies existing categories of the human world in a way described by Mary Douglas in *Purity and Danger* (1966): a source of pollution to be legally and ritually circumscribed and, if possible, eliminated. During the age of discovery, Keith Thomas (1983) tells us, a firm line was drawn between man and beast and between the domesticated world of controlled productivity and the vermin and predators that obstructed it; and this urge to distinguish the human from the animal world had implications for relations between human groups. "If the essence of humanity was defined as consisting in some specific quality, then it followed that any man who did not display that quality was subhuman, semi-animal" (41). It is instructive to see that in the imaginations of some writers in seventeenth-century England, the categories of human that occasionally crossed the line into the realm of not-man included, not just such groups as the Hottentots and American Indians, but also womankind, children, and the Irish.

From time to time conquering people have categorized indigenous populations not only in the realm of the subhuman but also in the realm of "vermin," inconvenient obstacles to the "productive" or "profitable" use of the land they occupy. The combination of competition over resources with category-defying differences has been a common background to occasional mass killings of indigenous populations, such as the systematic elimination of Indians in California during the Gold Rush of the late 1840s and early 1850s and the more contemporary low-intensity massacres of the Yanomamo in the rain forests of Brazil.

The starting point of ethnic cleansing, as the world has recently seen to its horror, can also be the activation of ethnic hatred in regions where the state (or an ethnic group with statist ambitions) is weak and has expansionist ambitions, as in East Timor, Rwanda, and Sierra Leone. These are conflicts in which the stakes, for those engaged in massacres, are largely political and only indirectly material. Rival peoples are dehumanized or portrayed as dangerous, or both. The path to mass killing is cleared by the rhetoric of hate. This, as we will see further in this chapter, is a form of mass killing occasionally experienced by some peoples that have recently identified themselves as "indigenous."

"Ethnocide," sometimes also called "cultural genocide," occurs more often where the state has a firm grip over a subject people but is still striving to secure its national identity. It is usually manifested in policies or programs of "assimilation" aimed at eliminating stark cultural differences and rival claims to sovereignty that arise from first occupation of a territory. Its goal is the elimination of knowledge of, and attachments to, distinct and inconvenient ways of life. In the nation building of the United States, Canada, Australia, New Zealand, and elsewhere, assimilation policies made use of what was referred to as the "tools of civilization"— the schools of the state, the churches of the Christian faith, and the households of "national families"—to eliminate the attachments of children to the "backward" and "uncivilized" ways of their families and ancestors.

Most dominant governments practiced such a minimally lethal expansionism as a way of removing "savages." Mass killing was piecemeal, fragmented, and separated in time, an apocalypse on the installment plan, not the kind of orchestrated campaign exemplified in the twentieth century's bloodbaths of holocaust and ethnic cleansing. What most colonial powers (especially the English) chose to do when faced with the "Indian question" was negotiate arrangements of Indian removal and colonial settlement. (Tocqueville notes this in *Democracy in America*, [1840] 2000: 325, where he contrasts the Spanish use of the sword with the Anglo-American tradition of dispossessing Indians with the pen.) The legacy of the resulting treaties is not easily dismissed. Given that the indigenous "beneficiaries" of treaties—despite the dishonorable circumstances in which they were usually negotiated, ratified, and implemented—hold them as testaments of the sacred trust obligations of the governments that signed or inherited them, there is perforce a legal core to many indigenous claims of uniqueness that cannot easily be ignored. But many states have opted to do just that. A fundamental error in the Indian policies of most Western governments has been to take on the obligations toward native groups, or peoples, as collectivities, while trying to meet (or avoid, as the case may be) these obligations by upholding the rights of *individuals*. The result has been some of the most shameful failures of state judiciaries and legislatures and the most serious compromises of fairness and the rule of law.

Ethnocide and ethnic cleansing are among the most significant markers or sources of indigenous identity. Indigenous representatives speak of the "gross violations" of their peoples' rights, if not in ways that make direct use of the abstractions of human destruction, at least in ways that reflect the meaning they encompass. For Mick Dodson (1998), the suffering of the original peoples of Australia and the Torres Strait Islands, is seen in "the runny eyes, the angry, frustrated faces, the lost knowledge, the desecrated land and the hopelessness" (18). Others boldly, and perhaps impoliticly, use the blunt verbal instrument directly, accusing states of perpetrating or condoning the genocide of their people.

But who is doing what to whom? One of the important matters raised by the indigenous peoples' movement is the global distribution of human rights issues, complaints, and contests. It is generally accepted that countries with dictatorships or unstable democracies, wide disparities in the distribution of wealth and opportunity, and vulnerable populations in areas of resource development will evince the clearest tendencies toward human rights abuse, most blatantly in the form of state-sanctioned violence toward the state's own citizens. The composition of international meetings on indigenous human rights does not reflect this assumption; a disproportionate number of delegates are from liberal democracies, from states generally recognized as highly "developed." The obvious explanation for this is that democracies are most likely to permit or encourage the development of civic responsibility and organized criticism of governments that would bring indigenous delegates together without intimidation or interference. But this still leaves us with the task of considering the distribution of human rights violations. How do the human rights violations of democratic states compare with those of unstable democracies or dictatorships? And if wide differences within and between democratic and nondemocratic states are confirmed, in what sense might there still be found commonalities in the history and experience of indigenous peoples worldwide?

I can only hope to touch briefly upon these questions. A full consideration of them would have to begin with the varieties of nation-states, the greater varieties of indigenous peoples living within them, and the plethora of histories of their interactions. Some of this ground has already been covered by Perry (1996), Maybury-Lewis (1997), and others. I am fortunate, however, in having undertaken research in two very disparate regions, northern Canada and West Africa, among peoples who today claim indigenous identity, whose experiences overlap and differ in ways that illustrate the variety of indigenous experience and the globalization of indigenous identity. In this chapter I will use this research to examine some of the common experiences of indigenous peoples, arrived at from within greatly disparate cultural and political histories.

GRIEF AND GRIEVANCE IN NORTHERN CANADA

By early May the waters of the boreal forest are strikingly scenic and dangerous. The winter's ice has usually cleared away from streams and rivers, except for stratified remainders above the water line. The season the Crees call "breakup" begins in April with dark stretches of open water appearing in the ice that in winter safely carries snowmobiles, cars, and even, in the coldest months, buses and heavy equipment. Eventually the open water takes over, and the last swaths of ice float along the shore of sheltered coves and inlets, treacherous to walk on but with their own musicality in the cold of early morning when small pieces of floating ice harden and jingle like wind chimes with the movement of waves. The water has now opened to boat travel; and Cree hunters come out of the villages, some to move with their families to summer camps, others to hunt and fish for only a day or a few nights before returning to the community. Many Crees don't know how to swim. An elder from the far north told me that before children had access to swimming pools in the city nobody swam because the water stayed cold all year long, a reasonable enough explanation. When I asked what he would do if his canoe ever capsized he said, "If that ever happens, you know your life is over."

In May 1994 two brothers, Ross and Bernie, were traveling by motorboat on a "forebay," a lake formed by a hydroelectric installation, some nine miles upstream from Cross Lake, a large native community in northern Manitoba. The hydroelectric installation and control structure had been constructed on their family's territory in the early 1970s without their consent. Their boat, traveling at high speed, struck the end of a barely submerged log that acted like a fulcrum, flipping the boat over backwards. Unlike the hunters from the far north, Ross and Bernie knew how to swim. Ross, the elder brother in his early forties, made it to the shore of a small island in the middle of the forebay, but Bernie struggled in the water, weighed down by his clothes, quickly going numb and unable to move in the water. Ross went back into the water to rescue his brother, and they both made it to shore.[1]

When a rescue party, alerted by the fact that the brothers were long overdue, found them later that evening, Bernie was shivering in a nest of spruce boughs he had somehow managed to pull together, but Ross had died of exposure. He had become too cold after his second entry into the water to make any efforts to warm himself.

At first the young hunter's family did not want to sue Manitoba Hydro for his death. Seventeen other drownings and deaths from exposure were attributed by the people of Cross Lake to the hydro project, but lawsuits were for them a foreign, painful, and in some ways frightening process. In this instance, however, the family did take Manitoba Hydro to court, and after several agonizing years of litigation won a decision in their favor. The decision by a Provincial Court held that the floating log that overturned the hunters' boat was associated with unpredictable and unsafe conditions caused by the hydro project for hunters who depended upon the waterways for subsistence.

This ruling presented Manitoba Hydro with a serious problem because, from that point on, every piece of floating debris was a potential liability, a lawsuit waiting to happen, and large stretches of shoreline were literally impenetrable tangles of stumps and dead trees, sometimes jarred loose into travel lanes by fluctuating water levels, while submerged stumps were occasionally coming loose from their moorings and floating to the surface (or, worse, just below), where they too became navigation hazards to Cree hunters and their families.

Resolution of this problem was the subject of a meeting I attended in Winnipeg in the summer of 1998, on the invitation of a four-member delegation from Cross Lake. Also attending were their lawyer, a mitigation manager and a lawyer representing Manitoba Hydro, and a representative from Manitoba's Department of Mines, Forestry, and Natural Resources.

After an exchange of pleasantries and an opening prayer (insisted upon by Crees for the opening and closing of all meetings), the representatives of Manitoba Hydro outlined their proposal for making the waters of the forebay safe. It consisted of hiring a six-man crew to clear floating deadheads out of a "safety zone" in the main travel corridor. Some thirty deadheads had been identified, their locations marked with Xs on a map. They would be hauled onto boats or towed to shore, and after this was done any new deadheads found in the water would be similarly dispensed with.

The objections of the Cree delegation to this proposal reveal the connection between rights and indigenous identity. One of Cross Lake's band managers approached the map and pointed to the dotted line signifying the boundary of the proposed "safety zone." He reminded his listeners that the main purpose of travel on the forebay was to reach the fish and mammals that were the Crees' traditional sources of food. "Are you going to ask the fish to come along this line?" he asked. "Are you going to ask the moose to come into this line? Are you going to ask the beaver to come into this line? Are we expected to exercise our treaty rights to hunt and fish only along this line? This is a racist standard. Do we not have treaty rights outside this narrow channel?"

The lawyer for the Crees followed up on this statement by pointing out that there had been four instances in the past two weeks of people from Cross Lake striking debris with their boats. He referred to the proposal as "Russian roulette."

Eventually it was agreed that Manitoba Hydro would finance a shore-line cleanup, starting with a crew of thirty laborers hired from Cross Lake. Within several days of these new jobs being announced, more than two hundred applications were submitted to the Band Office.

The argument used by the Cree representative in this meeting to extend the scope of an environmental mitigation proposal has another layer of meaning, a wider agenda that connects it with the global pursuit of indigenous rights. For the Crees, a safety corridor to protect hunters traveling on the reservoir is unacceptable because it does not accommodate the hunting rights protected by treaty and international law; the limited scope of the government utility's proposal is a rejection of legal difference, of those distinct rights that make native peoples different. Such a proposal rejects not only subsistence opportunities but also rights and the opportunity to exercise those rights. It encompasses the barest responsibilities of the utility toward individuals, regardless of their racial or cultural affiliation, who might wish to travel on the water. It therefore represents a denial of indigenous, native, and Cree identities; and, conversely, it represents an invitation to abandon those identities and their concomitant rights, to participate in the nation-state as citizens without the complications of distinct rights and identities. A tangle of logs along a shoreline can thus come to represent cultural assimilation and constitutional monism.

The safety zone speech has a fundamental point of similarity with many indigenous interventions in international forums. For example, Giichi Nomura (1994), in a presentation to the U.N. General Assembly on the occasion of Human Rights Day 1992, described the denial of his people's rights by Japan. This was expressed in Japan's long-standing (until 1986) claim to be the world's only "mono-ethnic nation" and was manifested in such actions as forced relocations, educational assimilation, prohibition of the use of the Ainu language, and the curtailment of subsistence practices through imposition of penalties for fishing and timber cutting. "What we are after," Nomura said, "is a high level of autonomy based on our fundamental values of 'coexistence with nature' and 'peace through negotiation'" (70). The Ainu and the Crees, addressing very different levels of government about struggles with very different nation-states, are nevertheless articulating basically identical grievances, rights, and aspirations.

When I arrived for a two-year stay in Cross Lake, Manitoba, in 1998, I had not the least inkling of the depth and prevalence of despair in the community. There were at first only hints that things were not as they should be. I watched a group of five children aged between six and eight crossing a grassy field near our home. One of them crouched beside a stagnant, muddy drainage ditch, ran his hand across the surface several times to remove floating particles, and took a long drink through pursed lips.

I later discovered that in the changed circumstances of village life children learn autonomy more from neglect than instruction. The local court docket is the busiest per capita in the province and the jail cells of the Royal Canadian Mounted Police are regularly filled beyond capacity, mostly with absentee parents who are nurturing addictions rather than their children. In the aftermath of almost communitywide drinking binges, women are swollen from beatings and teenagers talk about gang rapes as though they were a normal occurrence.

But the full extent of despair was eventually revealed to me, not through my skills as an observer or interviewer, but through a mounting death toll. There were nine suicides during my two-year stay, from 1998 to 2000, in this community of a little more than 4,500. Royal Canadian Mounted Police (RCMP) records show that in 1999 there were 144 requests for assistance involving attempts and/or threats of suicide. The nursing station, understaffed and unable to maintain records, estimates that they handled as many distinct cases of attempted suicide as the RCMP.

As this was happening, many people were casting their minds back to a similar rash of suicides in 1986–1987. During the course of this earlier crisis, which lasted a little more than a year, there were seven completed suicides and over fifty attempts. Cross Lake's suicides were therefore occurring mainly in "clusters." I began to understand why this was happening when interviews with survivors provided some of the details about how the suicides occurred. One man, now in his mid-thirties, talked about his own will to die, how he had attempted suicide four times, including driving his car over a bridge, and how this was connected to a pervasive hopelessness, not just in himself but in others. His entire circle of friends, he told me, had lost their connection with life. The first death among his friends was entirely unexpected.

> Real early in the morning, about seven o'clock [my friend] came and asked us for a cigarette. He seemed all right. Then he [started] joking around, kissing us on the cheek and those kind of things . . . and he said "I'll see you guys," and he left. I guess he went home, went to his room and then took a .22 and shot himself. One shot. He didn't fall right away or anything. He sat there. They heard the shot in the house, but as soon as he shot himself he picked up a guitar and started to sing. They thought they were just hearing things. I guess while he was singing he kind of fell over, and that was it. He died from internal bleeding. When I saw him at the nursing station there was just a little trickle of blood.

If there was already a generalized sense of hopelessness among the youth of the community, the suicide gave it a sharper definition. It provided a deeper sorrow, what was described to me as an emotional "numbness" and detachment. Soon, another suicide occurred, clearly connected to the previous one.

> For a couple of weeks there [my buddy] just spent a lot of time in his room. And then one day he was just, whew, all happy. I thought, "Great." He went out and was hanging around and he went to a few parties here and there visiting. [One day] I took him for a ride. . . .
> He told me to stop.
>   I said, "Ok."
> He said, "I'll see you," and he just got out of the truck. . . . There was a big party there and he went in, went right into the closet and shot himself [with a shotgun]. So they rushed him to the nursing station. . . . You could see the big hole . . . and when you turned him over you could see where the pellets came out on the other side. And then, everybody was kind of freaking out. . . . He had an IV and he kept yelling for his friend, the one that shot himself [with the .22]. And he kept ripping those things out of his arms, the IVs. And then there was [a preacher] there. He told him to pray, and he got him to calm down. He prayed. And he just died.

In close-knit native communities, where any unusual event attracts instant notice, suicide attempts and completions are directly witnessed by many, and the impact of them is felt by all. There is a tendency, therefore, for grief to be felt collectively, and for suicidal events to occur in "clusters" until the community as a whole finds a way out of its misery. The suicides continued this way for over a year, with one death connected to the next, each new bereavement feeding an entire generation's will to die.

Even under "normal" circumstances, suicide is difficult to understand. It is difficult above all for families and friends of the victims, but also for those looking more broadly for the social causes of such a high prevalence of suicidal behavior. As the two narratives show, there is a collective experience of hopelessness at work in Cross Lake. It is collective both in the sense of "contagion," with one suicide contributing to the emotional circumstances of another, and in the sense of a communitywide experience of despair.

In a global survey of the conditions and causes of poor mental health, *World Mental Health,* Desjarlais et al. (1995) find that mental health "is first and foremost a question of economic and political welfare. Although the links between social forces and ill health are complex and varied, close inspection suggests that mental health concerns almost always relate to more general concerns that have to do with the economic welfare of a family or community, the environment in which a person lives, and the kinds of resources that he or she can draw upon" (15). In Cross Lake's suicides, we are finding an expression of the cumulative histories of political annexation, suppression of knowledge, and economic disadvantage that motivate both self-destruction and a positive urge toward indigenous activism. In this way, indigenous leaders are an elite formed not from wealth or privilege, and not exclusively from education, but from the mere ability to remain emotionally stable.

This leads us to the question of the social causes of suicide, which can be approached through what might be called "historical pathology." With this starting point, several events stand out as relevant to an understanding of the community's crisis.

First, the people of Cross Lake were in the mainstream of residential education policy. From 1919, when the St. Joseph Christian School was established, until the early 1970s, when the school burned and residential education in other communities was phased out, the people of Cross

Lake experienced a form of "education" in which many students suffered brutal punishment, sexual abuse, loss of language, and disconnection from family. The testimony of those who are called "residential school survivors" is a harrowing reminder of the dangers inherent in removing a distinct people's sovereignty and imposing institutional efforts to change them. Being in school "put a lot of anxiety on me," one former student at St. Joseph's recalled, "because I thought I was in prison. I couldn't do anything. I was never free, even to think for myself."

Another elder who attended residential school in the 1930s remembered a sense of unfairness inherent in school conditions: "We weren't fed properly. We were strapped. But the priests and sisters, they had good food and beautiful sleeping quarters. The only thing that I got out of school was the ability to work."

Specific incidents become the focus of lasting bitterness for those who suffered brutality at the hands of school supervisors with complete power over them: "Usually the children got shoes in the spring, and they would hand them out one by one. You usually wouldn't get the right size. I told the sister that I couldn't fit my shoes. She turned around and took a shoe and started hitting me with the heel. She knocked me down to the floor, and some of the girls told the sister she had killed me. The girls had to look after me. The sister just left, just like that. The girls took care of me and cleaned me up on the bed."

Others find events that recall the loneliness they felt at separation from their families. A former student from a residential school in Norway House remembered catching a glimpse of her mother through the window. Her mother had come to the community unannounced for a medical reason but wasn't allowed by the school authorities to visit her daughter. "I saw her walking in front of the school and I was banging on the window because I was so happy to see her. I was screaming, and she saw me and she just waved at me. I opened the window, opened it a little bit. . . . And I felt somebody behind me pulling me by the hair, pulling me away from the window."[2]

Clearly such experiences, shared by enough people, can have implications for an entire community's well-being, for its *minowin*, as the Crees call it.[3] This is especially clear because, following the end of residential education in Cross Lake in 1969, there was no healing strategy put in place to enable affected individuals or the community to recover from the residential school experience.[4] But the schools are no longer in operation; the painful experiences are memories. Whatever lasting effects residential schools had for individuals and families, the object of their suffering has vanished, existing chimerically only in memories, emotions—and self-destructive behavior.

In 1996 the government of Canada acknowledged the serious, multi-generational harm done to aboriginal Canadians by the imposition of residential school education, which had resulted in the breakup of families and disruption of relations between generations and had contributed to the lasting effects of mental, physical, and sexual abuse. But for many victims of abuse in residential schools, the government response was too little too late.

The hydroelectric project on the Nelson River has become even more important than residential schools as a focus of indigenous activism in Cross Lake. The project is more tangible, embodied in the Jenpeg generating station nine miles upstream from the village. It manifests itself in water fluctuations, floating stumps and logs,[5] and ancestral remains washed out of graves and scattered on shorelines.

The hydroelectric project is a focus of grievance because it impedes the Crees' ability to hunt and to heal themselves on the land. The project is seen as a source of displacement and dispossession. It is an obstruction to identity.

The animals on which the Crees used to depend for food, clothing, and income also struggle with the changes imposed on their river system. A Cree hunter once told me about a time when he and his friends had stopped for lunch on the shores of the Nelson River and noticed something odd floating past. It turned out to be a duck sitting on a nest that had been dislodged by rising water, still gamely trying to incubate her eggs as she headed downstream. The people of Cross Lake will tell anyone willing to listen that the river is no longer able to provide its people with the same abundance. Muskrats are often killed in their dens by water fluctuations, and only some beavers have adapted to the new regime by constructing lodges with terraced "apartments" in which they can move their kits to different levels in accordance with the height of the water. Whitefish have all but disappeared, their spawning grounds destroyed, and predatory species of fish such as northern pike and walleye were contaminated by mercury when the project was first constructed. Those taken from the river are still suspect, despite assurances from fisheries experts that they are safe "in moderation."[6]

For some, the declining opportunities for subsistence from the land are compounded by a loss of connection with deceased relatives and ancestors. These ancestors were buried at scenic outcroppings near the water, the very places now most susceptible to water currents and shoreline erosion.[7] One Cross Lake leader told me about a dream he had before any loose bones were found: it began with him wading in the water, looking down and seeing submerged headstones, and then moving toward a sense of outrage at his discovery, on higher ground, of loose bones and a row of uncovered graves. It was a premonition that now motivates him in a single-minded advocacy for grave restoration.[8]

In almost every meaningful sense, the people of Cross Lake have been displaced. The sense of home, which once extended far into the rivers, lakes, and forests of northern Manitoba, has been rapidly narrowed to a centralized village. Much of their symbolic attachments to the past have been washed away, sometimes literally with the bones of the ancestors. Cross Lake residents who lived through the period of construction of the Nelson River project in the early 1970s uniformly report feelings of dislocation and loss stemming from the development's impact on the availability of fish and game and people's ability to travel safely on the affected waterways.

In one sense residential school and destruction of a river system are not at all dissimilar: both severely disrupted a way of life. Residential schools did it by physically removing children from their families and housing them in dormitories; hydroelectric development did it by permanently altering the river system, making it less productive and less safe. One removed the people from the land; the other removed the land from the people.[9]

The main impulse behind the activism of indigenous leaders, however, is not so much their sorrow from loss of life, land, productivity, and freedom, as the denial by governments and corporations that these losses have occurred and that the grievances are legitimate. The ultimate source of disaffection among the people of Cross Lake is an absence of validation, a lack of willingness on the part of governments to seriously acknowledge social suffering and a collective experience of injustice. Problems in the affected Cree communities, such as those arising from unemployment, poor health services, lack of recreation facilities, and poor water quality, only reinforce a more fundamental sense of isolation, a perception that those in government will not remedy or atone for the Cree people's suffering.

This perception was sharpened by the failure of compensation for the impacts of the hydroelectric project, amounting to what was widely seen in Cross Lake as an abrogation and extinguishment of treaty rights. The 1977 Northern Flood Agreement (NFA) between Canada, Manitoba, Manitoba Hydro, and the Northern Flood Committee (NFC), which represented five aboriginal communities affected by the project—Nelson House, Split Lake, York Landing, Cross Lake, and Norway House—began to be negotiated in 1975, several years after construction on the hydroelectric project had already begun. Colin Gillespie (1999), a former member of the NFC's negotiating team, remembers the thinking behind the decision to avoid one-time cash compensation in favor of the mitigation and community development standards contained in the NFA: "How could fair and equitable treatment be ensured, when so little was known about a development which could profoundly affect future generations? It came down to a choice: between a one-shot legal settlement, which would have certainty, and a long-term socio-economic relationship, which would require trust" (5).

The NFA opted for the latter, setting high standards of community compensation and development. Most ambitiously, it called for the eradication of mass poverty and mass unemployment. Manfred Rehbock, one of the consultants who drafted the NFA, was inspired by the Marshall Plan, having lived through the rebuilding of post–World War II Germany, and some of the ideals and choices of wording contained in Schedule E of the NFA arose from his perception that the Cree communities affected by the Churchill/Nelson River megaproject faced a comparable, though much smaller-scale, challenge of development to that of postwar Europe.

For the first eight years after NFA ratification in 1978, the government of Canada budgeted no funds for its implementation, and since then it has done so only on condition of extinguishments of NFA obligations (Gillespie 1999: 7). The focus on implementation became small claims, forced into arbitration and courts, a process that the NFC (1993) characterized as "adversarial and lengthy" (58), while the most important provisions of the NFA, notably the "eradication of mass poverty" promise in Schedule E, remained entirely untouched. Sadly, the mechanisms built into the NFA for conflict resolution became the primary means of its implementation.

In 1985, the governments of Canada and Manitoba and Manitoba Hydro made the first attempts to extinguish the NFA by offering the NFC $30 million to settle, in perpetuity, all resource-related claims resulting from the hydroelectric project. This was rejected by the NFC. "Global" settlements were also proposed by the governments in 1988 and 1990, culminating in a draft Proposed Basis of Settlement of Outstanding Claims and Obligations, offering $242 million in cash and bonds to resolve some 150 outstanding claims and to eliminate most of the government's NFA obligations (NFC 1993: 56). This was similarly rejected by the NFC, mainly because of concerns about the termination of rights intended to last "in perpetuity."

Then, in 1992, Split Lake, faced by a situation in which full NFA benefits were seemingly unattainable, became the first of the NFA signatory communities to enter into a "Comprehensive Implementation Agreement," which eliminated, clause by clause, almost all government responsibilities in the NFA, with the exception of injuries, deaths, and "unforeseen" impacts caused by the hydroelectric project. The Split Lake agreement established a process by which the governments negotiated individually with the Cree communities, with "finalization" agreements (or "termination" agreements, as they are called in Cross Lake) signed with York Landing in 1995, Nelson House in 1996, and Norway House in 1997.[10]

As Cross Lake's Comprehensive Agreement approached its final form it was closely scrutinized by some Band Office employees with the use of a *Black's Law Dictionary.* It was also submitted for an independent legal opinion to Manfred Rehbock and his colleague Betty Nowicki, who replied: "We take no pleasure in predicting that Cross Lake's Schedule E development entitlements . . . will remain unachievable targets under the current NFA implementation proposal. Why your rights and entitlements under the NFA . . . should be permitted to be treated with such contempt (especially by Canada as your trustee) defies our comprehension" (unpublished letter to Cross Lake Chief and Council, April 16, 1997). Ultimately, however, it was the elders who decided for the community. As Cross Lake's chief and council sat in their Band Office preparing to sign a copy of the Comprehensive Agreement, a small group of elders took them out of the room, one by one, to a community meeting in which the fate of the agreement was to be decided. The signing was postponed. The Comprehensive Agreement was the main campaign issue of an election for chief and council and was eventually discarded, publicly thrown into a trash can in October 1998, by Chief Roland Robinson during his inauguration ceremony.[11]

As we will see below in chapter 5, this decision was not arrived at without outside influence. In deciding to mount a campaign in opposition to the will of the state, Cross Lake had already allied itself with a wide cross section of indigenous, environmental, and religious organizations. Whether self-consciously or not, the community had entered into an active engagement with the politics of indigenism.

NORTH AND SOUTH

Cross Lake's experience of assimilation policy and imposed megaproject development is typical of the communities that first inspired and organized the indigenous peoples' movement. Nongovernmental organizations (NGOs) from North America and, as the scope of international meetings expanded, from the South Pacific and northern Europe were most active in the organization of the first international meetings of indigenous peoples at the United Nations. Peoples and organizations from Central and South America were at first less well equipped to form effective local and regional organizations and alliances but are now an effective, and often independently minded, regional bloc. Then, within the past decade, indigenous peoples from the former Soviet Union began attending meetings, represented largely by the Inuit Circumpolar Conference and the Russian Association of Indigenous Peoples of the North. At approximately the same time, but more contentiously (for reasons I will soon discuss), indigenous peoples from Africa and Asia established their presence in international processes and thereby globalized the category "indigenous peoples." As the regional scope of the movement has moved to new hemispheres, above all to the inclusion of peoples from unstable and/or undemocratic states, the form of grievance has also shifted from a more or less uniform pattern of ethnocidal displacement and assimilation to a more frequent inclusion of mass killing, the entanglements of ethnic rivalries, and efforts toward ethnic cleansing.

The extent to which there is agreement on fundamental issues in international indigenous caucus meetings is probably a product of necessity: states, secure in their position in international bodies and international law, can safely disagree—the system is designed for it—but indigenous peoples and organizations still stand on the outside looking in, and major disagreements are potentially fatal to their chances of entry at high levels in the U.N. system. The existence of an indigenous consensus on the issue of self-determination, particularly in resisting revisions of the draft declaration intended to limit or qualify self-determination, does not mean that all indigenous delegates agree at all times on all issues. This is only to be expected. What I find revealing is how those disagreements that do arise tend to be patterned and how they have evolved over the past several decades.

When the International Labour Organization's (ILO's) 1989 Convention on Indigenous and Tribal Peoples (No. 169) was being prepared, those indigenous groups that tended to be most vocal in consultations were from the Northern Hemisphere. A pattern emerged that was observed by Lee Swepston (1990) during the course of these consultations:

[A] noticeable phenomenon was a "north-south" split among NGOs, closely reflecting that between developing and developed nations.

"Northern" indigenous peoples' representatives were the most articulate and the best able to deal with the complex ILO structure, new to all the NGOs. They dominated, and were resented by, the few organizations of indigenous peoples from developing countries—the "south"—who could afford to come to the Conference. Further, those from the "north" were the most vocal in expressing dissatisfaction with the final text of the new Convention, as it did not respond to their highly political and ideological demands; while those from the "south" tended to see it as a working tool which could lend concrete assistance to the most disadvantaged people in the most disadvantaged nations. (226)

In the 1980s the "north-south" divide followed several basic differences between indigenous organizations. Those from the "north" had more commonly experienced assimilation-oriented education. They therefore possessed a greater technical capacity for adapting to unfamiliar bureaucratic settings and legal language. More significant is the fact that in the "south," until the end of axial competition between the United States and the Soviet Union, there were more military dictatorships actively repressing indigenous organizations, some by exterminating the indigenous people themselves. Antonio Millape, president of the Confederation of Mapuche (in exile), representing some nine hundred thousand Mapuches in Chile, presented the following testimony to the 1977 U.N. Conference on Discrimination against Indigenous Populations in the Americas:

In 1973 when the coup took place in Chile, my own house was surrounded by two police wagons with 16 military men who invaded my house without respect for anyone. . . . [From that moment on] I was detained at least ten times, not only myself but also the president and leaders of the 63 regional associations of Mapuches, more than 3,000 leaders of communities. . . . A massive extermination of the Mapuche occurred. In some places a hen or two only exists. People are starving. . . . Go to any Mapuche home today, and you will find that the dog outside will not bark, because it is too weak. If you go inside you will find one or more children lying sick, dying of starvation. . . . That is the form of extermination today under Pinochet. . . . All regional associations have been banned. It is difficult to organize now. Our most immediate goal is to stop starvation, this extermination. (International Indian Treaty Council 1977: 10)

The concerns of many indigenous societies were more often about protecting themselves from starvation, massacres, or returning from exile, concerns not always clearly reflected in the abstruse discussions involved in preparation of a legal document.

Since 1989 much has changed. Not all dictatorships have fallen. Not all repression of indigenous organizations has ended, but a significant number of transitions toward democracy have occurred, especially in South and Central America, making it possible for indigenous organizations to work more openly, sometimes in cooperation with state governments. In this sense the gap between north and south is closing. It has now become possible for formerly repressed indigenous organizations to begin thinking about their place in the world, their place in the state, and what it means to be "indigenous" with rights to self-determination.

THE AFRICAN/ASIAN CONTROVERSY

One of the principal arguments by which the claims of groups to be indigenous have been resisted by states and by groups and organizations with rival claims to indigenous identity focuses upon the history of decolonization. The "minority" peoples of Asia and Africa, according to one approach, cannot reasonably say they are indigenous, or at least act politically upon this claim, because they have already been liberated. The states that emerged through the process of decolonization are the mechanism through which indigenous identity has already been affirmed and given political substance. The cultural diversity of the colonial world necessitated the creation of multicultural states. True, there have been disappointments over the ways power has been abused and democracy suppressed in some newly formed states, but the answer to this must be found in national reforms, not further divisions, be they "ethnic" or "indigenous." Governments of nation-states liberated from colonialism have found various (usually indirect) ways of expressing this. The slogan of the government of Mali (posted on all government business such as visas, letterheads, and Web sites), "un peuple, un but, une foi" [one people, one goal, one faith], reflects a concern with securing equality within a typi-

cally heterogenous African state. A more direct expression of this sentiment was made by the government of Morocco in a 1985 statement to the
Working Group on Indigenous Populations: "The problem of the rights
of indigenous populations does not arise in Morocco since all citizens,
whether living in the town or the country, enjoy the same rights and are
subject to the same obligations" (1). The state is the bearer of a constitution providing all citizens with freedom and equality, with a regime
of benefits and duties that cannot be interfered with by the assertion of
"particular traditions."

In Asia, with more dense populations and complex histories of migration, displacement, absorption, and dispersal, greater emphasis is placed
by those resisting indigenous identity on the impossibility and inadvis-
ability of attaching distinct rights and benefits to the principle of "first
occupancy."[12] The government of India thus sometimes claims to represent nearly one billion indigenous people. All citizens are sons and
daughters of the soil; none may legitimately claim an identity based on
having occupied the territory first. Nothing is to be gained, and much potentially lost, by the revival of tribalism.[13] India has thus supplemented
the we-are-all-indigenous argument with concerns that a forensic in-
quiry into who occupied the land first, or an open definition that allowed
people to self-identify as indigenous, would, in either case, lead to chau-
vinist claims by groups all over India, some with significant local power,
even though they are minorities nationally (Kingsbury 1998: 435).

The emphasis by the People's Republic of China is on the powerful
orthodoxy that it has a national history of colonial victimization and has
already been liberated from colonialism by the revolution (Kingsbury
1998: 449). China generally supports the initiatives undertaken by the
United Nations on behalf of indigenous peoples, pointing out (truthfully
but without revealing the reasons) that China itself does not have any
groups or organizations claiming such identity.[14] This approach is consistent with the Marxist idea of liberation as a dramatic, once-only event,
an idea inimical to the pursuit of political autonomy by any distinct minorities. It is difficult, to say the least, to claim the need to be liberated
from a state founded with great ideological and political conviction upon
an already completed struggle for liberation.

The extension of indigenous identity to Africa and Asia has also been resisted by some indigenous leaders, mainly from the Western Hemisphere. These leaders argue that the struggles of those from the decolonized world do not truly represent the indigenous experience. To them the pivotal issue is a history of displacement by alien and dominant powers, not marginalization by others with equally deep ties to national territories.[15]

Nevertheless, there is a seemingly irreversible momentum behind claims of indigenous identity by peoples from Asia and Africa. Participants in recent meetings on the proposed permanent forum included Asian representatives from the Asian Indigenous Peoples Pact, the Asian Indigenous and Tribal Peoples Network, the Chittagong Hill Tracts Administration, and the Nepal Indigenous Peoples Development and Information Service Centre and African representatives from Tin Hinan ("Nomadic Women") and the Ancap-Tamaynaut for the Indigenous Peoples "Amazigh" of Morocco. A May 2000 seminar sponsored by the Commission on Human Rights, entitled "Multiculturalism in Africa: Peaceful and Constructive Group Accommodation in Situations Involving Minorities and Indigenous Peoples," held in Arusha, Tanzania, included indigenous representatives of the Berbers from Morocco, the Himbe and Herero peoples of Namibia, the Pokot people of Kenya, and the Hadza people of Tanzania. This was largely an opportunity for African indigenous leaders to present their peoples' history of oppression and survival. The Amazigh (Berber) spokesman, for example, told of the historic process of Arabization and French domination that led to the partial destruction of Amazigh culture. Although Amazigh activists had begun organizing NGOs for the defense of their language and culture as early as the 1960s, it was not until 1993, with their participation in the World Conference on Human Rights in Vienna, that Amazigh leaders first perceived their similarities with indigenous peoples from other regions. They have since "looked for the protection of their collective rights and recognition as peoples" (United Nations 2000e: 3).[16]

Those claiming indigenous identity from the "decolonized" nations of Africa and Asia point to the ongoing oppression and marginalization they experience at the hands of the state. The artificially created and centralized states of Africa and Asia care little about indigenous knowledge and cultures. The conclusion of struggles for national independence did not liberate those who continue to depend on forests and pastures for their livelihood.[17] This was the basic argument made by Moringe Parkipuny (n.d.), a Tanzanian Member of Parliament who spoke on behalf of the East African pastoralists (specifically mentioning the Masai) and hunter/gatherers (notably the Hadza, Dorobo, and Sandawe) in a statement before the Working Group on Indigenous Populations:

> The most fundamental rights to maintain our specific cultural identity and the land that constitutes the foundation of our existence as a people are not respected by the state and fellow citizens who belong to the mainstream population. In our societies the land and natural resources are the means of livelihood, the media of cultural and spiritual integrity for the entire community as opposed to individual appropriation. The process of alienation of our land and its resources was launched by European colonial authorities at the beginning of this century and has been carried on, to date, after the attainment of national independence. Our cultures and ways of life are viewed as outmoded, inimical to national pride and a hindrance to progress. (2)

The indigenous peoples of Africa thus point to postindependence continuities with their colonial subjection in support of their status as "indigenous" peoples in need of protection and liberation from oppressive states.[18] Customary laws of indigenous peoples were suppressed with colonization and not reinstated after independence. Land has been expropriated by dominant groups, while the people who depend on it have been removed and left without economic alternatives. Indigenous languages are not used in schools, creating the predicament in which indigenous people must choose between losing their identity through educational opportunity or remaining disempowered, without the knowledge needed to uphold their rights. The majority view in the international indigenous community is that the ways that indigenous peoples are losing their languages, their cultures, and their very lives in Africa and Asia are identical to those of indigenous peoples from other regions. Indigenous peoples from decolonized states can take little comfort in national liberation when they are themselves being excluded and thus rank among the most disadvantaged people within disadvantaged states.[19]

The common world outlook of those claiming indigenous identity does not conveniently follow the successful transplantation of immigrant peoples into new hemispheres. Indigenous identity is not contingent upon continued domination by peoples of European origin. It matters little to those claiming indigenous identity if their oppressors are historically successful immigrants or the recent beneficiaries of national independence. Indigenous identity, as the next case study reveals, has become a global phenomenon in recent decades because the experience of grievance and loss is in some fundamental ways the same for the victims of displacement in every hemisphere.

TRANSHUMANCE, SETTLEMENT,
AND SURVIVAL IN AFRICA

At first sight, the Tuaregs' self-identification as an "indigenous people" does not appear to be favored by history. Islam is by far the more obvious means, or rallying point, of expressing endemic dissatisfaction with the state. And the Tuaregs are Muslim to the core, proud of the sherifan ancestry that connects their clerical clans in a line of descent to the prophet Muhammad. It is true that past reformers tended to direct their energies toward what they saw as the abuses of the Sufi orders rather than overtly expressing their political ambitions. Abdullahi ag Mahmud, a puritan reformer of the Gao-based group the Kel es-Souk, who died in 1952, was opposed to many of the practices of the Qadiriyya order: the invocation of "saints" in prayer, the manufacture or use of amulets, and the attributing to "marabouts" (a term used throughout sub-Saharan West Africa for venerated clerics) of holiness that gives them the status of intermediaries between ordinary worshippers and God (Kaba 1974). In other times and places, however, these same ideas have created reformist communities, unified far-flung tribes, and inspired resistance to state hegemony.[20] Given this Islamic background, what is there in indigenous activism that makes it in some ways preferable to religion as a means of social and political reform?

The answer to this question underscores the basic appeal of indigenous identity and activism. If a people who do not fit the popular profile of what it means to be indigenous can find an active place in the international indigenous community, then we have an opportunity both to expand the limits of existing social and political categories and to understand them better.

The Tuaregs are not typical of an indigenous people, at least not the stereotype of one. They have a hierarchical and aristocratic social structure rather than a form of egalitarian or acephalous meritocracy more typical of hunter-gatherers. Under French colonial rule in the 1930s they were forced into the manumission of the Bellas, slaves at the lowest end of the social order, a process that resulted in chaotic disputes over cattle ownership. They are loosely grouped into federations of tribes; each tribe is further divided into "classes" that include nobles (*imoshar*), pastoralist vassals (*imghad*), clerical clans (*ineslemen*, meaning "Muslim"), and artisan castes. The *ineslemen* are similar in their way of life to other Tuaregs—cattle herding among those in the steppelike Sahel and camel nomadism in the central Sahara—except that they have traditionally had the status of social inferiors and they do not bear arms. Clerics who cannot aspire to a place in the nobility make ideal peacemakers between tribal groups locked in feuds.

Another feature that makes the Tuaregs, superficially at least, less than typical of indigenous peoples is that they are residents and citizens of postcolonial states. In a sense, all peoples of these states are "indigenous," having ancestry and permanence that extends beyond historical records, but there are those who share in the aspirations and ideals of the state and those who do not. Part of what determines political loyalties in Africa is the geography of independence. The landlocked nations of West Africa were created with the aid of a ruler, with straight lines scored across the map, especially across the desert where no rivers could mark natural boundaries. New frontiers were established on a land that was previously frontierless. Clearly, not all Tuaregs recognize the authority of these historically recent state boundaries. When I asked one herdsman what nationality he belonged to, he replied, "Our territory is included within four states." To survive in the sparse desert requires a pattern of transhumance that crosses several state borders—in this case, as far as

I can gather, Mali, Algeria, Niger, and Chad. The loyalties and laws of the new nation-states are at odds with the subsistence requirements and mobility patterns of desert nomads. The project of national construction does not seem to include the possibility of regional transnationalism or standoffish "a-nationalism."[21] The resulting policies of containment and assimilation mirror those imposed upon indigenous peoples in many parts of the world where mobile ways of life were predicated upon differences inconvenient to nation-states. Marginalization often proceeded with the same inexorability in the independent postcolonial states as in the "successful" colonies transplanted onto the Americas, Australia, and New Zealand.

I went to the Republic of Mali in 1984 with the impetuous enthusiasm of a doctoral candidate in social anthropology from Cambridge University. It did not occur to me then that I would encounter a social entity called an "indigenous people." During the ten months I spent in Gao, a remote administrative town of thirty thousand in northeast Mali, this category of people entered my world through the back door. Even then, the Tuaregs had not yet developed their own status as "indigenous." My original purpose was to study Arabic literacy among the Songhay, the agriculturalists living along the shores of the Niger River. I soon discovered a flourishing Islamic reform movement in the Songhay villages with (in retrospect) many points of similarity with the better-known Taliban of Afghanistan. My goal as a researcher was to scrupulously avoid the picturesque, to portray the impact of reformist Islam on a society usually described as "pagan," to understand a religious force that was portrayed in the ethnographic literature as either culturally destructive or overlooked because it was as ubiquitous as sand. The Tuaregs, by contrast, were picturesque. It was the Moors who fired Saint-Exupéry's imagination in *Wind, Sand and Stars* (1939), and a Bedouin who rescued him and his mechanic when they crashed in the Libyan desert, but a Tuareg would have had the same mysterious effect. During colonial rule, the French mythologized the desert nomads. At the same time, they hunted and executed their recalcitrant leaders. And because these people were so inherently fascinating, they didn't interest me in the least.

This, at least, was my early way of thinking. Things changed when

I made the decision to hire a Tuareg (an instructor in the local *lycée*) as my Songhay translator (who, not atypically, was fluent in French and three African languages) so as to avoid the friction that would inevitably have occurred if a Songhay had accompanied me to the factionalized villages. Ibrahim ag Muhammad, without my being aware of it, taught me a great deal about what it meant to be Tuareg. At the time, Ibrahim was in his mid-twenties but looked older, his light frame made more ample by a turban and the folds and billows of his clothing. He was familiar with French literature and talked about the possibility of immigrating to France, but he had never been there, never having earned enough money to travel. In some ways he was staunchly conservative. At twenty-one he had married a twelve-year-old girl and was disappointed that, despite their efforts, they were unable to produce a child until she was sixteen. He dismissed my congratulations when his wife gave birth to a daughter.

Ibrahim and I often exchanged thoughts and stories. He asked me once, for example, what snow was like. I told him a little about being a child in a small town in British Columbia's Rocky Mountains where in winter the tiny crystals of frozen water were piled higher than a man's head. It really wasn't cold if you dressed warmly, and could actually be fun with a sled or toboggan, sliding down the slopes of snow-covered hills.

He, in turn, told me stories of survival that showed the harsh side of life in the desert. One of his uncles, while riding alone from one camp to another, was unexpectedly thrown from his camel. When he got up, the camel skittered away, not letting him take the bridle. Every time he approached it, no matter how stealthily, the camel shied and trotted out of reach. He spent the entire night trying to get control of his beast, to no avail. Eventually, he ran out of water. With midday temperatures reaching 130° Fahrenheit, he knew he would soon die. In desperation, he found a suitably sized rock, stalked the camel as before, and, rather than lunge for the reins, hit it on the side of the head, killing it. He subsisted on the camel for two weeks, drinking its blood, roasting its meat, and crawling inside the carcass during the day to shade himself from the sun. He was found that way by a group of fellow Tuaregs, curled up inside the desiccated rib cage of his once-unbiddable camel.

I was also brought closer to the lives of the nomads by an Africa-wide cataclysm. There was no way to predict before I set foot in Gao that the rains would be reluctant and desultory for the second year in a row. When it did rain early in the season I was cheerfully optimistic, in keeping with the children laughing, dancing, and splashing under gutter spouts, and didn't quite understand Ibrahim's obvious lack of enthusiasm as he wet his palm in a downpour, as though not being given the right change. Unfortunately he was right. The rain was just enough to send up shoots that were blasted and scorched by the sun for days on end; the ground was barren by the time the next storm clouds gathered. And if that was not convincing enough as a harbinger of disaster, the desert sent us sandstorms that announced themselves with dust and dry lightning visible on the horizon. Then came walls of sand that swept toward the town with the speed of an avalanche, the tops of the nimbus clouds that generated them barely visible above their rolling crests. The first of the storms caused shouts and screams of panic as people scurried for cover: an enclosed room, a blanket to crawl under, or, if nothing else, a corner to crouch in and pull loose clothing over one's mouth and nose. The storms hit with suffocating darkness, leaving nothing visible, not even one's own hands or feet. Yet, like almost all disasters, the drought progressed with an air of normality. As the darkness of the fourth storm cleared into an orange-brown haze, there appeared in the street the silhouettes of young men, laughing and smoking with affected unconcern.

Soon the nomads came in from the desert. Most came on foot. Others, especially women, rode donkeys, some with young children swathed in dusty scarves. Only a few men came on camels. The abattoir filled to capacity with bony cattle, the surviving remnants of herds rushed to market and sold for a fraction of their normal value.[22] Conical hide tents appeared on the outskirts of town, and soon there was a disaster-relief village serviced by the White Fathers, Médecins sans Frontières ("Doctors without Borders"), and the Red Cross. Still, the nomads and villagers died by the thousands. There were no airlifts of food. Relief had to wait for international awareness and sympathy, and once the sacks of rice arrived at the docks of Abidjan and Accra, they had to be hauled overland by truck. The drivers, to make more money, often overloaded their vehicles and broke down on the unpaved northern route from Mopti to Gao.

It was a globally public catastrophe. Television outlets vied to find locations that best illustrated a disaster that encompassed almost the entire sub-Saharan region, and Gao was one of them. I once saw a well-known national newscaster from the United States, on her way from getting a municipal visa at the police station, struggling in the sandy street, surrounded by children tugging at her clothes, shouting "Anasara! Anasara! Donne moi cinq francs [give me five francs]!"[23] A while later I saw a Tuareg man, unsteady in the same manner but from exhaustion rather than inexperience, holding a child of indeterminate age, sunken-eyed and skeletal, with the fixed death-smile of one whose starvation has gone beyond the point of recovery. This was the image the media came to collect.

The developed world responded with an unprecedented outpouring of generosity. In the time before compassion fatigue, Africa was in a crisis that called for checks, food drives, and benefit concerts. The sympathy and relief funds that resulted saved countless lives. But, unknown to most donors, once the immediate crisis was over, many of these funds were used in a way that assumed the nomadic way of life was a thing of the past. "Progress" required that the nomads learn to farm.[24]

This was nothing new. For centuries overgrazing and climactic fluctuation in the desert periodically forced the nomads into the agricultural zones of the Sahel and in at least one instance led to a group's voluntary agricultural sedentarization (Maïga 1997: 164). Under French colonial government the first attempt, not to impose agriculture, but to contain the nomads, was put into effect in 1908, with a requirement of official authorization *(laissez-passer)* for movement from one administrative region to another. It was largely ignored by the nomads and certainly had little effect on their willingness, or lack of it, to farm.

Since independence, two successive governments tried to implement policies of sedentarization in one form or another. In 1963 the Marxist-oriented government of Modibo Kieta tried to directly legislate the settlement of nomads into riverine villages, a policy that sparked a revolt among the Tuaregs of the *Adrar des Iforas,* the desert region north of Gao. Troops were sent from Mali's capital, Bamako, to suppress the revolt, and order was restored only when the Tuaregs found they could escape across the Algerian border, out of range even of air attacks, well into the inhospitable desert (Lusignan 1969: 245).

The government of Moussa Traore, which took power in 1968, was the first Malian regime to use drought as a means to sedentarize the nomads. The drought that lasted through the early 1970s brought the nomads under political control, temporarily at least. With their cattle decimated and the government handling the distribution of food aid, the Tuaregs were in no position to resist efforts to settle them in villages (Decraene 1980: 85). This scenario was to repeat itself in the 1983–1985 drought, when instruction programs were set up to encourage young Tuareg men to take up farming, an occupation they usually disdained as "unmanly."

The Tuaregs consider themselves superior to the black administrators from the south, who came to dominate them through a process of decolonization and nation building that the desert peoples do not fully acknowledge. In precolonial times (almost within living memory), the Tuaregs collected tribute, usually in the form of millet and rice, from the Songhay and sedentary Fulani who farmed the alluvial plains of the Niger. And, from the Tuareg perspective, the farming peoples further to the south were equally their social inferiors. These, especially the Bambara, are now seen as the ethnic source of the powers of state.

Earlier, under the French, different methods of settlement were used. Once the last armed resistance to colonial rule was suppressed, the French set about educating the Africans, to make them "citizens" of the empire. Colonial education in French West Africa was consistent with the general goal of promoting Western values. The central goal of education was to make the schools a medium for the transmission of French language, culture, and "civilization." Secondarily, the schools were meant to train local auxiliaries, clerks, telephonists, and others to contribute to the functioning of colonial administrations. The model for this enterprise was naturally the educational system in France. The language of instruction was almost exclusively French, and pupils were given a literary and scientific education that differed little from that provided to children in France (Hiskett 1984: 293). This was especially true after 1946, when an educational reform reduced the adaptation of colonial schools to local conditions and cultures with the introduction of standardized metropolitan classical curricula aimed at assimilating students into French culture. One of the phrases in French recited by African students translates as "Our ancestors the Gauls were blond."[25]

Although some benefited from their education and achieved lower-level positions in the colonial administration and prominence in the independent state, French education was not an unmixed blessing, especially for rural peoples, who saw it as challenging their identity and sovereignty. Soon after the first independent government took power in Mali in 1960, an education policy was introduced that had much the same effect as that implemented by the French. An "education of quality, for the masses" was introduced, together with an economic five-year plan intended to bring about agricultural modernization and prosperity. Recruitment on a massive scale took many children away from Quran schools, which had provided traditional Islamic education based on rote memorization of the Quran, and into government schools, now opening their doors even in remote villages and semipermanent Tuareg encampments. By 1965, over six hundred new schools had begun teaching the rudiments of French for administrators and good citizens.

Despite more recent efforts to change school curriculums to make them more compatible with the lifestyles of rural students, national education still aims to teach skills, principally literacy in French, that are not essential to a subsistence economy and that presuppose involvement with, or in, the national economy and administration. And even a rural state curriculum cannot surpass the usual transmission of knowledge by watching and doing. The form of education that trains children out of their way of life, without allowing them to reach high standards in French, is seen by many nomads and villagers as nothing less than an effort to settle and control them by taking away the skills that help them survive.

State education is an anathema to mobile communities even more than to sedentary villagers. It imposes a choice of settlement and renunciation of migratory subsistence or separation from children and loss of the ability to transmit skills and knowledge to them. But rarely is the conundrum quite so stark. Noble Tuareg families managed to ease the transitions demanded by French education policy by sending the children of slaves or "commoner" classes to meet school quotas. They also sent their daughters more readily than sons, with the result that those qualified for administrative positions and political offices are today often women.

If formal education has turned out to have certain advantages, other political challenges to the survival of the nomads are more immediate and sinister. In Mali, Songhay militants, originating from the agricultural villages along the Niger River, have formed a movement called Ganda Koy, proclaiming themselves "masters of the earth" and overtly advocating the extermination of "white" Tuaregs and Moors. The fact that these nomadic groups once exacted tribute from the villages along the Niger and sometimes swept in from the desert to take by force what they needed or wanted might explain, but can hardly excuse, the Ganda Koy's more recent promulgation of racial antipathy and violence. In language strikingly reminiscent of European hate literature, they stigmatize the Tuaregs in terms of weakness, as "errant populations, without nationality, without a State, coming from the desert in miniscule tribes" (cited in Baqué 1995: 30) or as more forceful, dangerous opponents in descriptions that harken back to the not-so-distant days of village raids: "armed rebel-bandits . . . [and] slave raiders. Banditry is the normal state of being for a Tamashek" (30). The conclusion reached in Ganda Koy literature, expressed in an ominous mixed metaphor, is that the Tuaregs "are a foreign body in the social fabric" (30). Largely because of such hate, the Accord de Tamanrasset, a 1991 treaty between the desert tribes and the Malian government that provided the Tuaregs with regional autonomy, was scuttled. A similar 1992 peace agreement, the Pact National, avoided controversial reference to the term "autonomy" but was still widely seen by sedentary populations as accommodating the demands of Tuareg rebels and remains largely unimplemented (United Nations 2001: 8). Ganda Koy activists initiated massacres of Tuareg families living in urban centers. (One method of killing reported to me was by hand grenades tossed into crowded sleeping quarters.) Not all Tuaregs remained passive throughout this escalating interethnic violence. Some armed Tuareg groups initiated killings and abductions of civilians and government officials, including murders of those supporting rival Tuareg factions.[26]

Malian security forces responded brutally to Tuareg insurgency. When the Tuaregs staged an uprising in 1990, launching attacks on government officials and security forces in the northeast, the government initiated severe reprisals against the Tuareg community. According to Amnesty International (1991), "[A]rmy units attacked encampments, beat, raped or killed the inhabitants, and destroyed property. . . . In Gao, about a dozen

Tuareg men and one woman were said to have been publicly shot by firing-squad near the airport . . . after which their bodies were mutilated by onlookers and crushed by an armoured vehicle" (152). Between April and June 1994, more than six hundred extrajudicial executions of nomads took place in Timbuktu. This was a prelude to further warfare and systematic killings in the neighboring region of Gao (Baqué 1995: 30). These were the same herdsmen I had encountered in the 1980s whose cattle were dying and who had no other recourse than to gather their families in hivelike camps of hide tents, waiting, starving, for food aid to arrive. I described this experience to a Tuareg delegate representing the Tin Hinan at a meeting in Geneva. She listened without visible emotion, then remarked dryly: "When you were in Gao, we were dying of hunger. When I was there a few years later, we were being shot."

Even the most drastic measures to settle the nomads have ultimately been unavailing. The Sahara is a frontier almost impossible for states to control. The desert nomads live in a realm of largely imaginary borders, mere lines on a map that translate only partially and temporarily into legal reality. The miragelike evanescence of state control makes it possible for nomads to exercise their self-determination to a degree impossible for some states to either accept or eliminate.

More than anything else, attempts by the state to impose control and social change result in misery. But the course of Tuareg suffering during the past century of colonization and state marginalization has created the possibility of their identification with indigenous peoples elsewhere in the world.

Various attempts have been made to restrict their mobility, and hence their political autonomy, to make them better citizens of the state in ways that parallel the historical experiences of many indigenous peoples. The French fought and largely prevailed over them militarily and then educationally. The Malian government has since, in addition to developing French-language uniformity and military control (with occasional eruptions of punitive violence), added agricultural settlement to the policies designed to patriate and patriotize the nomads. This has given the Tuaregs, despite or in addition to their Muslim identity, a quintessentially indigenous history.

The grievances the Tuaregs have with states are thus consistent with those of many other indigenous peoples: state-sanctioned violence, forced settlement, loss of language, loss of territory, loss of identity. The Tuaregs seek the protection of their own means of subsistence, language, political autonomy, and control over the territories they and their ancestors have long inhabited. Their historical qualifications for participation in the indigenous peoples' movement make the distinctions sometimes drawn between indigenous and tribal societies seem superficial and meaningless. The ambitions of the state in attempting to create a coherent national culture and the simultaneous development of indigenous activism have each in different ways made such indigenous self-identity possible.

Although the Tuaregs have recently taken up indigenous identity and activism, we cannot expect to see concrete results from this for some time to come, if ever.[27] Securing their way of life will require not only a political change of direction on the part of states such as Mali and Niger and a change of attitude, toward tolerance, on the part of the Tuaregs' hostile neighbors but also the regional accomplishment of these changes, across state boundaries. The nomadism they seek to protect is as vast as the obstacles that confront it.

THE FOUNDATIONS OF INDIGENOUS IDENTITY

Comparing the vulnerabilities and grievances of indigenous peoples in northern Canada and Africa is one of the ways to describe the new identity based on indigenous activism. The comparison of such widely differing peoples winnows away those features that don't truly belong, leaving us with a digestible kernel, something that tells us the essence of how indigenous peoples, as an international community, are defining themselves.

Several decades ago, such a comparison would not have made sense. The Tuaregs of the West African Sahara and the Crees of northern Canada would have had little or nothing in common. One is a nomadic pastoral people of the desert and arid savannah, the other a hunting, fishing, and gathering people of the northern boreal forest. One is a people with rigid class distinctions and with chiefs drawn from a nobility, the other an egalitarian society with a tradition of leadership based on hunting skill. One is a people in conflict with governments that are ready to use deadly force to restrict their mobility and their suprastate exercise of self-determination; the other is in conflict with a liberal democracy subject to embarrassment and public censure for the unnecessary use of force. Even the range of temperature difference between the desert in the hot season and the northern boreal forest in winter is roughly equivalent to the difference between the freezing and boiling points.

Yet in recent years these two groups have somehow come together in the same meetings under the same rubric: as indigenous peoples. Under these circumstances the basic common features of their histories become more important than the contrasts of environment, subsistence, social structure, and politics. When we look for the things that indigenous peoples have in common, for what brings them together and reinforces their common identity, we find patterns that emerge from the logic of conquest and colonialism. These patterns apply equally to peoples otherwise very different in terms of history, geography, method of subsistence, social structure, and political organization. They are similarities based largely on the relationship between indigenous peoples and states. Of course, there is great variety in state behavior toward the distinct original societies within their borders; but whatever the specific arrangement, policy, or action pursued by states, it usually falls into one of three categories that arise almost naturally from the ways indigenous cultures are perceived within the policy-influencing sectors of a dominant society: assimilative state education, loss of subsistence, and state abrogation of treaties.

The most widely used mechanism of cultural reformatting among indigenous peoples, and the source of both common collective grievance and the technical abilities of leadership, has been compulsory *assimilative state education*. The global nature of this phenomenon is striking. Indigenous people from far-flung states and hemispheres understand what it means to be subject to efforts to remove their natal culture and language in an alien school environment. They often share experiences of abuse that stem from institutional control over children who are both powerless and seen to be socially inferior or defective. Direct or indirect efforts to absorb other societies have also included legislation against spiritual practices, desecration of graves and sacred sites, removal of artifacts (usually to be placed in museums), imposition of unwanted resource extraction, and imposed change to medical knowledge and practice, including the use of medical institutions as a source of both curing and cultural transformation.

The Crees and Tuaregs share the annexation of knowledge by formal state education. The French colonial experience was, surprisingly, less traumatic than missionary residential education among Canada's aboriginal peoples, but the objective was similar: to uniformly distribute the skills and knowledge needed to make "useful" citizens of those whose differences would otherwise represent multiplicity and the ever-present possibility of dissent. State education, more than the first uses of colonial force, was an exercise in pacification.

State education has similar effects among all peoples with subsistence economies.[28] Most immediately, it interrupts mobility among those who pursue game or pasture. It competes with oral knowledge, the primacy of myth, and the authority of elders. Loss of language contributes to loss of ability to describe the world and express emotion. Words describing natural phenomena in an apparently plain and direct way are, for fluent speakers, redolent with meaning and affect. Such words are absent from the truncated vocabularies of those raised in villages, who are fluent in the basic language but untutored in its nuances. Only the lucky few have had the opportunity to learn from elders, the dons of the forest, steppe, or desert, whose linguistic skill separates them from literate villagers as much as Latin separated the medieval clerics from their parishioners.

It would at first seem that the decline of such knowledge would result in a natural and gradual cultural slide in the direction of global convergence as people everywhere came under the influence of literacy and state education. Are all peoples soon to resemble one another in their uses of writing and bureaucracy, differing only in the outward expressions of language and reified custom? This is among the most pressing sociological questions of our age, and one for which the rise of indigenous identity provides at least part of the answer.

Ernest Gellner, in *Nations and Nationalism* (1983), argues that school-transmitted culture is the institutional centerpiece of nation-states, the main source of social mobility and cultural integrity in industrial society. "Exo-socialization, education proper, is now the virtually universal norm," he writes. "Men acquire the skills and sensibilities which make them acceptable to their fellows, which fit them to assume places in society, and which make them 'what they are,' by being handed over by their kin groups . . . to an educational machine which alone is capable of providing the wide range of training required for the generic cultural base" (37). As outlined in this passage, Gellner's model is more prediction than actuality, especially when we go beyond the few contemporary industrial powers and consider those times and places in which states are struggling to achieve educational control and uniformity. These are the contested zones of nation building in which the ethos of oral iteration and subsistence technologies overlap with the homogenizing educational ambitions of nation-states.

Among the world's indigenous peoples, state education has tended to be brutal and traumatic, imposing drastic transformations of collective knowledge, social arrangements, and identities. But it remains incomplete and contested. It has, contrary to Gellner's model, created the skills and conditions for marginalized "folk cultures" to resist state-sponsored nationalism and administrative control. A central paradox of modernity is the way that formal education, technology, and bureaucratic methods have shaped and sharpened social differences, resulting in more effective assertions of distinctiveness than ever before.

The desert nomads and hunting peoples of the boreal forest have both, in varying degrees, experienced a *loss of subsistence.* Among the nomads, this loss took the form of natural disaster—to good Muslims with an intact theodicy, this was an obvious manifestation of divine power. Grievance arose, however, when the state colluded with the dry winds from the desert to settle the nomads in permanent villages, to make farmers of them. Agriculturalists are always easier to manage than those who can leave, taking their herds with them, if they don't like the way they're being treated.

The way the nomads experienced imposed changes to their subsistence is unusual, taking the form of slow accretions of drought and settlement policies that have largely been resisted. Even ethnic and state-sanctioned violence has not entirely broken their means or their will to live in the desert. For many others, the shared history and experience of subsistence decline is more immediate. Almost all indigenous peoples worldwide face situations in which extractive industries, based on such activities as logging, mining, and harnessing the hydroelectric potential of great rivers, continue to erode the viability of subsistence economies, contributing to the social pathologies of dislocation without extending to these peoples the full benefits of ownership, revenue sharing, or employment.

This has important implications for indigenous governance. Subsistence on the land, for indigenous peoples, is the most important source of autonomy and power. Removing a people's control over the land, even while granting political freedoms, is a recipe for regional despotism. To give a people their own constitution, their own institutions, and their own forms of democracy, with no control over subsistence or local industry, creates conditions favorable to an insidious form of dependency, in which the only way for leaders to exercise power is to control and exploit the people themselves.

A final category of behavior toward indigenous peoples of widely varying cultures and regions has been *state abrogation of treaties*. Often states have dealt with the differences asserted by indigenous peoples by protecting their distinctiveness and recognizing their sovereignty through treaties, agreements, legislation, and/or constitutional reform. States are usually brought into their treaties and agreements with indigenous peoples unwillingly, against material (industrial) interests, against the drive toward constitutional integrity and uniformity, and against currents of populist intolerance. They are compelled to negotiate constructive arrangements with indigenous peoples because the circumstances of colonial encounter present state policy makers with civil unrest, violent repression, and, sometimes, genocidal destruction as the other alternatives. Once the state rejects the options of war and genocide as means of occupying the land, it must come to some form of accommodation with the original inhabitants. Treaties were a common way of reaching this accommodation, although a trust relationship could develop through less formalized policy actions.

Even those treaties negotiated when indigenous societies were at their weakest—dominated militarily, decimated by disease, no longer in control of subsistence and thus subject to starvation—were still built upon recognition of their status as self-determining and distinct. It is possible to remove a people from their land, isolate them in "reservations" or "homelands," and still recognize their differences and rights to self-determination. In more recent years, agreements between states and indigenous peoples, such as the James Bay and Northern Québec Agreement, the Nunavut Agreement, and even the Accord de Tamanrasset (had it been honored), have tended to go further into the details of regional autonomy and protections of cultural difference than, say, Canada's numbered treaties or other land surrenders of the nineteenth and early twentieth centuries. But all are based upon the understanding that those negotiating the terms of the document being offered or imposed by the state represent distinct societies and have rights that are different from those of ordinary citizens. Whatever they may surrender, yield, cede, or render to the state (including their political rights), the entire process is premised upon a mutual recognition of sovereignty.

Special rights, such as those built into the Accord de Tamanrasset and the NFA, exist largely because a people or sector of society faces extraordinary obstacles to prosperity. These rights do not stand in the way of comparable living standards for all citizens; they are a means toward it. Yet the tendency of many states has been to limit, diminish, and extinguish the distinct rights of aboriginal peoples. This is yet another source of common experience, unity, and identity among indigenous peoples and organizations.

Despite the development of "modern" treaties and agreements between indigenous peoples and states, the most significant sources of indigenous identity are broken promises, intolerance, and efforts to eliminate cultural distinctiveness or the very people that represent difference. Ethnic cleansing becomes an actuality or latent possibility when a minority people are seen to be significantly obstructing the unity and prosperity of the dominant society: claiming title to land that could be better used; practicing faiths laden with error and malignant powers; insisting upon maintaining traditions that contrast with those of the standard bearers of nationhood; and, by virtue of these differences, competing for political representation and power as a distinct society—such perceived faults lead to a general view of minority people as an obstacle to unity and collective self-actualization by those with power over them. More significantly, the minority is seen as somehow beyond the possibility of reform, unchangeable, stubborn, or, even when "properly" educated, subject to cultural recidivism.

With such perceptions as a starting point, dominant peoples, especially in frontier societies where there is competition over resources, sometimes assert their identities and interests by eliminating, one way or another, the weaker people who stand in their way. Such "cleansing" has taken a variety of forms, including forced expulsion, imposed hunger, and mass killing. The goal of total removal is inseparable from the idea, itself a companion of collective hate, that a subject population cannot be separated from its attachments to cultural differences and assertions of sovereignty. Ethnocide, by contrast, stems from the prevailing notion that cultures are malleable, that entire peoples are capable of guided transformation and therefore that inconvenient or threatening attachments to differences can be peacefully disposed of through strategies of cultural reform.

These basic approaches to eliminating cultural differences are not mutually exclusive. Ethnic cleansing and ethnocide can in fact be seen as complementary, since their main difference is that one has the goal of eliminating a people whereas the other has the goal of removing those features that make them distinct. But it is important also to keep in mind that colonial powers or dominant ethnic groups are not always politically homogeneous or coordinated in their actions, interests, and objectives. State governments can be perfectly willing to negotiate treaties with their indigenous inhabitants—or, more correctly, "neighbors"—while settlers are bent upon their extinction. It is thus conceivable, and realized on a number of occasions, that the sovereignty of indigenous societies can be affirmed through a treaty-making process at the same time that policies are put into effect to remove their cultural differences, all the while that they are being forced onto reservations or starved into submission or that frontiersmen are waging open warfare against them with impunity.

The category "indigenous peoples" has thus flourished through the combination of a broad legal definition of a nondominant form of society with global patterns (or their historical residues) of invasion, occupation, imposed cultural change, and political marginalization. The comparison made in this chapter of an aboriginal people in Canada and one of the recently emerged indigenous peoples of Africa reveals the ability of human rights processes to forge new identities, unifying those from disparate regions who experience the widest conceivable differences in their relationships with state governments and who are attached to widely divergent social formations and subsistence patterns. As I will discuss in chapters 4 and 5, their common identity is also based on what they hope to achieve in international forums—above all, formal recognition from states and interstate governing bodies of their experience of human rights abuses under existing international law and the need to enshrine their rights to self-determination as "peoples" in emerging human rights standards.

4 Relativism and Rights

This chapter deals with the two most important theoretical/philosophi-
cal problems facing the human rights movement: relativism and collective rights. The two are closely related. If we profess the relativist idea of
cultural contingency in moral standards, and conversely reject any form
of ethical universality, we are likely also to support the notion that discrete societies are themselves the best source of values, guidance, and
growth for individuals. Collective rights are an obvious corollary because cultures, as the collective embodiment of the most important human values, cannot be protected any better way. If, on the other hand, we
admit to a universal code of ethics, one that transcends all cultures, times,

and places, we become more interested in protecting individuals, making cultural affiliation a matter of choice, a product of individuals expressing themselves in freedom.

The indigenous peoples' movement, as the embodiment of human differences in action, forces us to confront these issues directly. Collective/ individual rights are a legal policy outcome of one's position on cultural relativism, an outcome that is even now being contested, with the political and economic stakes increasing, in efforts to set human rights standards for indigenous peoples.

To properly handle these issues, I have separated the legal and policy implications of collective rights from the more philosophical and, in practical terms, insoluble questions posed by relativism. But my arguments concerning relativism and rights are in many ways parallel and arrive at almost the same destination.

THE UNIVERSALITY OF UNIVERSAL HUMAN RIGHTS

The development of human rights standards represents an effort to achieve a universally applicable morality. This is to be accomplished, not through revolution or revelation (in fact the project struggles against some of the tenaciously held precepts of revealed religions), but through wide consultation, with a backdrop of bureaucracy and law. It is an extraordinarily routine and bland foundation for morality, arrived at through the consensus opinions (in so far as these are possible) of officials. For this reason, it actually stands a chance of success. Revelation and charisma thrive upon opposition and, while occasionally appealing to hundreds of millions, cannot universalize the harvest of souls, especially not where rival faiths present resistance and counterevangelism. The advantage of the universal human rights code of social conduct is that it is based, in principle, upon broad consensus and does not inspire the kind of exclusivism and hatreds so characteristic of religions. It is an effort to find a conceptual and moral orderliness out of the chaos of globalized differences, through structured consensus rather than the auto-da-fé or sword of truth. Its disadvantage is that without the sanction of spiritual devotion, it fails to inspire loyalty and conviction. Unlike other visions of universal, secular morality—implemented without success (in fact with descents into horror) in the French and Russian Revolutions—the human rights movement proceeds bureaucratically and without revolutionary passion. One can attribute both the success and limitations of human rights universalism to the fact that it functions through the pedantry of jurists, diplomats, and administrators rather than though the heightened emotion of prophecy. It has no place for saints, prophets, or revolutionaries. The information on which the most important discussions are based is gathered, collated, and presented by "technical experts." It is an attempt to achieve a morality beyond culture and religion, based on a system of knowledge that transcends both morality *and* culture. It represents an extension of the consensual foundation of scientific knowledge into the realm of ethics. It is therefore, for some, a rational source of moral consolation. It is the focal point of a vast array of noble aspirations: the liberation of racial minorities and women from discrimination and abuse and of children from suffering and exploitation; an end to religious and ethnic intolerance and violence; an end to torture, political oppression, and genocide; and an end to the marginalization and extinction of indigenous peoples. For some, separated from the moral untidiness of lobbying and the palace intrigues of international organizations, it is a source of extravagant hope.

But, like all universal systems of ethics, the human rights movement has its critics. There were many who objected to the Universal Declaration of Human Rights when it first appeared in 1948, saying that it did not truly represent all human expressions of social good and rightful conduct. The guiding hand of Eleanor Roosevelt, who chaired the drafting committee, was, they said, too firm and inflexible, above all in the Universal Declaration's adherence to representative democracy and its liberal emphasis on individual rights. Some state governments, particularly from Asia, have claimed that a right to development and economic progress should take precedence over free speech and democratic development, that a people cannot be free until they are fed, and that firm political control is the first requirement of prosperity. In their view, the priorities and limited scope of human rights are yet another form of imperialist arrogance.[1]

Defenders of human rights instruments occasionally point to the broad consultations involved in the drafting process, which, in the case of the Universal Declaration, went far beyond the core group of seven experts from different nationalities and religious backgrounds to include many contributors petitioned for their opinions and others whose submitted views were duly considered. The claim that human rights are not universally inclusive and legitimate is, according to some of their defenders, merely self-interested posturing, concerned not with rights but with regime maintenance, and not with development but with the personal interests of officials (Donnelly 1989: 189).

The process of setting the early human rights standards does, however, seem to have left one category of human society almost entirely out of the picture: oral societies in which communication only occasionally reaches far beyond natal groups or villages, and rarely beyond their territories of islands, tundra, forest, or desert. In the mid-twentieth century, when the United Nations was a new beginning for structured internationalism, before the accelerating influence of new technologies of transport and communication had reached into every corner of the globe, such societies were much more common. None of the representatives consulted for input into human rights instruments were from exclusively oral societies; all were from societies long accustomed to bureaucracy and law. This divide, by its very nature, did not make itself felt until indigenous peoples strove for recognition in international forums.

This feature of representation and of limits to inclusion in the drafting of human rights instruments again raises the question of the universality of universal human rights. Is the International Bill of Human Rights consistent with oral societies? Do oral societies need to change, in particular to develop literacy and formal education, in order to benefit from its protections and conform to its standards? And does this, in turn, imply the loss of a form of life—an end to myth and the wisdom of elders, to nurturing and socialization beyond the reach of states, an end also to the comfortable, narrow suspicion of strangers, the prejudices of closed societies?

When we begin to think about applying universal human rights to indigenous societies, we are thus immediately faced with a number of potentially far-reaching dilemmas. It is by no means universally agreed that indigenous peoples' claims to self-determination and other human rights are valid or worth the political sacrifice of supporting, but let us assume for the moment that, through a combination of political will and serendipity, indigenous peoples did receive the recognition many are seeking. Let us imagine them as being suddenly in a position of having their goals realized, their wishes granted, their claim to self-determination recognized, their rights to land affirmed and honored, their struggle against racism proactively supported, their health needs met, their fair share of prosperity assured. Would this be the end of human rights questions as they applied to indigenous peoples? No, because we can assume that, as self-governing peoples, they would be in many ways responsible for upholding the human rights of their own people.[2] Their share of responsibility would be determined in large measure by the specific constitutional arrangements they had with states, but responsibility would be there, in increasing measure as they became more autonomous.

This is the point at which dilemmas, ambiguities, and trade-offs begin. I remember sitting in a kitchen in Mistassini, Québec, as an elderly Cree woman told me about how she met her husband. She was at the river cleaning fish when her father called to her, telling her she had a visitor. She clambered up the bank and was introduced to a young man she had met several times as a child, the son of one of her father's hunting partners. Her mother and father explained solemnly that she was to marry him. A brief ceremony was performed on the spot, and the couple was joined. "That was my wedding dress," she said, "all covered with fish blood." The authority of elders in arranging marriages, and controlling the lives of junior family and community members, is a very widely distributed feature of what are variously called oral, subsistence-based, or kin-based societies. The Universal Declaration of Human Rights, with its emphasis on individual protections, opposes such exercise of authority, as in Article 16(2): "Marriage shall be entered into only with the free and full consent of the intending spouses." Does this imply that human rights for indigenous peoples mean more than protection from the state? Do human rights, in fact, imply dissolution of many features of indigenous societies widely seen as "traditional" and as the foundations of distinctive identities? And if human rights are vigorously implemented in a way that stretches the elastic limits of social change, does this not, in another form, reflect the assimilation policies that indigenous peoples are sworn to resist?

Matters are further complicated by the denial of basic rights on the part of some indigenous societies in ways that show more likeness to tyranny than attachment to tradition. While living in Cross Lake, I returned home from an errand to find my wife hosting a volunteer aid worker, whom I knew to have long experience in Asia and the Middle East, together with five women visiting from another Cree community, who were introduced to me as "dissidents." Through much of the afternoon they talked about their loss of rights in their own community, how their chief and council had effectively imposed control on all forms of political expression, how their campaign posters in a recent referendum were torn down by band employees as soon as they went up, how they were denied access to the local radio station to express their views, and how band members who opposed the "ruling party" were evicted from their homes, fired from their jobs, denied band membership, and physically intimidated. A band employee who had been especially active in publicly opposing the policies of his chief and council returned home from an absence of several days to find all his belongings jumbled outside, and his house, officially owned by the band, boarded up. The aid worker added her own observation: "It sounds like Burma, without the tanks." A national aboriginal grassroots organization, the Accountability Coalition, by assembling numerous letters of complaint and petitions from across Canada, has confirmed the pervasiveness of band council corruption and rights violations in many (though by no means all) aboriginal communities, yet there is no remedy for their actions, supported as they are by the Indian Act and the federal government's understandable reluctance to interfere in "self-governing" aboriginal communities. How can the denial of civil and political rights usefully be distinguished from "traditional" human rights violations? If, in principle, one kind of individual freedom is defended against the abuses of indigenous governments, can we avoid the more sweeping application of human rights?

The advent of indigenous village-states challenges value-neutral, relativistic approaches to cultural differences. Indigenous societies are more often adopting such things as written constitutions, formal electoral procedures, and pursuit of claims in international forums. But cultural relativism can contribute to a kind of residual political inhibition and vacuum of accountability. Under circumstances of (sometimes forced) political assimilation with nation-states, but without encouragement of civil liberties to provide a restless, creative, and unrestrained opposition, indigenous despotism can prosper; and relativism provides it with a made-to-order sanctuary.

PROBLEMATIZING RELATIVISM

Anthropologists have sometimes been vocal advocates of the particular communities in which, over periods often extending into many years, they developed relationships, and more than one court decision has gone against native plaintiffs in part because of the supposedly biased testimony of sympathetic ethnographers. One arrives almost automatically at the expectation that anthropologists would easily and without qualms work toward the development of human rights standards for the protection and prosperity of indigenous peoples, their research subjects.

In fact, some anthropologists have done so willingly and even with great conviction. But there is by no means a consensus among them that the human rights movement is worthwhile, or worth devoting one's efforts to. The participation of anthropologists in the human rights agenda has philosophical implications that are not widely recognized, implications that relate to one issue above all others: the possibility of truth and moral judgment in the encounter with (or between) widely divergent cultures. The position taken by most anthropologists, even some who, without reflection, support the human rights agenda, is against universal or dominant paradigms of truth. This issue is one that goes to the heart of current debates about human rights standards, and discussion of it can provide insights that go beyond the mere dominant paradigm of an intellectual discipline.

An association is often made between relativism and the discipline of anthropology. Anthropology has always also accommodated approaches that universalized in one way or another, whether through evolutionism, Marxism, or adherence to Enlightenment ideals of human progress, but in many people's minds to practice social or cultural anthropology means, almost by definition, to take a relativist approach to the question of ethical boundaries; as a cultural or social anthropologist one is expected, in other words, to support the view that there are no universal standards to human behavior, that each culture has its own natural integrity and should not be judged by the standards of another society (usually meaning the West). A textbook definition of anthropology puts this feature of the discipline succinctly: "Anthropologists believe that distinct cultures and lifestyles can only be understood in relation to their unique integrity, and they admonish against trying to judge the behaviors of one group on the basis of the values of another group. Early in their careers, anthropologists are advised to avoid their own ethnocentrism in attempting to understand the ways in which other people manage their lives" (Chambers 1985: 3). Cultural relativism is thus a salient part of the apprentice anthropologist's intellectual socialization.

This has by no means always been the case. Anthropology can be traced to the socioevolutionism of the nineteenth century, influenced significantly by the vision of human societies progressing through "stages" toward advanced industrial civilization. "Progress" in technology and industry was also widely associated with moral improvement. Non-Western societies were not always blamed for their backwardness, but for even those nineteenth-century ethnologists who reveled in human diversity, the sad fact was that so-called primitive societies were simply unequipped to make the kind of choices that would allow them to compete with civilized people. Their demise was therefore imminent. For Tylor and Frazer (and, in the early twentieth century, Lévy-Bruhl) they lacked essential concepts and had not developed a rational logic. For Morgan and Maine, it was more the undeveloped state of legal, social (mainly via kinship), and political institutions that helped us to understand human differences and, to some extent, the moral superiority of civilized societies.

Relativism in anthropology—guided by the notions that there are no universally applicable standards of human conduct and that, conversely, cultures or societies must be viewed in context with an appreciation of human variety and complexity—is usually understood to take one form only, a general rejection of anything too sweeping in its generality in the face of human differences, but there are in fact two distinct paths taken to arrive at this point, each with different implications for the claims of indigenous peoples. I will refer to them as empirical and self-reflexive relativism.

Empirical relativism emerged early on, starting in the late nineteenth century, in reaction against the evolutionist premise of the superiority of civilization. An American "school" of anthropology sometimes referred to as "historical particularism" rejected evolutionism and pseudoscientific racism, while ennobling fieldwork and ethnographic reporting of small-scale societies. Franz Boas, who led this intellectual movement, began cautiously with a postponement of the effort to find scientifically valid laws of cultural behavior, at least until sufficiently exhaustive and reliable data had been gathered by dedicated field researchers on a sufficient variety of cultures. Premature theoretical paradigms, lacking the proper body of factual knowledge, were inevitably flawed, or worse, socially destructive. The result was radical induction, driven by the conviction that only through description of the variety of human cultures could we ever hope to arrive at any idea of the paths of cultural transmission and the regularities of human history.

Somewhere along the line, the empirical, particularist study of cultures acquired a strongly flavored relativism. Cultures, isolated and reified by anthropological reporting, each had their own integrity, their own worldview, their own way of establishing order in a chaotic universe. Margaret Mead, trained as one of Boas's students at Columbia University, took this a step further and established her popularity in the 1960s with an approach that breathed life into Rousseau's imaginary natural man. A subtext of at least some of her work was that there are people different from ourselves from whom we can learn to live better, simpler, more innocent lives. This gave new nobility to fieldwork, endowing it with a sense of mission: to discover new human differences so that we may benefit not only from the knowledge but also from the cultural wisdom thus acquired.

At the same time, empirical relativism invaded anthropology from other quarters. British social anthropology, in its quest for pattern and order in social arrangements and human thought (with connections between the two) obliquely defended the moral integrity of its human subjects. Malinowski argued with particular conviction that no practice or thought is so strange that it cannot, from an informed perspective, be seen as contributing to social stability and order. This detachment to some extent pervaded British anthropology, even though the unadorned functionalism of Malinowski did not find its way into every nook and cranny. The main current of British social anthropology in midcentury was characterized principally by a steadfast adherence to the goal of scientific thoroughness in ethnography, striving to map the variety of human social worlds and organizational possibilities.[3] This was inconsistent with moral judgment, in much the same way that the research of the entomologist is morally detached from the violence of insects.

Empirical relativism was also part of ethnographic collecting initiated from continental Europe. The French ethnographer Marcel Griaule, for example, after leading a two-year collecting expedition that meandered from one shore of sub-Saharan Africa to the other, settled on the Dogon of the Niger Bend region (in present-day Mali) as his most interesting hosts and proceeded to search for a pan-African cosmology to rival ancient mythology and the Old Testament. His *Conversations with Ogotemmeli* (1977) certainly pointed in that direction, though the extent to which Griaule himself contributed to the final narrative is still in question. The underlying lesson of Griaule's work of ethnographic collection is that the simplest lives are rich in thought, wisdom, and mystery and therefore possess an inherent value at least equal to the moral achievements of the West. French ethnography during the colonial period reveled in a kind of *relativisme pittoresque* in which the value placed on alien cultures largely depended on their originality, richness, and color.

The predominant assumption in each of these schools of ethnology is that a society's moral responsibility increases with power, that relatively powerless societies, the colonized and oppressed, even those as yet unaware that they are colonized and oppressed, should be free from our judgments, and especially from our censure. This assumption does not just arise from benevolence, compassion, or a root-for-the-underdog kind of sympathy, but equally or more often from a hard-headed scientific pragmatism: societies subject to our judgments tend to change themselves accordingly and consequently lower their value as original, untainted specimens of human diversity. To others, more romantically inclined, reformed societies lose their luster of authenticity; but the main premise of all forms of empirical relativism begins with the knowledge value of human diversity.

Empirical relativism, by placing a high value on discrete cultures, was closely associated with the conviction that individuals can best realize their potential through the culture to which they belong. Despite the rational empiricism of most ethnographic research in the immediate post–World War II period, this moral priority given to cultures placed many anthropologists at odds with certain aspects of Enlightenment rationalism, particularly the individual rights tradition that dominates human rights discourse. Melville Herskovits, author of the American Anthropological Association (AAA) 1947 statement on human rights, made an early plea for the inclusion of cultural values in the emerging "Bill of Human Rights": "The individual realizes his personality through his culture, hence respect for individual differences entails respect for cultural difference" (AAA 1947: 541). Hence, any effort to codify a universal system of rights must "take into full account the individual as member of the social group of which he is part, whose sanctioned modes of life shape his behavior, and with whose fate his own is thus inextricably bound" (539). (It is interesting to note that relativism flourished in anthropology just after the twentieth century's darkest time of infamy. One might have expected the opposite: the widespread realization that there *are* universals, that we recognize immorality when we encounter it.) There is a predicament exposed by this unabashed relativism. On the one hand, anthropologists commonly feel a strong impulse to defend their research hosts against the destructive intrusions, and sometimes atrocities, of dominant societies. The strength of their fieldwork attachments makes it difficult not to stand up for their friends. Under these circumstances, who could object to human rights? How can one reject an effort to liberate humanity from the scourge of war and atrocity? On the other hand, universal standards of behavior arising mainly from a tradition in political economy that accords ultimate importance to the individual have every appearance of leaving culture in the cold, perhaps even undermining human variability, and hence the raison d'être of anthropology. Even with a view of culture as "contested, fragmented, contextualized and emergent" (Wilson 1997: 9) (which amounts, ultimately, to a regress of relativisms within cultural relativism), anthropologists who concern themselves with human rights have not found an unambiguous way out of this predicament.

Another trend in anthropology, which leads directly to self-reflexive relativism, has less difficulty with human rights because it rejects them utterly. Boasian anthropology was part, perhaps only a small part, of the varied pedigree that led to postmodernism, the transdisciplinary intellectual movement prevalent in the 1980s and 1990s, and into the new millennium when human rights standards specific to indigenous peoples were being developed. It was also shaped by global politics. Decolonization created ambiguity and challenges to anthropology in several ways: it radically shifted arrangements of power, giving the formerly oppressed new opportunities to oppress in their turn; eruptions of ethnocidal warfare made it difficult to take sides with any combating group; new security concerns and bureaucratic quagmires facing prospective researchers in newly independent states often made fieldwork a risky venture, encouraging a self-reflexive concern with the researcher's own doubts, intellectual and practical blind alleys, and the elusiveness of understanding (see Pratt 1986). Scientific goals and the moral certainties of victimhood faded from view, replaced by a greater awareness, even celebration, of ambiguity, dilemma, meaninglessness, the unattainability of truth, and the pitfalls of judgment. All political, moral, or intellectual claims to certainty and truth, including the universalism of human rights (based as it is on a political, moral, and intellectual foundation), were therefore suspect. Identities were historically and politically contingent, traditions were invented, and hegemony took the form of difficult-to-detect meaning.

The precise notion of "modern" behind the implicit rejection in the word "postmodern" is unclear (clarity is avoided in practice by postmodernists, for reasons discussed below), but for many anthropologists who adhered (or continue to adhere) to this trend, what seems most *démodé* consists of Enlightenment ideas of progress in the quest for truth and the possibility of universal, transcendent reason in the understanding of human society. The nuances of meaning behind ideas and practices in alien societies, and indeed within oneself, are ultimately unfathomable (which implicitly invokes a Freudian/Durkheimian notion of a cultural unconscious). Clarity of ideas and expression is therefore only a more certain indication that ambiguity is being falsely avoided and hegemonic meaning imposed. Anthropologists, no matter how sincere, skilled, or persistent, are never able to plumb the depths of an alien conceptual system. Moral standards are inescapably part of culture and, not being properly understandable, are incapable of being properly judged.

The idea that the most significant source of hegemony is in the *meaning* ascribed to things, that the real constraints on human lives, from which all other infringements on liberty flow, are in the realm of thought and imagination, gives to postmodernism a sophisticated allure of liberation. Escape from intellectual bondage may be impossible (or nearly so), but it is nevertheless the postmodernists' first order of business. This ignores the very simple fact that profound suffering and insecurity are inimical to any thought whatsoever, aside from those arising from the urge toward escape, survival, and security. Gellner (1992) points to the limited ability of postmodernism to deal with the most important political realities of the modern world: "If we live in a world of meanings, and meanings exhaust the world, where is there any room for coercion through the whip, gun or hunger?" (63). In practical terms, the constraints of symbols and discourses are poor substitutes for the sharper realities of an apparently growing human capacity for tyranny, brutality, and bloodshed.

A concern with meaning even finds its way into the work of those unfashionable anthropologists who take human rights seriously. Talal Asad (1997), for example, problematizes the prohibition of torture in the Universal Declaration, arguing in particular that the words "cruel, inhuman and degrading treatment" could easily slide toward cultural misunderstanding and, by implication, widespread injustice. Religious flagellation, for example, could be misperceived as practicing cruelty (or at least degrading treatment), especially since, he says, the Universal Declaration does not clearly distinguish between pain under compulsion and voluntary participation in acts that cause pain.[4] Asad does not argue, as would a good postmodernist, that the meanings of pain and cruelty in alien cultures, or his own, are unfathomable and indescribable. Rather, the variety of such meanings eludes the grasp of universal moral standards. "The modern dedication to eliminating pain and suffering," he argues, "often conflicts with other commitments and values: the right of individuals to choose, and the duty of the state to maintain its interests" (111). Further, "ideas of torture, cruelty, inhumanity and degrading treatment are intended to measure what are often incommensurable standards of behaviour" (112). The solution he proposes is a greater number of ethnographic studies dedicated to elaborating the myriad ways that humans experience and understand cruelty and pain.

This argument, though it stays close to torture, cruelty, and pain, is easy to apply to most articles of the Universal Declaration and the International Covenants, and even, for that matter, most other international instruments and other forms of agreement between people of different cultures or civilizations. Somewhere in each totalizing passage there is bound to be at least one point of possible cultural contestation and misunderstanding. While I do not wish to argue that drawing attention to such gray areas through cross-cultural research is pointless, I do wonder where this leaves the development and implementation of human rights. It raises the question of the priority to be given to cross-cultural understanding.[5]

Asad's approach to human rights does not accommodate such a concrete starting point because it contains elements of both self-reflexive and empirical relativism. Self-reflexivity can be found in the argument that laws are confounded by the cultural contingency of meaning; that which is intended as universal certainty is made arbitrary by conflicting perceptions and interests and the variety of human worlds. Empirical relativism comes through in the simplicity of his solution: greater, though not ultimate, certainty can be achieved through more research. The project of elucidating the world's various cultural meanings evoked by each area of human rights protection would be, if pursued with too much priority, a quintessentially Boasian project: before one can arrive at a legitimate universally valid law one must first have a detailed understanding of the rich variety of cultural forms and meanings associated with it. The result of such an approach to human rights would be, as it was to some degree for Boasian anthropology, inductive paralysis.

But to determine whether this is truly so, we should consider first whether cultural misunderstanding is really having an effect on the way the business of human rights is done. Clearly, no one is being prosecuted, indicted, or even publicly criticized by U.N. agencies for condoning or encouraging the supposed cruelties of fire walking or football. Cruel, inhuman, and degrading treatment means, *in practice*, something quite different, something more akin to the use of rape as a strategy of terror and "ethnic cleansing." Human cruelty can be so richly, imaginatively, and breathtakingly *cruel* that we have not yet arrived at the point of pursuing frivolous human rights complaints.

Thanks largely to his clarity and directness, Asad's concern with cultural meaning and misunderstanding exposes a wider problem in both empiricist and self-reflexive approaches to human rights: they deny, *in practice,* the possibility of universal moral standards. To his credit, Asad offers the caveat that he does not deny the existence of cruelty but is "merely skeptical about the *universalist discourses* that have been generated around it" (112). But it is difficult to argue that figures like Hitler, Amin, Pinochet, or Milosevic can be excused by the particular cultural or historical circumstances in which they lived. Asad's approach to human rights sets no bounds on the equivocation and uncertainty of cultural meaning. The argument that the meanings, and therefore moral resonances, associated with torture or cruelty are contextually variable can be used to justify virtually any outrage, any act of collective violence, any infringement, subtle or flagrant, by states or minorities, of human rights.

PROBLEMATIZING ANTIRELATIVISM

The contrast sometimes made between what has come to be called "applied anthropology" and postmodernism is, in one sense, incorrect: both are ultimately heirs of the Holocaust and colonial guilt. But while postmodernism eschews any notion of activism (oppression is meaning) and moral judgment, applied anthropology is guided by restless visions of development, prosperity, health, justice, and, occasionally, moral improvement. Applied anthropology is to some extent a reaction against the obscurantism and "ivory-tower" musings of postmodernism; thus its emergence at roughly the same time.[6] Economists, who deal regularly and comfortably with the policy implications of abstract thought, do not feel the need for a subdiscipline of "applied economics," but the cleavage in anthropology between theory and practice, especially between theory and policy, has long been sharper. This fissile quality of the discipline, however, conceals an essential commonality. Postmodernism and applied anthropology are rival siblings, raised in the same environment but making radically different choices when they each came of age.

Applied anthropologists usually define what they do in terms of cultural relativism: policy will not succeed without knowledge of the cultures of those it is intended for; development will fail without the contributions of local understandings of prosperity; the misunderstandings of administrators can be corrected by cultural advocacy; imposed transitions can be harmful without careful cultural navigation. In a general extension of such positions, cultures, in their own terms, are seen as the legitimate sources of human values, growth, health, and well-being. But applied anthropology implies not just an occasional researcher's descent into the horrors of extreme poverty, from which some beat a hasty retreat to academic shelter to concern themselves with writing and scholarly credibility, but a heightened sense of *responsibility* for conditions encountered in "the field." For this reason, some anthropologists have begun to voice the antirelativist opinion that tradition and culture cannot be used to justify repression or suffering. There is a readiness, not just to implement policy, but to criticize it—and to criticize not just states and corporations but also cultures gone astray in the transitions of modernity. The ambiguities and power shifts of globalization have eroded the sanctity and solidity of cultural boundaries, justifying intervention, making researchers more willing to stay the hand that strikes the child, more willing to assign responsibility, wherever it may fall, for communal violence, unhealthy behavior, corruption, and repression.

Such an approach can be found in the work of Nancy Scheper-Hughes.

In *Death without Weeping* (1992) she expresses moral indignation over the everyday experience of scarcity, exploitation, sickness, and death among the women of a Brazilian shantytown. Her main finding, one that throws her into ambivalence, is that, faced with adversity, the women of the village suspend their maternal generosity, approaching children without compassion, empathic love, or care, "suspending the ethical," as she puts it (22). Practices associated with fatalism and dependency, she argues, "are not autonomously, culturally produced. They have a social history and must be understood within the economic and political context of a larger state and world (moral) order that have suspended the ethical" (22). The women's common practice of child neglect, especially with young babies, disturbs the compassionate observer, gives reason to pause and to doubt. But the object of our doubt and censure (if any such object exists) is unclear. The state, the sugarcane plantations, local officials, rival politicians, even the women toward whom Scheper-Hughes clearly feels compassion, are implicated in a complex web of outrage.[7]

Although not writing about a community that identifies itself as indigenous, Scheper-Hughes gives us a problem to consider that does have a bearing on the human rights of indigenous peoples: In situations of moral complexity and ambiguity, how can we resolve questions of rights and responsibilities? How can indigenous peoples be given the justice they deserve when there is confusion, both in general and in specific cases, over their place as victims, responsible actors, and violators of the human rights of their own people or others?

Scheper-Hughes can be given credit for not allowing the extremes of state and corporate injustice and irresponsibility to stand in the way of a critical look at the way the people affected by it are described. All too often, especially in the literature of human rights activism, societies are portrayed two-dimensionally as victim-specimens rather than as human actors with powers, however limited, to shape their own destiny. The indigenous encounter with modernity is thus oversimplified, stripped of agency and the immediacy of suffering.[8] The distance of the observer from the observed could not be greater, resulting in a document, almost a genre in human rights circles, that provokes the same blush of regret as the shrinking of biodiversity.

Observer remoteness is of greatest concern when the discussion involves human rights violations committed *by* minority peoples, not only because it invites censure without contextual understanding (Asad's critique), but because it invites states to interfere in local practices. There are thus distinct dangers associated with the absence of human rights ethnography because state actors are precisely those most often implicated in the cultural or genocidal destruction of cultural minorities and indigenous peoples.

Such issues inherent in the human rights approach to cultural differences are brought out by the growing condemnation of a practice (or set of related practices) sometimes called "female circumcision" or, as many now prefer, "female genital mutilation." Although the Masai of East Africa and the Bedouin of North Africa are to my knowledge the only people actively participating in the indigenous rights movement who practice surgical removal of the clitoris as part of female coming-of-age ceremonies, the issue raises the possibility of wider critiques of a range of practices in indigenous societies that run counter to human rights standards, particularly those that apply to women and children.

Among those who have recently written on female genital mutilation, the views expressed by Catherine Annas are perhaps the most forthright, and for that reason ultimately the most revealing of moral ambiguity. The procedures referred to as female genital mutilation, Annas (1999) explains, take three basic forms: (1) "Sunna circumcision," involving the removal of the prepuce and tip of the clitoris; (2) excision (the most common of the procedures), involving removal of the clitoris and labia minora; and (3) the most invasive and harmful of the procedures, infibulation, in which the clitoris, labia minora, and parts of the labia majora are all removed, after which the two sides of the vulva are stitched over the vagina, as a way of ensuring a "closed bride" in cultures that place a high value on female virtue and virginity in marriage (337). These procedures are usually performed on girls between three and ten years of age. Female genital mutilation has extremely wide distribution, occurring in more than forty countries around the world—twenty-six in Africa alone—and involving fifty-five hundred procedures per day.

Although often associated with Islam, the practice is estimated to be more than six thousand years old, making it, strictly speaking, an "indigenous" practice that has only secondarily been given religious justification (for which, Annas points out, there is no evidence in the Quran or modern theological texts). Here, indignation is directed toward the "traditional," not the economic and environmental violence of states or multinationals.

Annas's case for the suppression of female genital mutilation is grounded in its violation of the fundamental human rights of the girls on whom it is practiced; and evidence of human rights violation, in turn, is found above all in the medical harm of infibulation. This is how she describes it:

> In Africa and the Middle East, an elder woman, often referred to as the "midwife," performs the operation. The woman is not a doctor and, in most cases, has no medical training. The midwife does the cutting, while two or three women (often the girl's mother and aunts) hold the child down and force her legs apart. No anesthetic is used, and the cutting instrument varies from a sharp razor to a knife or sharp stone. In many cases, the midwife circumcises a number of girls, one after another, without sterilizing the blade. In some cultures, dirt and ashes are thrown on the wound to stop bleeding. Barring any complications, the procedure may take only six minutes. The child's legs are then bound together to allow the wound to heal. In an infibulation procedure, thorns or a sticky paste are used to fasten together the bleeding sides of the labia majora, leaving an opening about the size of a "matchstick or fingertip" for the passage of urine and menstrual blood. The girl's legs remain tied together until the wound heals, which may take several weeks to more than a month. . . . The risks associated with female genital mutilation are numerous and severe. The child experiences severe pain and shock. Medical risks include the risk of exposure to HIV and other blood borne diseases from unsterile instruments used during the procedure, as well as the risk of death caused by infection and hemorrhaging. Septicemia (blood poisoning) can also occur.
>
> With infibulation, women almost always experience difficulties in urination and menstruation. Sexual intercourse can be very painful, and penetration is difficult. In addition, dermoid cysts often form in the line of a scar, and can grow "as large as grapefruits." Increased infertility and infant mortality are also consequences of this procedure. Difficulties during childbirth are frequent and lead to an increase in the number of chil-

dren born with brain damage because of anoxia [oxygen deprivation] during delivery. The highest infant mortality rates in the world occur in areas where female genital mutilation is practiced. In addition, 25 percent of infertility is attributable to female genital mutilation. (337–38)

Annas concludes with a passion that is unusual for a scholarly discussion of a cultural practice: "When the effects of female genital mutilation are honestly faced, nothing can justify it. Not culture. Not tradition. Not parental rights. Nothing" (351). Young girls are neither the property of the tribe nor the property of their parents. They are individuals—with rights. Other than an obvious empathy with suffering children, it is a depth of commitment that finds strength in two principal sources: medical ethics and human rights. Medical ethics are violated when doctors perform (perhaps even when they condone) procedures that serve no medical purpose, that are in fact harmful to patients who are usually unaware of their rights. An especially strong case can be made (though Annas makes it only in passing in the longer passage quoted above with her mention of AIDS) that the practice of female genital mutilation ceases to be the business of tradition when it contributes, however slightly, to humanity's burden of infectious disease. This opens the door to legitimate cultural critique. It is not only a matter of using sterilized instruments, for the same kind of argument can be extended in terms of a kind of human rights epidemiology: the systematic victimization of women does not occur in cultural isolation but affects everyone exposed to it. Human rights are grounded in the inviolability of the individual and the interconnectedness of human worlds. There is thus a close connection between the medical and human rights foundations for censure of tradition.

Having taken the step of rejecting a traditional practice as a gross, ongoing, and widespread violation of human rights, how does Annas proceed? There are, she informs us, encouraging developments occurring within Western democracies to which female genital mutilation has been introduced via immigrants: bills being introduced, such as U.S. Congresswoman Patricia Schroeder's 1995 Federal Prohibition of Female Genital Mutilation Act, that would make it more clearly and explicitly illegal for parents to inflict the practice on their children and doctors to perform the procedure on patients. And by way of challenging the practice in Africa, the Middle East, and other regions where female genital mutilation is concentrated, Annas favorably cites the pressure put on the government of Egypt following the airing of an act of female genital mutilation on CNN, timed to correspond with the 1994 Population Conference in Cairo. The Egyptian government promised intervention and arrested several of the men involved in the televised procedure; but the pressure wore off, the men were released, and a promised national ban was forgotten. This fickle quality of public outrage is to be regretted. It is, Annas tells us, only through sustained pressure upon governments that the power of international embarrassment can lead to meaningful reform (347).

Annas devotes most of her scholarly effort to making the case that female circumcision is a violation of universal human rights that must be excoriated and ended, but she pays little attention to the problem of controlling the harmful behavior in the cultures from which it originates. The important question, therefore, is not whether there are or are not universals—the strength of the cases against such things as slavery and infibulation tells us they exist—but what to do about universalizing them. How, in other words, should those who make a case for a universal truth set about reforming those who act in contradiction to it? In Christianity this is an old question, answered very differently in practice by, say, the Quakers and the Catholics in their missions among the Indians (see Niezen 2000b).

Her first line of defense against infibulation is the state. But assigning responsibility to states for the human rights violations of minority peoples associates the latter with national embarrassment and invites repressive intervention. This occurred, for example, in Mexico when the state government of Chiapas arrested indigenous leaders for their part in traditional governments acting in contravention of state laws and, it would seem, human rights standards. Shannon Speed and Jane Collier (2000) see this as a use of human rights as an instrument of repression: "The state government of Chiapas appears 'colonialist,' not just in imposing a literal interpretation of human rights documents on indigenous peoples, but, more importantly, in using the discourse of human rights to justify intervening in the affairs of indigenous communities whose leaders happen to displease government officials" (878). Assigning responsibility to indigenous peoples, without regard to sovereignty, has an oft-repeated association with denials of plurality and distinctiveness, realized in policies of assimilation. Bringing indigenous peoples into compliance with human rights norms is by no means straightforward, given that the task involves the complexities of their relationships with states.

The starting point in resolving this dilemma is self-determination. Ethical judgments of a collective nature, judgments that implicate tradition and identity, cannot be reasonably separated from political history. Here we can find a point of agreement with Asad. Human rights universals are not recipes for social reform that can be justly and fairly applied to all peoples, in all times, at all places, in the same way. Applying human rights as a tool of social reform involves contingencies and social nuances that can only be perceived locally. Asad, however, sees the problem of *meaning* as taking preeminence, whereas my preference is to look first for the uses of *power*—the whip, the gun, and the controlled imposition of hunger.

SELF-DETERMINATION AND CULTURAL DISTINCTIVENESS

Neither cultural relativism nor, in at least some forms, antirelativism is fully consistent with the goals of universal human rights. Above all, the usual positions on both sides of the relativist/antirelativist divide are inconsistent with the application of human rights to indigenous peoples.

Let us assume that human rights are the only peaceful way to respond to the scourge of war, to the genocidal impulses that have escalated with the sophistication of the technology of destruction and the violence of nationalist impulses, and to the disregard for human life in the pursuit of profit; let us set aside for the moment any Machiavellian pragmatism that tells us that human rights can never overcome humanity's unscrupulous pursuit of power and that asserts necessary connections between ruthlessness and peace. What we have arrived at is a universal secular faith based on reason, law, bureaucratic order, and the greatest possible international consensus on foundational principles. Human rights scholars are, according to this line of thought, like secular Jesuits, grounding their convictions in reflection, reason, and polished argument, flirting with doubt and returning to conviction. The human rights movement, by its very nature, is profoundly antirelativist. It transcends human differences with few qualms. Legitimate cultural, religious, and national differences can be accommodated within its vision, even encouraged, whereas unnecessary mass suffering, death, discrimination, and oppression are not to be justified or condoned.

As with all faiths, however, there are inconsistencies within the human rights vision as it is applied in practice. In practice the moral actors responsible for human rights are almost exclusively states. This is understandable, given the importance of states in the structure and goals of the United Nations, but state exclusivism corresponds very inexactly with the reality of intrastate conflicts and the proliferation of terrorists and guerilla groups.

The indigenous peoples' movement can be seen as a step toward resolving this practical inconsistency, toward universalizing human rights. This is an uncomfortable process because indigenous self-determination—the recognition of the moral and political agency of nations within states—intrudes upon state sovereignty, the bricks and mortar of the U.N. system.

To be a self-determining people involves accepting not only the benefits of human rights protections but also the responsibilities of human rights obligations. For an indigenous polity to be self-governing means developing constitutional ties to states and crafting, centralizing, and expanding new powers (in some cases to include the powers of the state). Under these circumstances, relativism can be used as a convenient justification for despotism. Tradition has been used as an excuse for female genital mutilation, "dowry killings" in India, and even political repression by states. Conditions of shifting power and the porousness of cultural boundaries have taken much of the persuasiveness from cultural relativism; more than this, relativism can be used to compromise the basic freedoms of indigenous peoples in the process of emergence of nonstate powers. The logic of universal human rights—rights that transcend the interests of states and apply to all peoples at all times and places—

thus leads to the conclusion that cultural relativism is inconsistent with self-determination.

If a self-determining indigenous people is discovered to be responsible for serious human rights violations, what is the best avenue of recourse? To answer this we must keep in mind the histories of extinction at the hands of states, histories that indigenous peoples everywhere have in common in one form or another. For this reason alone, despite some instances in which states have negotiated new constitutional arrangements with indigenous peoples, states lack legitimacy as the instigators or enforcers of human rights critique. Largely because of this hypocrisy-laden ineffectiveness of states, the erosion of democracy and destruction of peoples by nonstate actors can occur under the public gaze.

This underscores the potential significance of the indigenous peoples' movement, and in particular the development of a permanent U.N. forum for indigenous peoples. To maintain its credibility the indigenous forum will have to include within its purview not only the urgent problems of racism, loss of land, industrial degradation, and state assaults upon identity and cultural integrity but also the human rights abuses perpetrated by indigenous peoples themselves.

The international movement of indigenous peoples thus represents a new possibility for universalism, based largely upon the actions and aspirations of indigenous peoples. Indigenism represents widely shared ideals, an empirical global coherence that was (especially with nineteenth-century evolutionism) once imposed by imaginary, value-laden distortions of "savage" lore and life.

But the universalization of universal human rights is rife with secondary implications of cultural transition and disenchantment. In the context of international human rights standards, the question of ethical universalism versus relativism can now be understood this way: Does the adaptation or elimination of particular censured traditions through international norms have negative consequences for cultural continuity as a whole? Are human rights yet another agent of social convergence? And do specific human rights provisions unintentionally (or intentionally) encourage cultural assimilation?

For indigenous peoples, the human rights agenda entails a trade-off in which some (mostly ineffectual) protections against state and industry and some (largely unrecognized) rights of self-determination are gained at the expense of much self-sufficiency and distinctiveness. Self-governance entails more negotiation with states and international organizations, greater use of written law, and greater reliance on formal procedures of election. Tradition, in the sense meant by Weber, as reliance upon things-as-they-have-always-been, as a way of commanding people's respect and obedience through connections with ancestors and the authority of elders, has an ambiguous relationship with such formalization. The use of written law is a necessity, to be pursued by the educated and tolerated, perhaps, but not often preferred by traditionalists. Indigenism is therefore a political strategy that entails almost as much cultural transition as cultural preservation. But, under the circumstances, there is no other peaceful way for formally educated indigenous leaders to proceed.

THE CHALLENGE OF HUMAN DIFFERENCES

When, at the most important points in human history (and possibly prehistory), societies began to internationalize, to coalesce into regions, spheres of influence, or intercultural civilizations, a problem presented itself: How much freedom does one accord distinct groups of people, sometimes very different from one's own? Or, from a minority point of view, how much of one's life is to be changed by the presence of powerful but in many ways unenlightened and ill-mannered strangers? Each particular situation required an assessment of the degree of threat posed by adjacent human differences and how to respond to them.

In this context we find an important development in the European (notably English) colonies: the question becomes not only how to exploit and influence the societies under colonial rule but in some cases how to simultaneously liberate the individuals oppressed by the milieu to which they belong. How does one cultivate or impose the liberty of the individual on societies recklessly determined to suppress every outlet of enlightenment, creative energy, leadership, and romantic love? There was a strongly evangelical flavor to colonialism that saw every human soul as unique and the only hope for its salvation as lying in its liberation from the perfidy, superstition, and deception of "savage" lore and life. It is a mistake to see this kind of evangelism as an exclusively religious phenomenon. It stems from any and all systems of privileged knowledge, any striving toward a final triumph of reason or truth. The truly committed doctor, educator, politician, and saint alike find it difficult to possess the truth and stand by while the unenlightened flounder in the darkness. Nor was the edge taken away by good intentions and philanthropy. There was, ironically, a natural affinity between the voices of liberal values within industrial democracies and the misshapen liberation of colonial evangelism. If John Stuart Mill could view with concern the tyranny of the majority in British democracy, how much easier it was to see the tyranny of ignorance and arbitrary despotism in societies as yet unblessed with civilization and rights of the individual.

Colonialism, not surprisingly, has little affinity with collective rights. The evangelical urge to reach and uplift individuals encouraged their removal from what were seen as harmful or dangerous collective entities. This was also reflected in the values and priorities of the League of Nations. A self-fulfilling quality to the denials of indigenous sovereignty articulated in international law during the pre–World War II era is especially clear in the positivist approach to colonial domination: Indians do not have sovereign status because colonial rule is inconsistent with such status; they do not have rights as peoples because colonialism is predicated upon the denial of these rights. Rather than shaping and controlling the expansion of European powers in indigenous peoples' territories, international law provided justifications for it.

The upheavals and horrors of the twentieth century gave much greater stature to a rival, collective notion of human liberation. It became seen as an apocalyptically fatal error to entrust nation-states and colonial powers with the well-being of their own, usually heterogenous, citizens. In the twentieth century, national and colonial forms of power showed themselves in their true (or at least potential) colors: rapacious, oppressive, ready to pursue Procrustean impulses toward racial or ethnic purity, and above all possessing the technology and state organization to commit violence on an unprecedented scale. Most of the victims of the twentieth century's horrors, in fact, were victimized for the very reason that they belonged to distinct groups.

World government and the development of human rights were responses to this new level of intrastate violence. The legitimacy of colonial
empires collapsed as oppressed peoples and nationalities sought the status of self-government. Collective rights in international law are seen by
some as a logical and necessary extension of this movement, an outcome
of the need to protect actually and potentially oppressed groups within
states: ethnic nationalities, genders, children, professions, classes, castes,
races—and indigenous peoples.

Although the historical circumstances that encouraged the development of universal human rights consist mostly of the misery and destruction of entire peoples, the ideas that took precedence in the drafting of
these rights originated in Western liberal conceptions of individuals as
equal and autonomous members of society. One result is a mingling and
confusion of apparently incompatible foundational principles with origins in both the "West and the rest" divide of international politics and
contests within the Western intellectual tradition itself.

In human rights discourse, the most important underlying intellectual
divide centers upon the question of the universality of individual rights.
Two basic principles of liberalism are the notion of equality—intended
to protect every individual by providing him or her with claims to equal
treatment under the law and, as a check on tyranny, the same responsibility of everyone to obey the law—and the progress of human institutions through rational design in the direction of individualism. But are
these principles compatible with all systems of human governance at all
times? Or are there legitimate notions of rights that protect groups from
outside domination, that begin with the human need for collective identity and continuity of social allegiance? These questions come into prominence whenever the global emergence of systems of law and governance
is considered in the light of human differences.

FROM MONTESQUIEU TO MAINE

The work of two legal philosophers, Montesquieu and Maine, whose use
of such a global comparative approach resulted in very different conclu-

sions, illustrates the basic contest of ideas now prominent in the development and application of universal human rights. In outlining their main
ideas I am using social theory as metaphor; my intention is not to assess
the actual impact of each writer on the history of ideas or on political
movements (even though, especially in the case of Montesquieu, these
are not negligible).

Montesquieu's work of genius *The Spirit of the Laws* ([1748] 1989) is an
early treatment of the rules that govern human conduct, influenced by
the first accounts of peoples inhabiting previously unknown (to the Europeans) continents. His work was influenced by, and not prejudiced
against, those whose descendants later came to see themselves as "indigenous." While Rousseau's natural man was almost wholly a product
of the imagination (similar to what British social anthropologists, in barbs
directed toward evolutionists, called the "if I were a horse" approach to
human history), Montesquieu, more than his contemporaries, was attentive to the raw material of sociological knowledge and thus to the remarkable diversity of human social arrangements.[9] This is not to say that
he approved of every system of government or every political act he encountered in his literary explorations but rather that he saw every system
as being understandable in its own terms. He stressed that our judgments
are rendered meaningless by an intricate determinism. He drew examples of political determinism from an immense variety of sources (cit-
ing some three hundred works in three thousand references). Climate has
an influence on human passions and hence the proclivity to certain behavior and systems of law. He argued, in one of many vignettes, that sus-
ceptibility to famine in imperial China created an ever-present danger
of revolt and invasion, which impelled the central leadership toward a
wary, and to some degree benevolent, despotism. Terrain, mode of subsistence, and population density similarly exert their influence on human
institutions. Turning to the inhabitants of the Americas, he assumed that
the wide-open spaces would cause marriages to be unstable and people
to sometimes "mingle indifferently like beasts" (291), an observation that
anticipates nineteenth-century evolutionist assumptions of "promiscu-
ous hordes" as the first human family arrangement. But he also made
more astute observations. By using the same approach he came up with

a pithy and largely accurate explanation for the absence of any form of political domination among North America's Athapaskan hunting peoples: "If a leader wanted to take their liberty from them, they would immediately go and seek it with another leader or withdraw into the woods to live there with their family. Among these peoples, the liberty of the man is so great that it necessarily brings with it the liberty of the citizens" (292).

The main thing for Montesquieu is that these formative influences upon political behavior can be found; they are recoverable by an attentive observer; behavior and laws can be understood, their reasons decoded. And where there is no mystery of origin, there can be little moral censure. There is in Montesquieu little sense of ascent toward human perfection. The freedom and happiness of the subjects and citizens of benevolent monarchies and republics are not products of a great design of history, evolution, or divine will. On the crucial issue of the origins of human differences, he does not consider the possibility of a shift from the condition of "vagabonds" who do not practice agriculture to other "advanced" conditions of human life. There is no transition from mores to laws (as there is in Maine's similar concepts of status and contract, discussed below). "Savages" live in a simple state of freedom because a combination of circumstances made it almost inevitable that they do so—the climate, the abundance of the land, the ability of people to be mobile and still meet their needs. Montesquieu does not posit an inherent state of inferiority to explain the differences between the European and those newly encountered people in distant lands. There is no universal design, no system of government to which humanity will or should conform. Simply, "Laws should be so appropriate to the people for whom they are made that it is very unlikely that the laws of one nation can suit another" (8).[10]

A century or so later, the intellectual climate in Europe was quite different. Remarkable achievements of technology and exploration imparted to the main currents of thought a confidence in progress. Christianity and European values combined into an abstract moral universe referred to with strongly positive resonance as "civilization." Of those writing within this milieu, Sir Henry Maine was among the most historically oriented, and thus the most faithful to his evidence, with as much or more connection to the Enlightenment ideas of human progress as to the censorious, Eurocentric evolutionism of many of his contemporaries. His evolutionism is grounded in ancient history, principally the legal history of Rome, material very much like Montesquieu's, with similar, though less eclectic, forays into comparative material.

In the earliest form of ancient society, Maine ([1861] 1977) informs us, the group around which all rights and obligations revolved was the family, a particular kind of family in which the patriarchal power of the father was absolute. All other members of the household—wives, sons, daughters, and slaves—were subject to his will. Their gradual emancipation from this despotic authority occurred through developments in Roman law, such as the increasing privacy of testamentary arrangements of wills, the separation of private property from the collective claims of kinsfolk, and, above all, the development of the idea of contract, which increased the capacity of individuals to enter into agreements outside the ambit of patriarchal domination. The rigidity of what Maine calls "primitive law" was largely a consequence of its association with religion, which "chained down the mass of the human race to those views of life and conduct which they entertained at the time when their usages were first consolidated into a systematic form" (45). The liberation of humanity from this constraint of thought, social arrangements, and jurisprudence occurred within the Indo-European tradition when laws became codified in writing and the rights of individuals were made distinct from their duties to society. The general thrust of Maine's argument is captured in the aphorism that helped make *Ancient Law* famous: "[T]he movement of the progressive societies has hitherto been a movement *from Status to Contract* [emphasis in original]" (100).

Maine invokes a suspension of moral judgment toward present principles of law by calling into question the speculative approach to the Law of Nature; but he does not extend this suspension of judgment into the less intuited, historical past.[11] For Maine, the transition from status to contract is unequivocally a progression in human history, an advance from the arbitrary domination (and extended responsibilities) of family despots to the relative liberty of contractual arrangements and individual responsibilities. It is not appropriate to invent the past in the imagination, and the present is not to be condemned by comparison with a past ideal. The transitions leading to present conditions, he later deduces from his study of Greek and Roman law, are progressive movements toward a better state, toward greater individual liberties.

Maine's answer to Montesquieu's pluralism is an oddly narrow historical universalism, based on an assumption that the conditions found in the transmission of social practice and legal codes—from the predecessors of ancient societies through the Dark Ages to European civilization—is a universal history. Societies outside the reach of this process are inconsequential. Truly unusual social arrangements are "anomalies" or "relics of older stages of the race which have obstinately defied the influences that have elsewhere had effect" (69). There is, for Maine, only one documented instance of fully realized human progression and emancipation—that introduced by Roman judicial reform, carried dimly through six centuries of medieval stagnation, culminating in European (and above all British) legal codes—but the potential for advancement is nevertheless universal. What has happened outside the narrow confines of the ancient world and its successor states? There is a sense in which Maine's perception of history ceases when it encounters difference. Societies outside the influence of the Roman Empire's reforms are rigid, morally stagnant. Where emancipation begins, it runs into blind alleys and ceases its progress or retreats back to duty, conformity, and constraint. The story of almost every society is one of missed or wasted opportunity. The stationary condition of humanity is therefore the rule, progress the great exception.

The limits to the historical perspective of even such learned evolutionist historians as Sir Henry Maine were the product of their unwillingness or inability to consider the genuine universality happening all around them through the growth of merchant capitalism and colonialism in every corner of the globe. The exploration and trade that brought the challenge of human differences to both Montesquieu and Maine already had globalizing powers in the eighteenth and nineteenth centuries. And today this process is very nearly complete. Written laws (whether or not people are aware of the reach of the state) have since reached every society, and individual rights are built into most legal codes. What Maine described as a unique transition or progression from status to contract has since become a near-universal *overtaking and displacement of status with contract.* Colonialism and postcolonial state domination involved the suppression of mores with law, the imposition of state regulations on (initially) oral societies.

The North American fur trade is an example of the first inroads of this transition. The fixed prices for pelts and goods for sale in trading posts marked the beginning of standardized transactions that led easily into wage labor. The replacement of subsistence and trade economies with formal wage labor is today a common experience of indigenous communities everywhere. Private property is a further step in the process. A policy of the U.S. government in the nineteenth century was to replace the collective ownership and community connections of reserve lands with fee-simple title in individual allotments. This policy was pursued with particularly disastrous consequences on the Omaha and Nez Perce reserves, where many individually owned land holdings were sold (thus irrevocably lost to communal control) and many thousands of acres were simply appropriated by the government and transferred to settlers. One of the common features of all assimilation efforts directed toward easing the "inevitable" transitions of aboriginal societies is the imposition of personal duty and opportunity upon oral societies with use rights in land and with duty and honor derived from relations with kin. There is a strong element of compulsion involved in the transitions of indigenous societies. Environmental destruction, forced relocation, and compulsory state education are the salient aspects of a global process of cultural homogenization. In different ways, Maine and Montesquieu were both right, but it was the actual imposition of Maine's universe on Montesquieu's autonomous, internally coherent societies that brings us to a more complete understanding of our own world.

This transformation, however, is far from complete. There are many who, while being aware of technology and experiencing the pull of individual opportunity, are unwilling to give up what, in one of many paradoxes of modernity, has become the freedom of collective obligations. An anthropologist I knew in graduate school once amused himself, or so he said, by taking a group of Bedouin Arabs who had spent their lives in the desert to a new automatic teller machine in Amman, Jordan; and while they expressed surprise at his amazing ability to produce money from a wall, and were temporarily filled with the possibilities that such access to

wealth might bring, they did not for all that decide to forsake their kins-
men and herds for a new life in the city. The pull of opportunity draws
many, but not all. The world of Montesquieu is to some degree resistant
to the values that go with the world of Maine.

More is involved in this contest, however, than the destruction of ways
of life and the opposition of rival values. Those who have made a transition from one form of life to another, who have become skilled in the
technologies and bureaucratic procedures of complex society, are sometimes able to use this knowledge in defense of their societies of origin.
The indigenous peoples' movement involves a sophisticated use of law
and the protocols of advocacy in the service of communities otherwise
without protection against the encroachments of state and industry.
Lawyers, human rights organizations, and environmental groups are
mounting campaigns, with increasing frequency and success, against the
collapse of indigenous cultures. The indigenous peoples' movement, in
Maine's terms, represents the use of contract to defend social relations
based upon status. The individual relationships, processes, and obligations of Maine, with the recent innovation of appeals to public sympathy
and support, are being used in the effort to preserve a world of Montes-
quieuian diversity.

This brings into prominence the potential for the indigenous peoples'
movement, as the embodiment of human diversity involved in a process
of legal universalism, to alter human institutions. Indigenous leaders are
presenting claims of collective rights in forums built mainly around the
rights of individuals and the governance of states. This challenge has
the potential to pluralize and collectivize international institutions. At
the same time, it is important to recognize that the influence is mutual.
Notions of equality and individual rights are through this same process
being brought to societies organized around group honor and obligations. The worlds of Montesquieu and Maine are intersecting at the cross-
roads of individual and collective rights.

HUMAN RIGHTS INDIVIDUALISM

There are numerous strands to the history of Western liberalism, including the systems of land tenure and inheritance in preindustrial England;

the importance of private individuals separate from society in the industrial revolution; the urbanization, migration, and complex division of labor of developing capitalist economies; and the revolutions (most influentially the French Revolution) that swept away the remnants of feudal nobility in favor of a rising middle class inspired by the universal ideals of equality, prosperity, and liberation. Two features of liberal individualism, however, stand out as having continuing relevance for the development of human rights standards as they have come to apply to indigenous peoples. First, liberal individualism is one side of an intellectual divide in post-Enlightenment European thought, opposed at significant points by relativism and pluralism. The Western foundations of human rights standards are therefore not as starkly individualistic as might readily be supposed. Second, liberal individualism is a historically and culturally unique vision of justice and human good; and in the context of an equally unprecedented exercise in formulating universal moral principles it fits uncomfortably with the collective experiences of many, if not most, participants. The universal charter of rights that resulted is not unambiguously oriented toward individual protections and rights. Nor is the contest between collective and individual human rights complete: it continues with particular clarity in the aspirations of indigenous peoples and the limits placed on them by international organizations and states.[12]

The development of international law addressed to the protection and rights of indigenous peoples is sometimes seen in contemporary legal thought as part of a "third generation" of human rights, developed after the 1948 Universal Declaration and the International Covenants. Some features of third-generation rights appear inconsistent with the goal of maintaining a strong, consistent body of human rights law. The ease with which claims are made for the recognition of new rights, such as the right to development and the right to disarmament, creates the risk of legal proliferation and dilution; and the main beneficiaries of these rights appear, more often than not, to be states, often the very states whose ambitions, in the light of human rights standards, are suspect.

The broadening of the concept of human rights to include certain collective rights of society or "peoples" is a development that some leading scholars of human rights find troubling. Jack Donnelly, in *Universal Human Rights in Theory and Practice* (1989), for example, argues in favor of restricting human rights to individuals. Human rights, as embodied in the original 1966 covenants, he argues, "rest on a view of the individual person as separate from and endowed with inalienable rights held primarily in relation to society, and especially the state" (145). He makes the reasonable, if obvious, point that "to be human is to have human rights" (144), but the essence of being human to Donnelly is entirely distinct from any form of group membership or identity. "Any rights that might arise from solidarity would not be *human* rights," he says (144). There are more substantive implications of this approach to human rights. Collective human rights are seen to give states greater latitude for repression. An emphasis on collective rights translates easily into an overemphasis on collective duties. Even if collective human rights are developed with the intention of uplifting oppressed minorities, those rights will also accrue to states, the only likely result of which would be an encouragement of state control over individuals, a strengthening and justification of the state's resolve to repress its citizens. There is an acknowledged trade-off to avoiding this danger: the exercise of individual rights may run into conflict with collective practices and may erode or destroy social groups. But if this occurs through the free exercise of individual human rights, it is defensible, and even to be welcomed. Above all, "[I]f the group can persist only through the denial of the human rights of its members, it has no claim to our respect" (152). In the case of aboriginal peoples, the autonomy of individuals to choose a way of life is a sufficient protection of distinct cultures, and collective rights are a perilous redundancy. "[Individual] human rights, however uncomfortably they fit with the traditional social structures of such communities, offer powerful protections for the rights and interests of aboriginal groups and traditional communities" (153).[13] In other words, if the world community invests exclusively in individual rights, it gets collective rights for free. As Donnelly explains, "[I]n the case of individuals who define themselves not principally as individuals but as members of a traditional community, *that* choice of a way of life must be guaranteed" (153), unless, of course, the particulars of the cultural choice are in conflict with individual human rights.[14]

A variant of the argument for exclusively individual rights places greater emphasis on traditional cultures—and less on states—as the enemy of individual liberty. This is the premise of a short article by Michael Blake (2000) in *Civilization*, the official journal of the Library of Congress. "The proper focus of our moral concern," Blake writes, "is not the survival of cultures as collective practices and traditions, but rather the political, civil, and human rights of the individuals that constitute them" (53). Cultural survival creates artificial obstacles to the peaceful transitions of declining cultures and the freedom of individuals who belong to self-professed traditional societies; thus the negative value ascribed to assimilation leads to "a stifling insistence on cultural purity and conformity" (53). Cultures can and will inevitably change and disappear, and the best way for this to happen is through a quiet transformation, as individuals freely choose to take on new lives in a new culture, "until what is distinct is lost or lives only in romantic traces" (53).

But the actual practice of assimilation, long part of indigenous peoples' legacies of oppression, has nearly always taken the form of imposition rather than dispassionate offering of assistance and improvement. How can people toiling under allegiance to a narrow, hidebound way of life, out of step with the times and, because of it (so it is often assumed), suffering in poverty and sickness, be left to cope on their own? Does not an enlightened and compassionate society have a moral duty to ease the inevitable transition, to bring the benefits of superior knowledge, faith, technology, and bureaucratic method? Therefore, let the most promising individuals of an unpromising society be changed and in turn bring about change. Bring us their children, and we will make honest, hardworking men and women of them.

The implications of exclusively individual rights, taken further than reasonable people might intend, are thus disturbingly reminiscent of discredited Indian policies with origins in the socioevolutionism of the nineteenth century. Where liberal approaches to the human good have consistently failed is in their methods (or lack of them) of bringing new values to stateless societies. Their predicament stems from ambivalence toward evangelism. How do those wanting to bring the virtues of democracy, tolerance of human differences, and freedom of the individual proceed in the context of societies that have never wanted or needed these virtues? How does one, in a tolerant and democratic way, impose tolerance and democracy? To counteract absolutism, pluralism must be absolutist. A product of this paradox has been that the inculcation of liberal ideals in indigenous societies has been piecemeal, erratic, indirect, and destructive. These ideals, in various forms, can be found in the thinking behind the imposition of band councils, urban relocation programs, the division of reserves into individual land holdings, the abrogation of distinct rights in treaties, and the assimilative orientation of state education. However much we agree with liberal values, liberal solutions to the challenge of universalizing the truth have been unsettling and ultimately self-defeating. One cannot teach men and women to be honorable by nullifying one's obligations; one cannot teach them to be tolerant by imposing a new way of life; and one cannot teach civic virtues by arbitrarily replacing consensus politics with new forms of election and representation.

STATISM

Advocating, directly or by implication, the assimilation of minority cultures raises a basic question that few contemporary exponents of the idea bring themselves to ask: Assimilation into what? What constitutes a receptacle culture? What privileged entity is to absorb the world's anachronistic, worn-out cultures? The answer that comes most easily, that most often lies in the background of assimilationist ideas and policies, is the culture(s), identity (or identities), and institutions of the nation-state.

It is easier to see where the prerogative of states came from than to anticipate where the nation-state is going. (While the more difficult latter question is impossible to address without resorting to historicism, the relevance of the indigenous peoples' movement for assessing the impact of globalization on the nation-state is to be taken up in chapter 6). In *Lords of All the World* (1995), a masterful survey of three centuries of Spanish, British, and French imperialism, Anthony Pagden distinguishes between two interdependent histories of European empire building. The first (his main subject) took place in the European discovery and colonization of the Americas, beginning with Columbus's voyage in 1492 and ending with the defeat of the Spanish royalist armies in South America during the 1830s. A second phase of imperialism involved the "indirect rule" of the British Commonwealth, the French in West Africa, and other European colonies whose legacy was the bloodshed of decolonization and the current relationships between the "First" and "Third" Worlds. We can extrapolate from and simplify Pagden's survey with the observation that the colonization of the Americas led to disaffection among the exploited expatriate colonizers, who then, through revolution or (particularly in Canada) comparatively gradual devolution of powers, acquired independent statehood; while in the empires of indirect rule, it was the indigenous inhabitants—paid but not enslaved, living under "tutelage" but not direct rule—who rejected colonial domination and acquired statehood themselves, in keeping with European recognition of the colonies as civil societies. This, in a nutshell, is the history behind the ubiquity and influence of states.

State dictatorships and the ambitions of secessionist groups to acquire statehood have to such a great extent come to be associated with political vexations and bloodshed that it is difficult to imagine how, in the years just following World War II, the assumption came to be made, most prominently in the thinking behind the U.N. Charter, that states were the legitimate embodiment of "peoples" and the most important political vessels for human liberation. The integrity of states was seen as an antidote to empire building, to the hegemonic reach across oceans and continents to recover the lost splendors of the ancient world in another, more technologically advanced, form. The greatness of a state was no longer to be measured by the number of nations it encompassed. Such, at least, was the new ideal, however imperfectly it accorded with the realities of postwar expansionism and ethnic nationalism. In responding to Nazism, the U.N. Charter with its "We the Peoples" confirmed the illegitimacy of colonialism and offered statehood as the means of acquiring a correspondence of political and cultural frontiers.

The postwar consolidation of statism is replete with implications for the development of human rights. Individual human rights cannot exist in a vacuum. Their obverse is a collective, constitutionally organized entity responsible for protecting and upholding these rights. And in practice this entity has been, with overwhelming predominance, the nation-state. Although the development of human rights law in recent decades has to some extent challenged the deference to state authority, international law remains organized around the consent of governments and a statist conception of rights (Falk 1988: 17). Statism is not limited to the United Nations, even though the United Nations clearly represents an international concentration of state authority. In Seattle, Prague, Genoa, and elsewhere protests against the secretive, undemocratic nature of the World Trade Organization, the World Bank, and the International Monetary Fund are a sign of popular idealism running up against the ability of states and industry to make decisions in closed rooms that affect billions of lives. Statism is also a fact of life in agencies with more humanitarian goals. Many indigenous delegates to the first International Consultation on the Health of Indigenous Peoples held by the World Health Organization (WHO) in Geneva in 1999, for example, seemed unaware, until they were told, that the WHO cannot involve itself in a crisis unless a request is made by a state government and that the WHO has no official grievance procedure through which complaints can be made concerning government failure to provide adequate health services. Richard Falk (1988) is correct in his assessment of indigenous rights as a serious challenge to the view of international law as an extension of state legitimacy and practice: "Indigenous peoples, to the extent that they centre their grievances around encroachments upon their collective identity, represent a competing nationalism within the boundaries of the state. Such claims, posited in a variety of forms, challenge two fundamental statist notions—that of territorial sovereignty, and that of a unified 'nationality' juridicially administered by governmental organs" (18).

THE RIGHTS OF (INDIGENOUS) PEOPLES

The supposed incompatibility between individual and collective rights stems from a false dichotomy. Both individual and group-specific rights are built into the International Bill of Human Rights. Although states were long recognized as the bearers of identity and obligations contained in the U.N. Charter, this monopolization of benefits and responsibilities is increasingly being called into question. The important issue being raised by most U.N. reforms is this: Who qualifies as a "people" with (among other rights) collective rights to self-determination and the concomitant obligation to uphold individual rights?

Ian Brownlie (1988) takes a legitimately cautious approach to collective human rights. Like Donnelly, he is dismayed at what he calls "the proliferation of academic inventions of new human rights and the launching of new normative candidates by anyone who can find an audience" (12), and he cites the "right to tourism" as one of the more absurd of these candidates. But he does not associate all collective human rights with this body of "emerging" rights or the proliferation and dangerous dilution of human rights in the "enthusiastic legal literature." The claims by indigenous peoples to adequate protection of lands and rights in traditional territories, in particular, challenge the exclusively individualistic approach to human rights and stand "apart from the usual prescription of human rights on the basis of individual protection" (4). Another group right, the right to self-determination, is situated in the ever-widening recognition of the right of a distinct community to have its character "reflected in the institutions of government under which it lives" (5).

This makes the indigenous spokespeople's insistence that the world community affirm their collective rights easier to understand. States have not always been friendly or honorable in their dealings with them. The promotion of exclusively individual human rights thus has dangerous implications because many nation-states have vested interests in controlling and usurping the collective rights (including the collective *human* rights) of indigenous peoples. Individual human rights are insufficient to protect collective treaty rights. Emphasizing exclusively individual human rights leaves states with an opening to interfere in group identity, to provide only those cultural choices that weaken both indigenous societies and the distinct collective (principally treaty) rights that are part of their relationship, as sovereign entities, with states. To do otherwise than to recognize indigenous rights of self-determination is to invite the continued repression and marginalization of indigenous societies.

Such claims of self-determination and international recognition of collective rights can be seen as an international equivalent of the problem of identity affirmation in the context of multicultural states. Multicultural-ism implies a plurality of identities brought together within a single state or other political body. It can therefore be seen as a solution to the prob-lems posed by the demands for rights and recognition on the part of dis-tinct minorities. Ethnic groups and indigenous peoples, we might as-sume, should be appeased by inclusion in multicultural enterprises. The best solution to minority conflicts is constitutional reform and other le-gal protections of those with distinct minority cultures; and the only rea-sons the world is witness to ethnic conflicts in so many regions is because of ethnonationalist stridency and state intractability, unwillingness to share power, and centralist agendas dominated by single parties and ma-jority populations.

The principal multicultural goal of states inclines toward equalizing the conditions of life and opportunities of all individual citizens. Those who are especially burdened by poverty and disease are often those who are also the targets of racism, sexism, and other forms of discrimination. Liberal states and organizations take pride in combating these scourges of equal opportunity. Those who have been relegated to second- or third-class status can be defended, and their lives improved, by greater inclu-sion and equality, reinforced by identical rights and immunities, as ex-emplified by the American civil rights movement.

This simple approach to cultural pluralism and demands for recogni-tion, as Charles Taylor (1994) points out, is inconsistent with the diverse origins and orientations of multiculturalism. One of the defining features of modern identity, according to Taylor, is a decline of hierarchical, fixed modes of social recognition and self-definition in favor of unstable iden-tities in which social agency depends upon recognition by others. The transition from honor, derived from a position in a social hierarchy, to dignity, based upon social recognition and affirmation, means that "in-wardly derived, personal, original identity doesn't enjoy . . . recognition *a priori*. It has to win it through exchange, and the attempt can fail" (34 – 35). In Western thought, a new discourse about dignity, which Taylor at-tributes principally to Rousseau, seeks some form of perfectly balanced social equality and reciprocity to take the sting out of the otherwise com-petitive other-dependence of recognition. The search for a politics of equal dignity, however, brings with it the temptation to align equal free-dom with the absence of differentiation and thus invokes the danger of homogenizing tyranny. This tendency toward uniformity does not nec-essarily take such extreme forms as the Jacobins or communist dictator-ships. In some modern societies, the search for balanced equality results in a form of liberalism that is merely inhospitable to institutionalized so-cial differentiation, to any "distinct society" preferences. It insists on uni-form definition and application of rights and has corresponding diffi-culty accommodating the aspirations of those societies seeking special protections for cultural survival. This is an approach to liberalism in which all citizens are guaranteed equal freedoms, including equal free-dom to choose their collective attachments, through the guarantee of ba-sic rights. Jürgen Habermas (1994: 112–16) supports this individualistic approach in his commentary on Taylor's essay when he asserts that liber-alism need not be blind to unequal social conditions or cultural differ-ences when it upholds exclusively individual rights and freedoms. "All that is required is the consistent actualization of the system of rights" (113), which will often, Habermas admits, require the sparks of social movements and political struggles.

The struggle for recognition by ignored or deracinated distinct groups occurs in the context of wider differences in the politics and ethics of lib-eral societies, between the universalization of individual rights and the affirmation of cultural differences. The politics of difference creates an-other form of liberalism, which sees collective identities coming into con-flict or competition with rights to equal individual liberties. There is a tendency in the search for balanced equality to respond favorably to all claims of recognition that come along. This, according to Taylor, is another homogenizing approach to cultural differences because cultural claimants seek affirmation from a central source, from the standards of North Atlantic civilization. This form of liberalism makes few judgments but provides affirmation, solace, recognition, and esteem encouragement to all who demonstrate a need for greater social inclusion.

A variant of collectivist liberalism, espoused cautiously by Taylor (1994), is hospitable to some claims of distinctiveness and some of the special rights that follow from them, but within the strict limits necessary to protect the most important universal guarantees of liberty and protection of individuals. "Liberalism is also a fighting creed" (62), Taylor argues. It cannot take a position of complete cultural neutrality without diminishing its core values. It cannot free itself of all judgments and accept the equal worth of all cultures in response to preemptory demands of recognition. Liberalism can, however, take a position somewhere between "the inauthentic and homogenizing demand for recognition of equal worth, on the one hand, and the self-immurement within ethnocentric standards, on the other" (72).

Indigenous peoples' claims to self-determination do not fit comfortably into any of these paradigms of liberal society. A widely held approach to liberal multiculturalism, one based upon individual rights and universal equality, cannot accommodate the fundamental demands of many ethnic minorities or indigenous peoples. The claims of some indigenous peoples pose significant dilemmas not only for multicultural states but also international organizations that are today striving toward greater pluralism and inclusion of the marginalized, disenfranchised, and oppressed. Demands for respect, restorative justice, and protection of distinctive ways of viewing and living in the world are accompanied by more far-reaching demands for self-determination and autonomy that transcend, in various ways, legal arrangements based on the equal rights of equal citizens. Indigenism looks for ways to conceptualize and pursue the good that may or may not harmonize with state constitutions. This is because indigenous struggles for recognition and actualization of collective goals are taking place largely at the suprastate level, through international networks and within international organizations. Indigenism is a social movement with a strategic focus outside of states that seeks to activate rights to autonomy *within* states. In so doing, it imparts a new meaning to pluralism and a new challenge to the liberal project of recognizing differences.

Recognizing the rights of self-determination of minorities, including indigenous peoples, however, raises the possibility, or rather inevitability, that some of them in turn will violate and undermine the human rights of their members. Liberalism, including its human rights variant, cannot protect individual liberty while taking an uncritical approach to collective demands of recognition, especially those based on claims of self-determination. For this reason, one of the most important challenges for the human rights project is creating conditions favorable to the protection of distinct societies without sacrificing too many of the rights and protections of individuals. To what extent might indigenous peoples themselves become oppressive states within states, purveyors of small-scale nationalist chauvinism, xenophobia, intolerance, and—almost as a corollary—strident repression of those, weaker still, with whom their vision and identity are at odds?

Kymlicka (1995) avoids this problem by positing a differentiation between a society's external protections against domination and its internal restrictions of its own members. He distinguishes the specific rights extended to collectivities that protect them from the external abuses of states from those group rights that give national minorities internal powers (often used abusively) over their individual members. A national minority can thus claim a need for group protection from the dominant society and a need for protection against internal dissent from individual members (such as those who malign or refuse to follow traditional practices or customs). These two kinds of claim are distinct and should not be conflated. Kymlicka argues that "liberals can and should endorse certain external protections, where they promote fairness between groups, but should reject internal restrictions which limit the right of group members to question and revise traditional authorities and practices" (37). There is thus no necessary contradiction between collective and individual rights, between external protections and the individual rights of group members.

This still brings us to a terrible dilemma stemming from the realpolitik implications of collective rights for national minorities: if we create and affirm the group-specific rights of peoples, we run the risk of encouraging some states to energetically and despotically exercise jurisdiction over everyone within their territories, including those with potentially rival claims of self-determination. Competition between states and national minorities would increase. At the same time, states would be given a more complete tool kit of justification for imposing national loyalty. On the other hand, if only individual human rights are recognized by the world community (as is nearly the actual state of affairs), states can claim to be upholding these rights, but through repressive policies in such areas as education and formal employment; in other words, states can allow individuals to freely choose their culture, religion, and mode of subsistence in accordance with the letter of human rights standards, while working to restrict the range of viable choices within these categories. Either way, states can, if they choose, easily circumvent the pluralistically oriented human rights statutes while falsely claiming to encourage within their borders the self-determination of all peoples and liberty of all individuals.

The indigenous representatives who attend international meetings are apparently willing to take whatever risks might be inherent in their group-specific rights. There is a movement afoot to accomplish the recognition of indigenous peoples as "peoples" with group-specific rights, one that still faces resistance but is nevertheless steadily gaining momentum. Indigenous spokespeople have often argued that, like it or not, collective human rights already exist, that states are the main beneficiaries of these rights, and that such rights should be extended to indigenous peoples through formal recognition of their status as "peoples." The right of national groups to self-determination has already been given some recognition in international law. The International Covenants, for example, affirm the right of all peoples to self-determination: "By virtue of that right they freely determine their political status and freely pursue their economic, social and cultural development"; and Article 1.2 of both covenants states that "in no case may a people be deprived of its own means of subsistence." These are examples of human rights that apply to collectivities—"peoples"—not exclusively states and not individuals; they therefore have the potential to greatly increase the leverage of indigenous communities in resisting unwanted development and purposive assaults on cultural integrity. The United Nations has not, however, defined "peoples," other than through application of the principle of self-determination to overseas colonies (that is to say, colonies created through what is sometimes referred to as "salt-water colonialism," a term that originates from meetings of the "Group of 77" developing nations to distinguish European settler colonialism from state practices that might in some ways resemble it). It has not extended recognition of self-determination to the national minorities internal to states, even though these minorities have usually experienced the same sort of oppression as bona fide "colonies." Recognition of collective rights in the Universal Declaration and the International Covenants has been extended only to those who, besides making a case for legitimate "peoplehood," also make a case for full membership in the community of nation-states. The door has not yet been fully opened to recognition of peoples with rights of self-determination within states. There are no visitor's permits or qualified memberships for stateless peoples in the General Assembly, and intruders are not welcome; crossing the threshold into the community of nations requires a badge of statehood.

Indigenous representatives (in common with spokespeople from other national minorities) have expressed the view that this restricted application of the term "peoples" is arbitrary, inconsistent, and discriminatory. They insist that they too are nations with identical rights to self-determination as states and that their powers of self-determination were not relinquished by their incorporation (usually by force) into nation-states (Kymlicka 1995: 27). The denial of collective rights, particularly rights of self-determination, for indigenous peoples is seen by the latter as an attempt by states at monopolization, a reluctance to extend to others legal principles that already exist for them. (It follows from this argument that the resistance of some state representatives to recognition of the collective rights of indigenous peoples does not involve complete rejection of the very notion of collective rights: states themselves are collective entities with specific rights in international law. The League of Nations was established to regulate those rights in the aftermath of World War I.) This argument further implies that the risks inherent in recognizing collective human rights—the greater leverage these rights give states in imposing repressive measures on nondominant peoples—already exist; the genie has already been released from the bottle, and the best way to respond is to offset state powers by also recognizing the collective rights of indigenous peoples.

It is impossible to tell if the United Nations' conservative approach to self-determination actually contributes, or may contribute in future, to the frequency of zero-sum secessionist conflicts. Very likely, few ethnic minorities that currently aspire to statehood would be satisfied with less. In the case of indigenous peoples, the experiment has not been supported by some states, ostensibly because of concerns that it would inflame similar secessionist passions. But leaving statehood as the only way for a people to achieve recognition of their right to self-determination is, on the face of it, *more* likely to encourage strident irredentism.

The idea of recognizing collective rights of indigenous peoples was initially met with strong resistance by many states; and some continue to object to a broad interpretation and application of collective rights, particularly rights to self-determination. Does this resistance stem from a widely held and slowly dissipating misunderstanding, or are there significant interests at stake? To approach this question, it remains for us to see how, in practice, indigenous peoples, states, and international organizations maneuver through the challenges and opportunities presented by "peoplehood" and the rights that flow from it. But before I take up this question in the next chapter, I will make one more point about the implications of individual rights and legal processes for indigenous societies.

THE WEBERIAN DILEMMA

So far in this chapter we have considered some of the predicaments inherent in relativism and the recognition of indigenous claims of group rights, especially the problem faced by some advocates of an exclusively individualist approach to rights, problems arising from the collective claims of disenfranchised aboriginals: holding fast to the opposition against these claims forces liberal thinkers into a rejection of pluralism, or at least an unsound defense of it. Liberal monism thus comes to share some of the assumptions behind policies of assimilation and the destruction of lives and lifeways through misguided philanthropy.

But indigenous leaders pursuing an institutionalized framework of legal remedy face a related paradox, stemming from the encounter of traditional societies with a legal system based largely on formal procedures and individual rights: What do international bureaucracies, bastions of state interests and legatees of Enlightenment rationalism, have to offer people struggling, seemingly against the current of modernity, to maintain honor and family obligations, nature spirituality, subsistence economies, and the authority of elders in governance? What is the possible connection between individual rights and individualism, between legal recourse and political routinization, between bureaucratic development and bureaucratization? Do these social transformations begin with a consensual choice of values, or is there a strong element of inevitability and irrevocability to them? Does the formal protection of unique cultures, even through the mechanisms of collective rights, have the effect of formalizing processes of cultural transmission that are in essence informal? Does not the strategy of working within alien systems of written law in itself bring about some of the erosion of traditional values it is intended to protect?

We might call this the Weberian dilemma. Max Weber, perhaps more compellingly than anyone before his time (the late nineteenth and early twentieth centuries) or since, described the social and personal costs and consequences of modernity. For Weber, one of the defining and most compelling features of modernity is the overwhelming power of bureaucracy and law over tradition and charisma as means of legitimating authority, of motivating men to act without recourse to duress. Charisma, in such forms as the gift of religious musicality of prophets or the inspired cruelty of war leaders, leads people to loyalty and action through the regular performance of extraordinary acts: miracles, uncommon valor, inspirational oratory. Tradition reposes on conservatism, the authority of elders, the comfort of things as they have always been. Legal or bureaucratic authority adheres to rules, professional hierarchies, routine decision making in accordance with prescribed formulas made permanent by systems of writing and record keeping. And while these forms of legitimacy can exist in combination, and although societies can change their form in accordance with the forces of history, it is in the nature of bureaucracy to challenge the arbitrariness of tradition and dim the luster of charisma. Weber saw the dynamics of legitimacy as leading to social convergence, a terminus to human history in which all societies resemble one another in their basic organizational structures and motivational forces. Although convinced by bureaucracy's durability and growth, Weber saw it as at the same time leading to gray ubiquity, atomization, loneliness, and a thwarting of the human search for spiritual meaning.

The same basic idea has been expressed in countless different ways, most recently in a pessimistic trend within the burgeoning literature on globalization. But as it applies to indigenism, the Weberian dilemma remains essentially the same: the pursuit of justice has its costs; for everything one gets from it, a price is exacted in return; there is no way to defend traditional societies without in some way transforming them—without, above all, taking on some of the trappings of bureaucracy and written law; the advent of genocide is only the most explicit of the conformist impulses of modernity, for to mount campaigns of either violent or peaceful resistance requires mastery of techniques and technologies that similarly lead toward the same symmetry of social roles, social identities, and social units.

If the pursuit of self-determination through various levels of legal remedy and reform does not necessarily preserve the integrity of tradition, what are the benefits of legal strategies? What, if anything, is in the plus side of a trade-off that requires sacrificing much of the authority of elders? Answers to these questions can only be attempted once we have a more complete description of the aspirations and strategies of indigenous leaders and organizations, my task in the chapters that follow.

The connections between relativism and rights, especially as they relate to indigenous peoples, are rife with ethical dilemmas, ambiguity, and conflicting interests. Conditions of modernity no longer allow Montesquieu's world of cultural pluralism to thrive without compromise. We must now add to the ingredients that contribute to cultural differences and make people who they are. In particular, the destructive and assimilative forces of environmental degradation, state domination, and ethnic rivalry are changing the world's cultural landscape. The landscape is also being changed by the very tools—the legal and political tools of multiculturalism—used to surmount obstacles to autonomy.

It is testimony to the human genius for adaptability under circumstances of want and oppression that the concept or category "indigenous

peoples" has been taken up by indigenous leaders as a form of legal ref-
uge, identity, strategy of resistance, and source of self-determination. But
as a concept connected intimately with the International Bill of Human
Rights, and the development of human rights standards, "indigenous
peoples" carries certain baggage. It is certainly not the same thing as, say,
Cree, Sami, or Tuareg identity. It has wider implications even than the
various state-sponsored forms of identity—Indian, native, aboriginal, *in-
dígenas*—which also carry legal meaning. Human rights standards, even
while protecting or accommodating cultural differences, are universalist
in intention. They are, in essence, antirelativist in orientation, with their
method based in the laborious, and at times seemingly futile, pursuit of
global consensus.

Human rights are thus at odds with most forms of cultural relativism.
Relativism is often invoked to set unique cultures apart from other influences, to preserve the vestiges of human differences. It strives to show
that human integrity is so closely connected to cultural belief and practice that judgment can stem only from ethnocentric views and standards.
Reform cannot be imposed without cultural unraveling and social catastrophe. Human rights universalism, by contrast, implies not just a tool to
be used in defense of cultures but a selective critique of them based upon
antirelativist standards, standards derived from philosophical and legal
traditions alien to many distinct societies. An implication of this view is
that by seeking shelter in human rights, indigenous leaders are unintentionally invoking a form of universalism poised to bring about as much,
or more, cultural change as protection.

It would not be giving indigenous representatives much credit to say
that they are unaware of this dilemma. Rather, it appears that many have,
in their own way, come to a realization that human rights are not closed
to change by a final revelation; there remains room for reform, not only
in their own societies, but also in the laws, procedures, and organization
of human rights and international politics. This is why (as we will see in
more detail in chapter 5) indigenous peoples are at the forefront of human rights standard setting, invoking above all their collective rights to
cultural preservation and self-determination, while pressing for genuine
multicultural (not just multistate) participation in international forums.

Despite the statist orientation of international organizations, the full implications of human rights universalism are held at bay by the possibility of legal and institutional reform.

Another serious dilemma arises from the very process of legal remedy and reform: that is, the functional uses of writing, law, and bureaucracy that have become necessary for the preservation of distinct cultures are in some ways antithetical to them. In other words, as formal strategies of defending distinct ways of life are increasingly relied upon, they penetrate societies more deeply, and, as the logic of Weber's schema on legitimacy suggests, they ultimately erode many of the distinct qualities of minority—once exclusively oral—cultures. The pursuit of collective rights through legal strategies thus unintentionally harbors individualism.

The power of bureaucracy and law to transform societies cannot be denied. At the same time, however, it is important to recognize that if indigenous peoples do not control these powers, they are subject to them. Bureaucracy and law have become much like climate and geography: facts of life in the environment of all societies. Those who claim indigenous identity set themselves apart by, among other things, their tendency or ability to accept such circumstances as they are and, in keeping with their methods of subsistence, to closely read the conditions in which they find themselves and to build their strategies for survival around them. The conclusion that most indigenous representatives have arrived at from reading the signs in their legal environment is that their survival depends upon the pursuit of self-determination, one of the topics in the chapter that follows.

5 The New Politics of Resistance

In the previous chapter the issues of relativism and collective versus individual rights revealed the pervasiveness of sovereignty as a point of contestation between indigenous peoples and states. Antirelativism does not commonly consider parties other than states to be moral actors, at least not in the practice of human rights, and thus it unintentionally denies the self-determination claims of minority peoples through a limited vision of moral agency and responsibility. The individual rights argument is similarly statist in orientation, reluctant to see beyond states as the parties responsible for respecting (or violating) individual human rights. Neither the antirelativist nor the individualist tendency in human rights is fully able to come to terms with indigenous peoples' claims of difference, especially of distinct rights, or, from another perspective, *equal* rights of self-determination.

In this chapter I consider some of the ways that self-determination has become a source of indigenous resistance to the centralizing tendencies of states, especially to prevailing notions and policy implications of individual rights, as affirmed and defended by states. Indigenous leaders often see sovereignty as a matter of immediate concern, upon which other rights—such as rights to land, subsistence, and health care—depend. It is a matter revealed in what people say to each other, in resistance through political uses of language, oral and written. The dialogue I have paraphrased in notes at international meetings is, unlike most contents of the recent anthropological literature, unashamedly and directly about power, expressed in an odd assortment of legal language and metaphor.[1]

The term "self-determination" encompasses every conceivable aspiration of politically organized societies. James Anaya (1996: ch. 4) finds various elements of self-determination elaborated in international instruments, including nondiscrimination, cultural integrity, control over lands and resources, social welfare and development, and self-government. The U.N. International Covenants alone articulate rights of peoples to self-determination in their political status, control of resources, practice of subsistence, and cultural development.

The ways that indigenous leaders envision self-determination reflect this variety of interconnected possibilities. In a paper entitled "The Right of Indigenous Peoples to Self-Determination," presented to the 1999 Midnight Sun Worship in Inari, Finland, Ted Moses (2000) stated, "[W]hen I think of self-determination, I think of hunting, fishing and trapping. I think of the land, of the water. I think of the land we have lost" (162). For Juan Léon of the Defensoría Maya of Guatemala, one of the most important aspects of his organization's work is the reconstruction of the Mayan legal system to make the administration of justice less punitive and corrupt, more consistent with what Francisco Raymundo (1997: 5–6), in a Defensoría Maya Web site, describes as the Maya's oral, preventive, conciliatory, restorative, and flexible approach to social conflict. There are nearly as many indigenous visions of self-determination as there are possibilities for economic, political, and cultural development.

In chapter 6 I will discuss whether (and if so in what form) indigenous goals of self-determination are likely to include exercising the right of nationalist secession. But first it is necessary to draw out the implications of the significant fact that there is a consensus at work among internationally active indigenous leaders concerning the strategic approach to be taken in forwarding their claims of self-determination. Whether or not this consensus proves to be unshakable, the fact that it has influenced the work of the U.N. Commission on Human Rights for approximately a decade gives us leave to consider the development of human rights standards as an emerging form of indigenous political resistance. Unlike any other form of indigenous resistance, the pursuit of self-determination through human rights standards is global in its ambition; at the same time it aspires to effect reform at a variety of levels: in international organizations, the constitutions and laws of states, and the organization and values of indigenous polities themselves.

One of the concerns expressed by elders in attendance at international meetings is the erosion of their peoples' sovereignty by what they see as an alien and illegitimate state legal system. Tony Black Feather, spokesman for the Tetuwan Oyate, Teton Sioux Nation Treaty Council, for example, told his listeners in Geneva that "[a]s long as our people seek a solution in the American federal system, we will be subject to the corruption the system imposes" (Tetuwan Oyate 2000: 1). This point of view is shared by the James Bay Crees: "Although we find ourselves in our own homelands, our own territories, living in the places we and our ancestors have never left, we are confronted by a legal system that is not ours. None of the indigenous peoples have any recollection that they have ever revoked or abrogated their own system of law, or that they have ever consented to have their rights determined by European or colonial legal systems" (Moses 1996: 1). Such rejection of state legal systems does not imply a rejection of formal laws altogether. It is rather an indication of awareness that the formal system in the control of states cannot be relied upon as a mechanism to redress grievances. This rejection of state legal systems, while recognizing the usefulness of law, is what constitutes a new approach to indigenous resistance: there is no longer a clear contrast between formal redress of grievances and the informal "ordinary" politics of resistance. New opportunities have become available for indigenous peoples to use written laws for their own purposes. One of these is the international regime of human rights, which supersedes state laws internationally; another is the development of written indigenous constitutions and laws, which supersede state systems locally. There are thus two principal ways in which the indigenous peoples' movement challenges state sovereignty: One is at the international level, pressing for reforms within international law and eroding the statist orientation of the international system; the other is as a pluralistic force within states that presses for realization in practice of the notion, uncomfortable to many, of nations within nations, of peoples who have rights to self-determination nested within their rights as citizens of states.

Formalizing indigenous codes of behavior in the form of written laws and procedures is by no means the only option available in times of inevitable transition, but it certainly has its advantages over the alternatives. Maintaining oral traditions in the face of encroachments from state and industry has become increasingly untenable; time and again, contests between mores and law have been decided in favor of the latter. And acquiescing to all the political arrangements and codes of conduct imposed by the state has fragmented communities, led to crises of identity, and delegitimized local governance. Inherent law making, on the other hand, has the advantage of connecting tradition with state constitutional and institutional arrangements, with many of the terms dictated by local practice. This does not arrest change, but controls it, gives it some shape and direction, keeps it from spinning out of control, holds it as much as possible within the orbit of legitimate and recognizable social arrangements.

This does not mean that indigenous nationalism is inherently or inevitably innocuous. If we have learned anything about nationalism since the French Revolution, it is that the development and reinforcement of loyalties based upon race, class, language, or religion are not without their costs. It is becoming ever more widely understood that indigenous societies—the victims of xenophobia, racism, and intolerance—are not immune from the risks of imitating the faults of their oppressors. "One of the unresolved dilemmas of basing indigenous claims on self-determination," Kingsbury (2000) writes, "is that in encouraging groups to mobilize as 'nations,' some groups or their leaders may take what to outsiders (and to some insiders) appears the path of nationalist excess, oppressing dissenters, mistreating and even creating minorities in order to create a clear majority and reinforce the dominant identity" (35). There is a small step between national restoration and nationalist retribution.

How, then, can we expect indigenous nationalism to be any different from other forms of nationalism, to be free of chauvinism and counter-hate, even if it develops within existing nation-states and is entirely or largely without secessionist ambitions? The answer to this question is not to be found in the centers of international politics, where displays of in-tolerant indigenous nationalism would be counterproductive, but in the local revival of self-determination, the untidy politics of micronational-ism, and the use of self-determination as an instrument of indigenous resistance.

THE GRAND COUNCIL OF THE CREES
AT THE UNITED NATIONS, 1981–2000

The Cree campaigns for implementation of the James Bay and Northern Québec Agreement and against forcible inclusion in a sovereign Québec in the event of the province's secession from Canada were far more suc-cessful than Deskaheh's attempted petition to the League of Nations.[2] Not only did the Crees receive hearings at the United Nations, they achieved redress of some grievances and built on their access to the organization to press for improved human rights standards for indigenous peoples generally. They are one among many politically active indigenous peo-ples involved in human rights standard setting, but their story in many ways illustrates the achievements and remaining obstacles in the inter-national promotion of indigenous rights.

The background to James Bay Cree involvement in international poli-tics is almost identical to the recent history of Cross Lake outlined in chapter 3, with an imposed hydroelectric megaproject leading to rapid, mostly unwelcome changes to the Cree lifestyle. In 1971 Robert Bourassa, then premier of Québec, announced the province's and Hydro-Québec's intention to construct a $6 billion[3] hydroelectric project in the north-ern James Bay region. Bourassa's conception of this region corresponded closely with the idea of *terra nullius*, the uninhabited or unimproved "wasteland" commonly described by early European explorers and settlers in North America and other regions inhabited by aboriginal peoples. "It has long been my belief," Bourassa (1985) wrote in his autobiographical account of the James Bay project, "that Quebec's economic strength lies in the development of its natural resources, the most outstanding of which is its rich hydroelectric potential. And further, I have always believed that to develop these resources would require conquering and taming the North" (13). In his announcement of "the project of the century" he made no mention of the approximately nine thousand Crees living in the region,[4] pursuing a lifestyle based largely on hunting, fishing, trapping, and gathering. Nor, until legal action was taken by the Crees, does he seem to have seriously considered the impact of the project on their way of life or the necessity of providing compensation for the imminent loss of land and resources. The Crees, after hiring lawyers and arguing in court for over a year (while construction on the La Grande project continued), won a decision in their favor, only to be overruled soon after by a higher court, which reasoned that indigenous rights were subject to a "balance of convenience" of the majority population in the south that wanted electricity.

The temporary victory of the Crees in the Québec court system, however, prompted the Canadian and Québec governments and Hydro-Québec to negotiate an agreement with the Crees and Inuits of northern Québec, seeking the surrender of territory necessary for the completion of the planned hydroelectric installations. The Grand Council of the Crees came into being in the course of these negotiations as an organization representing regional Cree interests. A submission by the Grand Council to the fourth session of the U.N. Working Group on Indigenous Populations in 1985 summarizes the Cree perspective on the negotiation of the James Bay and Northern Québec Agreement, signed a decade earlier.[5]

> Faced with the inevitability of the changes that were being forced upon us, we attempted in the negotiations to establish the basis for a Cree community where there would be a viable choice between continuing a traditional life on the land, or participation in the new wage earning economy that was being imposed. The Crees fought for an environmental

protection regime, protected hunting and fishing rights, and certain modification in the project. But we also wanted Cree controlled educational facilities and access to modern Cree controlled health services. . . . This was the only opportunity we had to alleviate the harm caused to our people by the sub-standard education, and poor or non-existent health care provided to Indians by the Canadian government. (3)

The resistance of the governments of Canada and Québec to implementing the James Bay Agreement resulted in new hardships in the Cree communities and prompted the Grand Council of the Crees to seek redress at the United Nations. The actual event that impelled a change in strategy was the death of seven Cree children during an epidemic of gastroenteritis in 1980. Medical help came only after repeated requests to government authorities, and a subsequent study revealed that the outbreak was caused by water contaminated as a result of inadequate sanitary facilities. This situation, in turn, was traced to the fact that specific provisions in the James Bay Agreement for the construction of water systems and sanitary facilities had not been fulfilled (Grand Council 1985: 4). Abel Bosum (1994) summarized the reasons (including the 1980 epidemic) that led the Crees to bring their case to the United Nations: "When an indigenous treaty is violated, when an indigenous territory is flooded to provide hydroelectricity, when an indigenous forest is clear-cut . . . our people are forced to turn to authorities who have a vested interest in the outcome. We must pretend that they are purveyors of neutral and unbiased justice" (2). International lobbying began with the goal of seeking high-profile, nonprejudicial forums to which grievances with governments and state-owned corporations could be addressed.

At this point the Grand Council had developed into an effective regionally based negotiating, lobbying, and public relations body with established connections to non-Cree lawyers and consultants, carefully monitored networks of communication with constituents, and an experienced leadership, including an elected grand chief and deputy grand chief. This leadership consisted of a small number of individuals, some sharing long-standing relationships that had begun in Indian residential schools, who struggled against all odds to continue their educations in high schools and colleges outside the Cree region in the 1960s and 1970s.

The Grand Council had the resources and personnel necessary for effective lobbying at the international level, and it now had issues to bring before international judicial and governing organizations. When representatives of the Grand Council first went to Geneva as participants in the second International NGO Conference on Indigenous Peoples in 1981, their main issues of concern were the violations of the James Bay Agreement by Canada and Québec and the specific conditions that resulted in a fatal epidemic. Press coverage of the Cree submissions to this conference was soon followed by Canada's implementation of the specific provisions of the James Bay Agreement concerning water supply and sanitation.

From this point on, Cree leaders cultivated a prominent place as representatives of their constituents and other indigenous peoples at the United Nations. In 1987 they applied for and were granted NGO consultative status by the U.N. Economic and Social Council, and today they are one of seventeen indigenous peoples' organizations worldwide to hold this position.[6] There are, in addition, approximately one hundred indigenous peoples' organizations accredited to the Commission on Human Rights Working Group that do not have status with the Economic and Social Council.[7] This more limited form of recognition at the United Nations gives organizations only a right of participation in the discussion on the Draft United Nations Declaration on the Rights of Indigenous Peoples. The Crees have therefore been in a privileged position, not only in bringing international attention to Canada's failures in meeting existing obligations toward its First Nations peoples, but also in participating actively in the formulation of human rights standards and draft principles and in proposals for the establishment of a permanent forum for indigenous peoples at the United Nations.

One of the matters that the Grand Council has brought before the Working Group on Indigenous Populations—an issue that speaks directly to the possibility that secession may become a normal outcome of indigenous assertions of self-determination—is the right of aboriginal peoples to determine their own political destiny in the event of Québec secession. This issue illustrates some of the central differences between indigenism and ethnic nationalism in the potential use of self-determination, in particular the pursuit (or absence) of statehood.

Richard Handler (1988) describes in detail the subjective sources of group unity, which he sees as providing the major impetus to Québec nationalism and the drive to secession. Nationalism, according to Handler, "is an ideology in which social reality, conceived in terms of nationhood, is endowed with the reality of a natural thing" (6). Strong historical and cultural convictions, combined with a negative vision of Anglophone outsiders intent on eroding Québec's linguistic and cultural integrity, lead Québécois nationalists to objectify their ethnic boundaries, to see national character as a concrete entity or being. Such cultural objectification is expressed by René Lévesque (1968), who led the province in its first referendum on independence in 1980, when he writes of the potential benefits of secession: "We finally would have within our grasp the security of our collective 'being' which is so vital to us, a security which otherwise must remain uncertain and incomplete" (28). It is the perceived need to give this nation of Québec its full freedom of expression that most consistently inspires the *indépendantistes* in their bid for a concrete nation-state.

The uncompromising pursuit of secession and sovereignty by Québec nationalists, and resistance to it by federalists and other provinces, has shaped the most important events in Canada's domestic politics over the past several decades. Two constitutional agreements intended to mollify Québec, include the province in the constitution, and head off attempts at secession—the Meech Lake Accord of 1987 and the Charlottetown Accord of 1992—were scuttled, mainly due to disagreements over concessions (or lack of them) to Québec's distinct status and self-determination. The Parti Québécois, upon its accession to the provincial leadership in 1976, led the first full-blown attempt to secede from Canada with a referendum on sovereignty in 1980. In 1995, under the leadership of Jacques Parizeau, the Parti Québécois held a second referendum on secession, this time with very close results. After the defeat of the "Yes" vote by less than 1 percent, the Parti Québécois promised not to let the matter rest until a fully independent Québec state was a reality. Clearly the Parti Québécois became emboldened in its uncompromising stance on secession, with Bloc Québécois leader Lucien Bouchard (later to become Québec's premier) rejecting a distinct-society alternative prior to the 1995 referendum and describing his response as one of "deep boredom, deep boredom. It will be hard to hold back the yawns" (cited in Guglielmo 1997: 207). Even after Bouchard's 2001 resignation, due largely to the declining fortunes of Québec separatism, party officials vowed to maintain their focus on the goal of sovereignty (*Le Monde* 2001: 4).

An investigation of the implications of Québec secession on Cree rights commissioned by the Grand Council of the Crees raises some of the aboriginal leadership's objections to the unilateral inclusion of their people in an independent Québec: "On what basis could Québec claim it can simply take over existing federal treaty obligations and unilaterally determine that the Canadian government would no longer be a party to the treaties concerned?" (Grand Council 1996: 5). The potential impact of secession on existing services in education, health, and justice also raised concerns, especially in the light of Québec's and Canada's poor records in the implementation of the James Bay Agreement. And, as the Cree position paper asks, "If Aboriginal peoples choose not to subject themselves to such impacts, how can a secessionist Québec government forcibly include them and their territories in a separate new state?" (5).

Québec sovereigntists have insisted on maintaining the present borders of the province in any independent state, despite the fact that much of the northern region is occupied by native peoples who do not speak French, who share none of the cultural convictions of Québec sovereigntists, and who do not wish to be included in a sovereign Québec. David Cliche, special Parti Québécois ambassador to Québec's native people, made it clear that the province was unwilling to compromise on this issue: "We are thinking of co-management of our lands and waters. We are envisaging and thinking of sharing royalties and sharing of natural resources. This is all on the table. What is not on the table is the division of the territory of the province of Quebec and the eventual division of the territory of Quebec as a state" (*Globe and Mail* 1994: A2). The Parti Québécois, moreover, denied the legitimacy of Cree and Inuit referenda, implemented in part with mobile ballots flown by helicopter to remote bush camps, which showed more than 95 percent of respondents in favor of remaining with Canada in the event that Québec seceded.

The Crees have used the U.N. Working Group on Indigenous Populations as one of many venues for the defense of their rights to self-determination in the context of Québec's intention to secede. Cree statements in international forums challenged Canada's position concerning the use of the term "peoples" in the draft declaration. To avoid the implications of international law, which confirms the right to self-determination for all "peoples," Canada had been pressing for alternative phrasings, including "populations," "groups," and "people" in the singular. Ted Moses (1993) stated at the 1993 World Conference on Human Rights in Vienna that "[Canada has] decided that our rights as peoples will not exist if they simply avoid referring to us as 'peoples'" (3). Later Cree arguments pointed to double standards in Canada's position on self-determination, including its unqualified recognition of Québec's self-determination but refusal of self-determination for the aboriginal "distinct societies" of Canada, and its use of the word "peoples" in reference to Canada's First Nations in the constitution but its refusal to use the word in reference to indigenous "peoples" in international conventions. As Moses (1994) stated to a 1994 meeting on the draft declaration: "Why should Canada recognize a right of self-determination for the various populations of a province that threatens secession, and yet oppose the recognition of that same right to indigenous peoples, who make no such claim to independence?" (7).

At the same time, a picture of grim chaos resulting from indigenous self-determination was portrayed by spokespeople for the Québec government. David Cliche, for example, stated in a press interview: "If the Crees in Quebec go their own way, the next will be the natives in British Columbia, and then the Ojibwa in Northern Ontario, and eventually every native nation on three continents" (*Globe and Mail* 1994: A1). A similar concern over microsecession as a potential outcome of broad recognition of aboriginal rights was expressed by Claude Bachand, a Québec member of Parliament, when presented with Cree objections to inclusion in a sovereign Québec. Given recognition of their rights as peoples, "Aboriginal nations would be free not only to choose self-determination but also to secede. . . . Canada and Quebec might then become like a piece of gruyere cheese, full of holes, with pieces of legislation that are not necessarily consistent.[8] The situation would become ungovernable" (Canada 1996b: 9).

Matthew Coon-Come (1994), as grand chief of the Grand Council of the Crees, attempted to minimize the impact of such statements in an address to the Center for Strategic and International Studies in Washington, D.C.: "We Crees are not 'nationalists.' That concept does not exist in the Cree language. Our tie to the land is not just political, it is also physical. We are part of our lands" (2). Ted Moses (1994) repeated this point to the Working Group on the Draft Declaration: "The Crees have no interest in secession from Canada. We want self-determination to be recognized so that we can finally become part of Canada" (7). Cree spokespeople had to perform a delicate balancing act to allay fears that the Crees would declare independence if self-determination for indigenous peoples was formally recognized at the United Nations.

Canada's contradictory position on indigenous self-determination does not make sense unless it is considered in the context of Québec's bid for secession. In order to claim all of the present borders of the province, Parti Québécois leaders insisted upon inclusion of all residents of the province in their proposed state, including the Cree, Naskapi, Innu, and Inuit peoples of the North. Canada's position on indigenous self-determination was thus an avoidance strategy, intended to prevent aggravating hard-line Québec sovereigntists in the period leading up to the 1995 referendum. Québec's denial of collective rights resonated in Canada's response to the draft declaration.

The strength of the Cree position in domestic constitutional debates depends largely on the progress of the self-determination issue in the United Nations. Even though this progress has proven to be laborious, the Grand Council has been guardedly optimistic in its hope that the United Nations will be an important source of support for aboriginal self-government and self-determination: "Further recognition of indigenous rights by the U.N. is now considered by everyone to be unstoppable, and it seems possible that 'indigenous rights' may become the next major issue to occupy the U.N. If that is indeed the case then Canada will be forced to completely rework its Indian policy, which in its present state is proving to be a serious source of international embarrassment" (Grand Council 1988: 12). Even though this statement is now more than a decade old, it seems to still hold true and to be closer to realization—an indication that the inherent possibilities in the pursuit of indigenous rights at the United Nations just might not wither on the vine.

ELDERS AND STATESMEN

There are basically two kinds of leader who travel to international meetings: elders and statesmen.[9] It is a sign of global change and an indication of the nature of indigenism that the two are distinct. One of the international roles of Cree elders from the James Bay region of Québec has been to present testimony on the flooding of their land by a hydroelectric megaproject to a variety of venues within Canada and to annual meetings of the U.N. Working Group on Indigenous Populations in Geneva. Their presence and testimony have occasionally been used to ground the efforts of the Working Group in the realities of forest life in its encounter with dramatic, industrially imposed destruction of lands and waters, and the realities of people used to living from the land in their encounter with loss.

According to an Inuit woman I once met in Chisasibi, the one thing that seemed to consistently disconcert Inuit and Cree elders when they first traveled to large cities, aside from the numbers of cars and people, was their introduction to riding elevators. After no perceptible motion in the small room, the doors open upon a new scene. The moment of disorientation was, in a way, a summary of their life experience: unaccountably the world seemed to have moved, while they remained in place. But from another perspective their sense of stability was illusory; it was just that the forces of change had been long unseen—until a new reality suddenly imposed itself.

There are elders who have successfully participated in international conferences, who traveled by air without too much difficulty, who managed to cope with the pace of life in a European city, and who were not visibly intimidated by the large meeting rooms, the microphones, the translators peering down from their glass booths, or the numbers of people they were addressing. But for all their ability to adapt, most indigenous elders have experienced the abrupt opening of doors onto a changed

world. And this experience is reflected in their sense of urgency, the priorities they set, and the way they define sovereignty.

For David Monongye, a Hopi elder from Hoetevilla, Arizona, in an address to the 1977 Geneva Conference, grievance and hopes for greater
self-determination are both to be found in the contest for control of land:

> This is our mother earth, so, therefore, I say that we might not let go of
> our land. Again, I will say that [we will] hold onto our land. Now I have
> heard, many of you have already spoken, how things were taken away
> from you people. We all have similar problems, discrimination, our hu-
> man rights are being denied, our sovereignty has been denied. Now the
> Indian bureau is trying to get all of our land that belongs to us that was
> given to us by the Great Spirit. They want to get ahold of all our land
> for themselves, but do not give it up. . . . Some of you may have eaten
> cracker jacks. What does it say outside the crackerjack box—"the more
> you eat the more you want." He has eaten up our land already, but he
> wants more. (International Indian Treaty Council [IITC] 1977: 11)

Another perspective from elders emphasizes dissatisfaction with the
proceedings of international meetings, above all with what they see as
the unwillingness of state representatives to treat indigenous peoples as
equals. This was the view expressed by a Lakota elder, Eli J. Tail, Sr.
(2000), to the Working Group on the Permanent Forum: "The first day I
was here . . . I thought that this was what the Permanent Forum was to
be—a place where all people would be on equal terms. And now I understand it is just in the early stages of being proposed, much less a real
forum. . . . Most of the indigenous peoples are from areas which the states
claim to have conquered. Why do you continue to fear us? You could just
kill us all" (1). Such disappointment is largely a product of hopes that
grow to proportions inconsistent with the political realities of international organizations.

Other indigenous delegates, whom we might call "statesmen," are
more comfortable with this new reality, more active negotiators, more
at home in meeting rooms. These qualities emerge from the necessities
of leadership. It has become quite simply impossible to defend indigenous interests without negotiating with states, and almost impracticable
not to transcend the state/indigenous relationship through international
lobbying.

THE NEW POLITICS OF RESISTANCE

The politics engaged in by the Grand Council of the Crees reflect the formal educations and worldly experience of the organization's leaders. The Grand Council thrives on strategic multiculturalism, above all the appropriation of state symbols of sovereignty. The Grand Council office in Ottawa is referred to in official correspondence as the "Cree Embassy." From the late 1980s until he was elected grand chief in 1999, Ted Moses was accorded the title "ambassador" of the Grand Council. This was not officially conferred by any one authority but was started informally by the Grand Council delegation and was eventually picked up by other indigenous delegations, state representatives, and U.N. officials. Sovereignty was pursued by the Grand Council through successful imitation of the most powerful symbols of statehood.

Another strategic use of identity goes in the opposite direction, toward minimization or denial of possible similarities between indigenous polities and states. This takes the form of representations of cultural isolation and purity and a corresponding denial of the influence of dominant languages, technologies, and political strategies. Sovereignty is thus asserted indirectly, by declaring cultural differences to be wide and insurmountable.

There is still a seemingly unalterable core of popular romanticism that makes it advantageous for indigenous leaders to embody in every aspect of their demeanor the picturesque qualities of indigenous life. David Stoll, in *Rigoberta Menchú and the Story of All Poor Guatemalans* (1999), argues that the pressure to make indigenous campaigns stand out from competing causes encourages leaders like the Nobel Prize–winning Rigoberta Menchú to distort the realities of their communities of origin and life histories, encouraging them to give in to popular demand for the exotic side of indigenous life. In the book *I, Rigoberta Menchú* (Burgos-Debray 1984), she describes her youth as more or less typically "indigenous," including exploitation and abuse by a wealthy ladino family and active participation in a guerilla movement. It was the consumer-driven demand for authenticity, Stoll argues, that led Menchú to significantly distort her past in such ways as to claim that her knowledge of Spanish was recently acquired, concealing the fact that much of her youth was spent in an exclusively female *internado,* or boarding school, run by Catholic nuns.

Refutation of the specifics described by one person, even a Nobel

Prize–winning person, does not call into question the suffering experienced by the Mayan peasants during Guatemala's brutal civil war. And notwithstanding Stoll's account of Menchú's life history, those indigenous leaders who are literate and familiar with international law do not often conceal their abilities in the meeting rooms of international forums. It is in the course of public outreach, the lobbying for popular support for specific indigenous causes, that the desire for "authenticity" is most likely to be expressed—and one way or another most likely to be fulfilled.

Indigenous leaders attending U.N. meetings, however, do not seem to be concerned with concealing their abilities behind a veneer of indigenous authenticity. The issues they are dealing with require them to use all their abilities. This is especially true of the struggle with states over sovereignty. In Switzerland, chosen as a site for international meetings because of its long-standing constitutional pluralism, there are few reminders of the potentially lethal nature of this competition. In some parts of the world, indigenous claims of sovereignty can still provoke threats of death, still send guerillas or state soldiers through the countryside shooting livestock, burning crops, and emptying villages through fear of their brutality or through actual acts of mass killing. In the meeting rooms of the Palais des Nations in Geneva, however, the matters that in other times and places provoke bloodshed are merely discussed before a chairperson, with everyone kept to turns of five minutes or less.

THE BATTLE OF THE "S"

The "battle of the 'S'" has been fought in one form or another, and with varying degrees of intensity, at every gathering of indigenous peoples and states under the auspices of the United Nations. It continues to be one of the most important sources of disagreement between indigenous peoples and states, although, on the state side, the lines have shifted and only a minority remains entrenched against the forays of the "S." If the called-for use of the "S" is left out of any human rights standard-setting exercise, indigenous delegates immediately raise the issue, to which recalcitrant states reply from their trenches.

In fact, the "S" does not always stand alone but, written in possessive constructions, marches in unison with an apostrophe, the position of which is vitally significant: an apostrophe placed to the left of the "S" is fatal to its plurality. Only an apostrophe on the right affirms the collectivist authority, the inherent pluralism, of the "S."

On the surface, the controversy surrounding the "S" appears to be a mere product of the pedantry of jurists; but hanging upon the "S" is the question of whether indigenous peoples are the same "peoples"—with an "S"—so prominent in the Charter of the United Nations (the preamble of which is formulated in the name of "the Peoples of the United Nations"), and who therefore must be recognized as possessing all the rights that flow from that status, including the right to self-determination. So the "S" in "peoples" represents something quite important: the unfettered right of self-determination, as given pride of place in Article 1 of the Covenants and Article 3 of the Draft United Nations Declaration on the Rights of Indigenous Peoples.

A right to self-determination covers a spectrum of political choices, from assimilation into a dominant state to independent statehood (Nettheim 1988: 118). Between these poles is a range of options involving arrangements of self-government or regional autonomy with the state. If anything, the United Nations has exercised a bias in favor of independent statehood as a way of resolving conflicts stemming from colonial situations. This in itself has inclined states toward resisting the "S" favored by indigenous peoples because it raises the specter of uncontrollable indigenous secessionist claims and conflicts. The debate over the "S" has therefore led to an impasse at the Commission on Human Rights, one result of which has been little progress on the approval of the Draft United Nations Declaration on the Rights of Indigenous Peoples.

The "battle of the 'S'" also made an appearance at the International Labour Organization (ILO) during discussions leading up to final drafting and passage of the Indigenous and Tribal Peoples Convention of 1989 (No. 169). Here, the "S" emerged as part of a wider debate between those who favored a bold and comprehensive statement of rights and aspirations, including an explicit statement of the indigenous right to self-determination, and those, particularly the employers and a segment of governments, who saw any mention of self-determination as potentially destructive of the sovereignty of nation-states (Swepston 1990: 223–24). This controversy emerged most sharply in what Lee Swepston, human rights coordinator of the ILO, described as "an arcane international battle akin to debating the shape of the table" (228). Meetings on the ILO convention struggled for three years over replacing the word "populations," in the Convention No. 107 of 1957, with "peoples" in the instrument being developed. A conference on the document was reduced to using the term ["peoples"/"populations"], with brackets reducing its potency. The issue was resolved with the unhappy compromise of using the term "peoples" in the ILO convention, but with a proviso placed in Article 1.3 intended to remove its legal authority: "The use of the term 'peoples' in this Convention shall not be construed as having any implications as regards the rights which may attach to the term under international law." In effect, the ILO, in the interests of realizing a convention that would meet the immediate needs of indigenous peoples, postponed the debate on indigenous self-determination by handing it over to its parent body, the United Nations.[10]

As we have already seen in a discussion of Cree opposition to the proposed terms of Québec secession, the "S" issue has been more contentious in Canada than elsewhere for two related reasons. First, Canada's constitution, revised and repatriated in 1982, makes reference to "aboriginal peoples." This gave prominence to Canada's rejection of the "S" in the context of international human rights standards for indigenous peoples, making the reluctant states appear inconsistent and hypocritical. Second, the likely motives for Canada's position on the "S" also emerged with particular clarity—relating to concerns about possible Québec secession—thus confirming the idea that the position of governments on the "S" had little to do with justice or consistency in law and a great deal to do with vested state interests. For these reasons the government of Canada was a primary target when indigenous delegates realized the significance of the "S" and began to challenge states on their position toward it.

In annual meetings of the Working Group on Indigenous Populations, Canada used and supported phrasings that avoided the "S," including "populations" (as in the name of the Working Group), "groups," and "people" in the singular. In a paper submitted to the 1987 Working Group, some of the thinking behind this approach was made explicit: "It should be noted that references made to Canada's aboriginal 'peoples' are consistent with the terminology of the Canadian Constitution with respect to Canada's domestic situation. They should *not* be interpreted as supportive of the notion that Canada's aboriginal groups are 'peoples' in the sense of having the right to self-determination under international law [emphasis in original]" (Canada 1987: 1).

At the 1993 World Conference on Human Rights in Vienna, indigenous delegates became aware that some states, including Canada, were avoiding using the "S." In response, they drew large "S"s on sheets of paper and pinned them to their clothing. When Canada's delegates spoke, they removed the sheets and raised them over their heads, a gesture that underscored the absence of the word "peoples" from everything being said.

It was only after the narrowest possible victory of the "No" vote in Québec's 1995 referendum on secession that Canada began to revise its position on the "S." On October 31, 1996, at the fifty-third session of the Working Group on the Draft Declaration on the Rights of Indigenous Peoples, a qualified recognition of indigenous self-determination was presented in which the government of Canada (1996a) accepted "a right of self-determination for indigenous peoples which respects the political, constitutional and territorial integrity of democratic states" (2). (It is worth noting that the qualification "which respects" gives Canada room to maneuver in the event that a secessionist province were to claim indigenous territories as part of a new state.)

This did not by any means put an end to the general controversy at the United Nations. Although such states as Australia, Denmark, and Canada changed their positions, other states, such as India, China, and the United States have remained adamantly opposed to use of the term "indigenous peoples" in any official U.N. document. This focal point of state/indigenous disagreement finds its way into almost every conceivable issue under discussion. On the first day of the 1999 World Health Organization Consultation on the Health of Indigenous Peoples, indigenous delegates made a connection between their health conditions, their control of land and resources, and therefore their need, above all else, for self-determination. At the 2000 meeting of the ad hoc working group on a new permanent forum, controversy flared up, among other things, over the name to be given the forum. When some states made it clear that they would not accept the word "peoples" in the name of the forum, and proposed instead that it be called the "Permanent Forum for Indigenous Issues," some indigenous delegates placed yellow signs with bold letters in front of their desks reading "WE ARE PEOPLES, NOT ISSUES." Milelani Trask (representing Na Koa Idaika O Ka Lahui Hawai'i), seated behind such a sign, stated, "The chair is conceding and caving in to the states that are twisting his arm," and a representative of the Assembly of First Nations said, "It is a shame that the state governments cannot recognize the world's indigenous peoples as such. . . . We are peoples, not issues. Issues may go away, but peoples do not."

After these statements had been heard, a proposal was made by the International Indian Treaty Council to draft a clause that would limit the implications of the word "peoples" in international law, thus meeting state concerns, while acting to "preserve position" for the indigenous delegates. An IITC spokesman cited the precedent set by Article 1.3 of ILO Convention No. 169 and suggested the following wording: "As it is beyond the mandate of this Working Group to provide judicial interpretation, the interpretation of the word 'peoples' and its meaning under international law should be left to competent U.N. bodies."

A resolution sent by the Commission on Human Rights (United Nations 2000b) for adoption by the Economic and Social Council two months after this meeting took place made no reference to this debate or the proposed compromise on "peoples" but referred in its heading to "Establishment of a Permanent Forum on Indigenous Issues." This veto by the Human Rights Commission of the indigenous position lends credence to the kind of frustration expressed by a Lakota elder: "[T]he work is dictated, without the indigenous peoples' input even being given consideration, with changes made outside of public discussion. . . . It is cruel to invite input and then completely disregard it" (Tail 2000: 1). At the same time, it reveals a continuing caution on the part of the United Nations toward the issue of indigenous self-determination. Such contests over sovereignty, if we look more closely, can be found throughout many of the discussions that take place under other headings.

DIALOGUE ON SELF-DETERMINATION

Battlefields, legislatures, and courts, with so much hidden behind their main adversarial goals, do not reveal human interests quite so clearly as tasks of cooperation. When people resist one another while pursuing a supposedly common purpose, the tensions revealed usually tell us something about their characters, the core of their personalities, what makes them tick. When we see political organizations resist one another in a cooperative venture, we usually know we have found something that can reveal their basic motives and orientations.

When indigenous and state delegates sat together for ten days at the U.N. headquarters in Geneva during February 2000, they had such a common purpose, revealed in the name given to the meeting in a U.N. document: "the ad hoc working group established pursuant to Commission on Human Rights resolutions . . . to consider the establishment of a permanent forum and to submit concrete proposals to that effect" (United Nations 2000b: 2). The permanent forum is to be the centerpiece of the International Decade of the World's Indigenous People and the principal mechanism for "furthering partnership between Governments and indigenous people" (2).

The question of self-determination for indigenous peoples pervaded the discussions of this meeting, not just in the explicit controversy over use of the word "issues" rather than "peoples" in the name to be given the forum but in matters related only indirectly to concerns about sovereignty. The methods by which indigenous representatives would be elected or appointed to the forum, for example, fed directly into indigenous claims to self-determination. Indigenous delegates were concerned that too much involvement from states in the procedures for appointing indigenous representatives would emasculate the forum by making its principal decision makers reliant upon state authority. The very discussion of state proposals for election or appointment of indigenous representatives seemed to be understood by indigenous delegates as an inappropriate intrusion into matters of concern to indigenous peoples as self-determining nations.

A Spanish proposal for setting up the indigenous representation at a permanent forum, for example, contained one element that provoked disapproval from many indigenous delegates: "Each Member State having indigenous populations on its territory will accredit two delegates for the plenary meetings: one representing the government and the other freely designated in an autonomous way by the Indigenous Peoples" (United Nations 2000a: 3). Indigenous delegates almost uniformly reacted with concern to this aspect of the proposal, seeing in it an attempt to "domesticate" and control state relations with indigenous peoples. The issue of representation was, for them, deeply implicated with self-determination. A representative of the Teton Sioux Nation thanked the Spanish delegation for presenting a concrete proposal for the membership of the forum but then offered a blunt criticism of the idea that indigenous members should be accredited by states: "Any attempt at linking membership in the forum with some sort of a formula between nation states and indigenous cultures from within the borders of those nation-states would be a real problem for us. This is the same kind of paternalism and the same kind of dominance that has brought us to the United Nations in the first place." Spain's position paper was probably not intended to weaken indigenous representation at the United Nations. It was a set of proposals to facilitate the establishment of a new forum in an organization dominated by states. Nevertheless, the suggestion that states should accredit the forum's indigenous representatives was broadly rejected by the indigenous caucus. The subtext of their objections seemed to be that indigenous sovereignty would not be secure in a system in which state governments had any part in the process of approving indigenous representatives.

The matter did not end here. A few state delegations grew impatient with the apparent inability of the indigenous caucus to arrive at a concrete, uniform system for electing or appointing indigenous representatives to the future permanent forum. Argentina's representative clearly felt that states were the most experienced at the international political game and should be closely involved in the appointment of indigenous members to the permanent forum: "What we want is for these communities to be properly represented. And the formula that we propose is the one which we think would best ensure representation for those communities." The government of Venezuela recommended the "homogenization of indigenous election procedures in order for there to be transparency," and others called for the indigenous caucus to arrive at the election procedures before the meeting's end. One indigenous delegate, however, shifted the blame for the slow progress being made on the election procedures by recalling the global impacts of colonization on indigenous political systems: "Governments are already highly organized. . . . But indigenous peoples are not in that situation. In fact, if we had been allowed to practice our own indigenous social, political structures, then maybe we would be in that state also. But those were the things that had been destroyed during colonization . . . and nation-state building. We have not been allowed to really develop and nurture our own indigenous social structures and political structures." An indigenous spokesperson from Bangladesh pointed to the practical and financial constraints of formal elections of indigenous representatives, modeled on the procedures of democratic states: "Are we going to say that each community is going to vote? Who is going to organize this kind of nomination procedure? Is there an election commission in the country which is going to nominate these kind of indigenous representatives? If that is the procedure, then we are talking about financial constraints. If the state wants to ensure that [all indigenous communities participate in the election process and is] willing to contribute money . . . the same money could be used for development of the indigenous communities."

The Commission on Human Rights, following up on this meeting, decided that the permanent forum would consist of sixteen members, eight to be nominated by governments and elected by the Economic and Social Council, and eight indigenous members "to be appointed by the President of the Council . . . on the basis of broad consultations with indigenous organizations taking into account the diversity and geographical distribution of the indigenous people of the world as well as the principles of transparency, representativity and equal opportunity for all indigenous people" (United Nations 2000b: 2). The United Nations was apparently neither in a position to accede to the will of some states to control indigenous representation nor able to recognize indigenous claims to complete control over procedures for determining indigenous membership of the forum. It gave ultimate authority over representation to the Economic and Social Council and left to one side the question of democratic mechanisms.

Another revealing difference between states and indigenous peoples that arose in discussions on the establishment of a permanent forum centered upon reference to the Charter of the United Nations in the mandate of the forum. The chairman of the previous year's meeting on the permanent forum pointed in his report to Articles 62 and 63 of the charter for possible guidance in setting out this mandate. Article 62 in particular points, in an apparently innocuous way, to the power of the Economic and Social Council to "make or initiate studies and reports with respect to international economic, social, cultural, educational, health, and related matters" and says that it "may make recommendations with respect to any such matters to the General Assembly, to the Members of the United Nations, and to the specialized agencies concerned." More of the same apparently bland material is found elsewhere in these articles, nothing that could easily be seen as a threat to state interests. But the prospect of referencing the Charter of the United Nations in the mandate of the permanent forum for indigenous people did indeed become contentious for some states. Their objections were not expressed so much in open plenary sessions as in the behind-the-scenes work of state and indigenous "facilitators," appointed to summarize the conclusions reached in closed caucus meetings. One indigenous delegate objected to this procedure, calling it "bad faith" on the part of governments to use facilitators to make objections to the indigenous peoples' positions without putting them on the floor. "They're not being forthright," he protested, "and they're saving their objections for the facilitators. We believe that's a corruption of the process." An indigenous delegate from Bangladesh insisted on the reasonableness of the indigenous position: "We're not at this meeting asking for a buffalo and hoping to get a goat," he said. "We want a goat and are asking for a goat."

As with many seemingly arcane but hard-fought controversies, the real issues of contention are general and far-reaching. Those states that objected to the very idea of an indigenous forum in the first meetings on the issue were faced with a growing consensus in its favor that they were no longer able to obstruct. With the forum itself now apparently a fait accompli, the strategy that remained to them was to limit its powers in every way possible. For some states, therefore, it became important to prevent the establishment of a forum with a mandate that could establish policy in the U.N. system, that could create compulsory instruments or standards, or that was able to intervene in internal violent conflicts. For these states, reference to the Charter of the United Nations invoked such possibilities. For the indigenous delegates, on the other hand, the charter embodied their most cherished aspirations. The goals set out in the preamble of the charter, "to save succeeding generations from the scourge of war" and "to promote social progress and better standards of life in larger freedom," seemed to resonate with particular force for one of Hawaii's indigenous delegates, Milelani Trask, who stated in a plenary session: "For [states] to object to peace and prosperity, that leaves us with war and poverty." In an indigenous caucus meeting one participant suggested that the indigenous delegates walk out of the meeting and call a press conference and urged others to "be strong and stand up against it" and to "fight for peace now, before they come with guns on our land." Others, who argued against a boycott of the meeting, prevailed.

A compromise between the indigenous and state positions was eventually achieved in a report of the facilitators with their recommendation that reference to Articles 62 and 63 of the Charter of the United Nations should be situated in the preamble of the document that would establish the indigenous forum. In this way, the mention of the charter would not be binding or operative. The states would be free of the risk of an indigenous forum with the power to intervene in violent conflicts.

Despite numerous disagreements between indigenous peoples and states, the 2000 meeting on the permanent forum brought out important points of agreement between the indigenous and state caucuses. The first of these was the general will to establish a permanent forum. This had not been a given in previous years, and the near-consensus among states that it be given a green light was something that caught some indigenous delegates by surprise, as though they had been bracing themselves for more confrontation than they actually encountered. Further, it was generally agreed that it be established as a subsidiary organ of the Economic and Social Council, putting it at a very high level within the U.N. system, as a body on the same administrative level (though not with the same power) as the High Commission on Human Rights. This would give the permanent forum an authority of its own, an ability to be seen and heard within the U.N. system, and therefore in the world at large. It would be in a position to attract requests for its help—from indigenous peoples, certainly, but also from governments and other agencies within the U.N. system. The dialogue on the permanent forum revealed deep differences between indigenous peoples and states, the expression of which indeed showed the United Nations to be largely controlled by states; but the points of consensus and compromise that were established showed the indigenous peoples' movement to be succeeding, in its own manner, in making the United Nations, as one indigenous delegate put it, "more human."

THE EXERCISE OF INHERENT JURISDICTION

Inherent-jurisdiction lawmaking involves the development of written laws based on the political rights of peoples. Its use by indigenous peoples does not necessarily involve the direct participation of the state. As I intend to show, it can, and occasionally does, take the form of a unilateral indigenous constitutional exercise based on local consultation and approval, originating from community-based reassertions of inherent governance. The use of legal language in this legislative process represents a reversal of the usual flow of cultural expertise and political control. Inherent-jurisdiction lawmaking is thus a use of legal language to reinforce the political and cultural defenses of an indigenous society and ultimately to create a form of constitutionalism that stands outside the statist paradigm.

A few examples will serve to illustrate this more clearly. In 1977 the Six

Nations delegation traveling to Geneva to attend the International NGO
Conference on Discrimination against Indigenous Populations in the
Americas decided not to carry American or Canadian passports. Instead,
they printed and issued their own. The Swiss immigration authorities
were persuaded to recognize the Six Nations passports prior to the 1977
meeting and have done so ever since. Chief Oren Lyons, who traveled
to Geneva with the Six Nations delegation, explained this gesture as
more than a symbolic act of sovereignty: "If a nation feels like a nation,
acts like a nation, then you will be a nation" (First Nations 1996: 71). The
exercise of inherent legal authority is thus not only an assertion of self-
determination but also part of a process of reconstituting sovereignty, of
indigenous nation building.

Two decades later, Chief Lyons was an official witness before an unusual assembly, an assembly that provides another example of indigenous use of inherent authority. On September 28, 1995, an indictment
was prepared by the Registrar of the First Nations International Court of
Justice and served via registered mail on the Prime Minister of Canada
and the Governor General of Canada. The indictment stated, in part, that
"Her Majesty the Queen in Right of Canada did, contrary to the original
laws and customs of the First Nations, the principles of international law
and its treaty obligations, unlawfully interfere with the free and unfettered exercise of jurisdiction by the First Nations through the forceful
application and enforcement of Canadian laws within First Nations territories" (First Nations 1996: 16). The government of Canada was duly requested to appear at an appointed time (9:30 a.m. on April 2, 1996) and
place (Ballroom "A" of the Radisson Hotel in Ottawa) to answer charges
before the First Nations International Court of Justice. Not surprisingly,
representatives of Canada did not appear and did not prepare a defense.
Instead a "friend of the court" was appointed by the First Nations Court
to represent Her Majesty the Queen in Right of Canada *in absentia*. Six
judges presided over the proceedings, representing the Anishinabeg,
Tanganekald, Ngati Kahungunu/Ngati Porou, Seneca, Xicano-Nahuatl,
Okanagan, and Blood Nations. The court first heard from John Borrows
of the Chippewa Nation, who summarized his understanding of the
sources of aboriginal legal authority: "it is found within the ceremonies,

it is found within the stories, it is found within the relationships, it is found within what we observe as we look at all the different orders of creation" (First Nations 1996: 3). The "trial" then proceeded to outline, through the testimony of elders and legal experts, the ways that native sovereignty had been illegitimately and illegally encroached upon in Canada. An Interim Order issued several days after these proceedings concluded "that in view of the fact that clear violations of First Nations law have occurred, First Nation [sic] be encouraged to impose a moratorium on the conclusion of any treaties, negotiations or other arrangements with the governments of Great Turtle Island until such time as this Court delivers its final judgment" (Chiefs of Ontario 1996). The First Nations Court subsequently ran out of funds and did not continue its proceedings. That an exercise of inherent aboriginal legal jurisdiction should be manifested in such an impeccable reproduction of the judicial process of international tribunals does not appear from the transcripts to have struck any of the participants as at all interesting or noteworthy.

Other indigenous societies pursuing similar goals of formalizing their powers have tended to be more compromising, going much further toward accommodating state structures. The Sami Parliaments of Finland, Norway, and Sweden, for example, have all, to varying degrees, limited their autonomous lawmaking powers through arrangements with state structures. None of the Sami Parliaments are vested with legislative powers or far-reaching independent decision-making powers (Myntti 2000: 204). The right to vote and run as a candidate in elections of the Finnish Sami Parliament (founded in 1973) follows a definition of "Sami" that is not approved of by the Sami Parliament itself but is based on criteria approved by the Finnish Constitutional Committee of Parliament—criteria that include "descendants of Lapps" as beneficiaries of political rights. The Sami Parliament feared that this definition would include a large number of people who had lost all meaningful ties to Sami language and culture; on these grounds, it rejected 1,128 applications to the Electoral Board of the Sami Parliament based on descent from Lapps (211).[11] The purpose of the Sami Parliament of Sweden is similarly defined almost entirely by the Swedish Riksdag. It is a state administrative body acting under the state's jurisdiction and bound by its rules, essentially giving it no

more scope than the Sami national organizations had before its inauguration in 1992. But the parliament's powers to distribute funding for Sami
culture and organizations and to launch initiatives such as a compensation regime for damage to reindeer herds caused by wolves, bears, and
wolverines are widely seen as contributing to Sami needs for self-
determination. The Norwegian Sami Parliament, founded in 1989, has
greater autonomy than those of Finland and Sweden. Although it is
funded from the state budget, it is free to set priorities, take initiatives,
and pursue its own decision making in particular cases (214). It has not
used its powers, however, to set out on a radical course of independent
law making. None of the three Nordic Sami Parliaments have been able
to address issues relating to land and resources. Competition with non-
Sami reindeer herders and extractive enterprises over lands essential for
reindeer husbandry has remained essentially unchanged during the past
thirty years.[12] The parliaments have been able to develop cultural initiatives but not resource protection. They remain closely tied, in mostly cooperative ways, to state administrations and distribution of authority.

By contrast, a lawmaking exercise initiated in Cross Lake took place
in a context in which the government of Canada lacked credibility, was
perceived by many as dishonorable, and was largely held responsible for
the community's high rates of joblessness and welfare dependency, inadequate health services, underfunded local government, and even its high
rate of suicide. As the outline presented in chapter 3 of the history of
Manitoba's hydroelectric development and the failure of Northern Flood
Agreement implementation suggests, Cross Lake's venture into inherent-
jurisdiction lawmaking might never have happened without a widely
shared sense of grievance and a corresponding conviction of the law's
power to change the behavior of governments. At the same time, a climate
of political liberalism allowed these sentiments to be expressed without
overt repression, fear, or intimidation—even to the point of tolerating an
exercise of indigenous nation building and autonomy not sanctioned by
the state. Grievance and liberalism are rarely found in such extremes.

The most significant result of Cross Lake's lawmaking was the passage
of the Pimicikamak Okimawin Trust and Hydro Payment Law, ratified
on October 30, 1998. With this law, the residents of Cross Lake went be-

yond lobbying and protest to the application of punitive sanctions. This law, in effect, provides the residents of Cross Lake with the option of paying their electricity bills directly to Manitoba Hydro (as usual) or of taking advantage of a new option created by the law: paying into the Pimicikamak Okimawin Trust, controlled by a community-elected board of trustees and administered through Royal Trust, a major Canadian financial institution. The idea for this law stemmed from the contradiction, obvious to many, of Cross Lake being owed so much by Manitoba Hydro (although a precise dollar amount has never been attached to the unfulfilled obligations under the Northern Flood Agreement) while the households and institutions of Cross Lake collectively pay more than $2 million annually in electricity bills. Councilor Nelson Miller invoked the sentiments behind this law when he remarked, "We're basically paying Hydro to destroy us and keep us in poverty" (*Winnipeg Free Press* 1998: A3). The Hydro Payment Law is thus a form of "creditor's possession," a written aboriginal law applying punitive sanctions to a state-owned utility.[13]

Manitoba Hydro, not surprisingly, did not embrace the law. Glenn Schneider, spokesman for Manitoba Hydro, bluntly stated his opposition to it: "In their view, it might be legal. In our view, it won't be" (*Winnipeg Free Press* 1998: A3). In 2001 Manitoba acted upon this view by filing suit for the recovery of $2 million in "unpaid" bills, an action that is likely to be tied up in Canada's court system for some time to come.[14] In a less open expression of Manitoba Hydro's resistance to the law, some Cross Lake residents who paid their bills into the trust received red disconnection notices, despite the fact that Manitoba Hydro received and accepted receipts forgiving its debt to Cross Lake in amounts equal to every trust payment. Despite the utility's initial reluctance to recognize the law, however, no Cross Lake household paying into the trust was cut off; and despite the dampening effect of disconnection threats, several institutions (notably the Band Office, Education Authority, and Arena), and more than three hundred out of approximately eight hundred households in the community, paid more than $1 million into the trust in its first year.

Cross Lake's exercise of inherent lawmaking authority was accompanied by a resurgence of nationalist sentiments and symbolism. Part of this is attributable to the legal necessity of separating the community's inherent authority from its ties to the federal government through Indian Act governance. Hence, the administrative body called Cross Lake First Nation was irrevocably connected to the Indian Act, whereas local lawmaking proceeded through a separate legislative body, Pimicikamak Cree Nation. In practice, separating the two orders of government proved nearly impossible. Residents of the community wished to identify themselves unambiguously as one nation, with one name and one set of symbols. The name "Cross Lake First Nation" fell into disfavor, seen by many as a holdover from an earlier, and misguided, regime, while "Pimicikamak Cree Nation" was rapidly popularized. Trucks and vans of the band police were repainted with a new logo and the words "Pimicikamak Cree Nation Police." Cross Lake Health Services became Pimicikamak Health Services, and Cross Lake Education Authority became Pimicikamak Cree Nation Education Authority. Despite the importance of separating inherent authority from existing ties with the federal Department of Indian Affairs, the dam could not be held against the politics of identity.

The community's reinvention of itself also found its way into a Web site (www.pimicikamak.ca) reflecting the newly articulated combination of grievance, rights, and national identity. "Our Nation is our people in our lands," the Web site tells its readers, "Our lands are the heart of the northern boreal forest—the greatest ecosystem of mother Earth. . . . Our Nation is our culture. Our culture is what has enabled us to survive in our lands. We are an oral people. We listen, and we speak. Our culture is our language. Our ancestors and elders speak to us the wisdom of thousands of generations." In Minnesota, an organization calling itself the American Friends of PCN established a Web site (www.unplugmanitoba hydro.com) which, under the heading "Washing Away a Way of Life," provides a summary of the community's history, based on presentations by spokespeople from Cross Lake: "For hundreds of generations, members of Pimicikamak Cree Nations (PCN) hunted, fished and thrived. . . . Today Cross Lake is a community in crisis. Unemployment rates are astronomical. Poverty is endemic. . . . A shocking number of people here perceive suicide as their only escape." The apparently contradictory messages within the presentation of national self—of a community destroyed, "washed away," and yet living in harmony with nature in accordance with the wisdom of elders and ancestors—are in fact very commonly invoked by Cross Lake's leadership. Grievance and pride are the main ingredients of identity, even if they are sometimes uncomfortably juxtaposed.

Cross Lake's lawmaking and nation building also brought out social cleavages. The process left a minority of the community's residents profoundly dissatisfied. These were the people who identified more strongly than others with that part of their ancestry connected to Scottish fur traders and mariners, who for years were labeled—sometimes scorned—as "nontreaty," as not taking part in the rights and benefits of Treaty 5 because of their mixed ancestry. When federal legislation gave them the opportunity to restore their Indian status, some chose to remain outside the fold, an affront to the true believers in Cree identity, while those who opted for "treaty status" became known by the federal bill that enabled the change: "Bill C-31 Indians." Many "Bill C-31s" did not find inspiration in the (re)creation of Pimicikamak Cree Nation. Their leader was a Pentecostal minister who looked upon the sweat lodge ceremonies attended by a majority of the newly elected local politicians as spiritually dangerous, consorting with dark forces, and a danger to the whole community. He made his views clear on Sunday radio sermons.

The cultural and political cleavage came to a head shortly after a local election in which the opposition found itself without power. They tried occupying the Band Office, removing the councilors, managers, and staff from their offices under a hail of abuse and intimidation, but were soon removed in their turn by the Royal Canadian Mounted Police because of the risk of damage to government property if the occupation were to turn into a siege. When federal government representatives were flown into Cross Lake to attend a televised community meeting, attempting to calm the situation with an explanation of the federally approved procedures of Indian governance, they were met with a flat denial of the legitimacy of Pimicikamak Cree Nation by its Pentecostal opposition leader: "What authority do you have in your regulations?" he asked the government representatives. "There's nothing wrong if we establish our own Chief and Council and establish our own reserve."

A federal government representative, after a brief conversation with the colleague seated beside him, replied, "Sir, if you did that, the Chief and Council you established would not be recognized." This was, from a government that in other ways had appeared cynical and callous as it failed to honor its obligations, an indirect after-the-fact affirmation that an aboriginal government was legitimately setting a course of unilateral self-determination.

There was, besides a sense of grievance and a felt need to recover traditions,[15] a process of legal validation from international and state legal systems at work in Pimicikamak Cree Nation's development of inherent-jurisdiction lawmaking. From a legal point of view, the validity of the Pimicikamak Cree Nation lawmaking program received confirmation from Section 35.1 of Canada's Constitution Act of 1982, which recognizes and affirms aboriginal and treaty rights. The constitution, in turn, is elaborated on in Canada's *Gathering Strength* policy statement as affirming "the inherent right of self-government for Aboriginal people" (Canada 1997: 7). At the same time, a recent body of case law from the Supreme Court of Canada cumulatively broadened and solidified the exercise of these aboriginal rights.[16]

During my first visits to Cross Lake's Band Office I was asked several times over a period of weeks to lend assistance in printing the Draft United Nations Declaration on the Rights of Indigenous Peoples from the Internet. Soon the curiosity of band employees extended to the Universal Declaration, the International Covenants, and, to my mixture of dismay and admiration, my own collection of books on human rights. The number of people reading this material could not have been more than a small handful, but this proved to be an influential group, closely involved in the process of developing the community's written laws.

The international legal principle that had a significant influence on developments in Cross Lake is the right of self-determination of peoples, the right to "freely dispose of their political status and freely pursue their economic, social and cultural development," expressed in Article 1.1 of the International Covenants and Article 3 of the Draft United Nations Declaration on the Rights of Indigenous Peoples. These articles were presented and explained by lawyers and band officials to community members in public meetings, local radio broadcasts, and local-access television call-in programs.

In a community the size of Cross Lake, a heavy investment in electronic media is an inescapable necessity for restoring a consensus-based decision-making process that looks for guidance to the values of a hunting way of life. This is not to say that concerns about media dysfunctions affecting democratic processes are unfounded or that mass media inherently function as stewards of public awareness and political accountability. There is something to be said for the view that mass media tend to be controlled, popularized, subverted, and reduced to the lowest common denominator of public entertainment and have correspondingly given up the responsibility of politically informing and interacting with the citizenry (Entman 1989; Katz 1998). And yet the local-access television channel of Cross Lake is of an entirely different order than the twenty-three major network channels within which it is nestled. It has almost no journalistic filter. Other than a few short documentary videotapes assembled to provide a record of the environmental destruction caused by the hydroelectric project, there has been no editorial intrusion into the record of public life. Public meetings are broadcast live, without commentary to cover the minutes, sometimes hours, of "dead air." In this unusual manner, Cross Lake's inhabitants are introduced to the functioning of their nation and are to the greatest extent possible becoming citizens of it.[17]

Human rights instruments have had several influences on indigenous lawmaking. One of these is the effect of international norms and standards on domestic law. In liberal democracies such as Canada, the United States, Australia, New Zealand, and the Nordic countries of Europe, courts are influenced in their development and application of domestic law by some willingness to conform to international standards, mainly to avoid putting the state at odds with its international obligations (Anaya 1996: 138). Changes in international law have thus probably made some states more willing to support or tolerate the exercise of indigenous self-determination. At the level of indigenous communities, international law, especially its affirmations of the self-determination of all peoples, has confirmed the idea that a viable system of community governance can be founded on the practices of the ancestors. A policy paper developed by

Pimicikamak Cree Nation (1998) in collaboration with its lawyers points to this connection: "The Cree people have never surrendered their aboriginal right to self-determination. It has never been legally extinguished. Now it is protected by both domestic Canadian constitutional law and by international law" (40).

Inherent-jurisdiction lawmaking is a possible outcome of recognizing indigenous peoples as "peoples." That it should be taking place especially defiantly in Canada is not surprising. It would be starkly contradictory to constitutionalize aboriginal self-determination and then deny its exercise in practice, although of course states behave this way with great frequency. But the exercise of inherent lawmaking authority is one of the possible outcomes of reinvigorated self-determination. The lawmaking process that I encountered in Cross Lake is an example of what can be expected from the growing international recognition of indigenous peoples' right of self-determination. It has a natural affinity with human rights; both are used as strategies in defense of tradition, above all through traditionally legitimized sources of power grounded in the procedures of written law.

THE POLITICS OF SHAME
IN ENVIRONMENTAL LOBBYING

The effectiveness of indigenous use of the politics of shame—the effort to influence a decision or policy through dissemination of information to an audience that is a source of political power, information that exposes the inappropriateness, harm, or illegality of a course of action—derives largely from a socially and politically active public that tends to perceive indigenous societies as living in perfect harmony with the natural world. This is a counterpoint, not only to environmental degradation, but also to the pace of life imposed by expanding global economies. At a time when the prevalence of stress in postindustrial society is causing staggering burdens of employee absenteeism, failed careers, broken families, and mental illness, indigenous peoples have come to represent an alternative, a form of life based upon patience, simple goals, and suspension of temporal imperatives.

Milan Kundera, in his novel *Slowness* (1996), juxtaposes such an alien-
ating and rushed reality, empty of intimacy and joy, with an idealized
portrayal of time-consuming intrigues and sexual liaisons among the
prerevolutionary French nobility; but he might just as well have used a
group of indigenous protagonists as his model of the atemporal "other."
Anthropologists can be strongly drawn to this aspect of the people they
work with. When Rigoberta Menchú spent a week with Elizabeth Burgos-
Debray in the latter's apartment in Paris narrating the life story that was
to become a best-seller in several languages, it was the deliberate patience
of the Guatemalan *indígena* that made one of the strongest impressions on
the anthropologist. "She came to my house one evening in January 1982,"
Burgos-Debray (1984) remembers. "She was wearing traditional costume,
including a multicoloured *huipil* with rich and varied embroidery. . . . On
her head she wore a fuchsia and red scarf knotted behind her neck. When
she left Paris, she gave it to me, telling me that it had taken her three
months to weave the cloth" (xiv). The gift was above all important because of the time it embodied. Almost everything about indigenous
people can become a reminder that they represent virtuous slowness: the
patience needed for traditional subsistence, their casual flouting of the
rules of punctuality, the length of their meetings and ceremonies, the art
objects and clothing that are often commodified, seen to embody (among
other things) time and creative serenity. It is the nostalgia some feel for
such temporal liberty that makes indigenous lifestyles the subject of romantic imaginings.

Urgency is applied to these imaginings by the understanding that these
ways of life are disappearing, succumbing to environmental destruction
and drawn into the vortex of a fast-paced, resource-hungry global civilization. Many assume that the world has already dispensed with its Indians and aboriginals, that those who remain with indigenous identities
are only the afterimages of destroyed societies; but there are others who
remain concerned with the fate of extant—and endangered—peoples.
This has some parallels with concerns about shrinking biodiversity, but
with more direct implications for human society.

When the Cross Lake Crees decided to campaign for restoration of
their rights and honoring of broken agreements, they looked to the pub-

lic that was exporting hydroelectric power from their territory. Above all they looked to the public in Minnesota, the customers for whom 90 percent of Manitoba Hydro exports were purchased, constituting 30 percent of the utility's gross revenue. If enough voters and ratepayers south of the border could be convinced that the energy they were exporting was responsible for human rights violations (or as one Cross Lake resident put it, that "there is blood in that power that turns on the lights"), then Manitoba Hydro's exports might come into jeopardy. This, in turn, might make the government more willing to redress the community's grievances.

But Cross Lake's human rights story fell largely on deaf ears. Poverty, relative to the rest of Canada, was not enough to command attention, not the kind of story that could compete with the human rights catastrophes happening in other parts of the world.

Cross Lake's leadership then hired a full-time lobbyist (with funds from the trust established with the Hydro Payment Law) to promote awareness of the environmental catastrophe happening at the other end of their power supply. Support began to grow, especially when Cross Lake's issues were connected with grassroots resistance to a proposed transmission line to improve the power grid between Minnesota and Wisconsin that threatened farm lands and wildlife habitat in the Midwest-Northeast corridor. It is too soon to tell if this campaign will have much of an effect on corporate and political behavior in Canada. Its strategic viability, however, is indicated by its support from a variety of environmental organizations, including the Sierra Club, the Audubon Society, the Clean Water Action Alliance of Minnesota, Save Our Unique Lands, and Minnesotans for an Energy Efficient Economy. Articles, mostly written by local journalists in response to presentations made by Cross Lake delegates in Minnesota and information provided by their information officer, appeared in the *Merriam Park Post, Southside Pride* (Minnesota's "neighborhood" newspaper), the *Wausau Daily Herald,* the *Pulse of the Twin Cities,* the *Minnesota Daily,* and the *Capitol Times* (Madison) and from Native American journals such as *News from Indian Country* and *The Circle.*

Throughout this campaign the emphasis was on how Cree culture, once in harmony with the environment, had been destroyed by the environmental catastrophe wrought by hydroelectric development. But little or no attention was given to the question "What next?" If environmental devastation significantly prevents hunting, fishing, and trapping, what do the Crees plan to do to subsist? If the government's solution—welfare—is unacceptable as the foundation for a replacement economy (and all agree that it is), where will the hoped-for prosperity come from?

Clearly the greatest—if not only—possibility for Cross Lake's economy lies in resource extraction from their territory, the timber and minerals coveted by outside "developers." The people of Cross Lake clearly sense that this possibility is within their grasp. Hopes and visions of the future, sometimes expressed in dream narratives or in stories told to children in classrooms, take the form of jobs, houses, stores, expansion of the town "as far as the ferry crossing" some nine miles down the road. Even though the Crees would probably be more environmentally careful with their own projects on their own territory than multinational corporations acting more or less alone, these are not the kind of visions the outside world wants to hear about; consequently this is not the kind of positive message that is communicated to environmental lobby groups. The high—or one might say impossible—expectations of environmental stewardship applied to indigenous peoples have a tendency to intrude upon their rights and thus their ability to prosper.

THE POLITICS OF SHAME IN INTERNATIONAL FORUMS

One of the creative uses to which the human rights forums of the United Nations are being put is as a launching point for the politics of shame. The release of information and opinions from the offices and press rooms of U.N. organizations can greatly raise the profile of a cause—so much so that U.N. agencies have taken to putting their facsimile cover sheets under lock and key to prevent NGOs (not just indigenous ones) from using their letterhead to command the attention of journalists.

The connection between U.N. meetings and indigenous lobbying is nowhere more apparent than at the annual gatherings of the Working Group on Indigenous Populations. Here attendance is open, and a wide variety of indigenous peoples and organizations, not just those experienced in standard setting, come to present information to the gathering. A broad base of attendance is also ensured by the establishment, as part of the International Decade, of a Voluntary Fund, which pays for those from indigenous organizations with small budgets to attend U.N meetings, albeit on a shoestring. (The Office of the Secretariat notes the frequent incidence during the working group meetings of inappropriate requests for coffee and doughnuts, a sign of the relative inexperience of those in attendance.) And the broad topics covered by the working group—such as indigenous peoples and land, treaties, and indigenous children—provide wide latitude for the expression of grievance and opinion.

A large and varied attendance at working group meetings is further encouraged by an open definition of "indigenous peoples," essentially allowing any to speak who define *themselves* as indigenous. I witnessed only one instance in which an exception was made to this openness. In the 1996 working group meeting a Hutu delegate took the floor and spoke— off the topic—about the circumstances and causes of the genocide in Rwanda. He was "gaveled" by the chairperson, ostensibly because his case was already being considered, as a matter of great urgency, by the International Tribunal for Rwanda.

One of the appeals of working group meetings, especially to delegates experienced in lobbying, is the international attention given to news that emerges from the U.N. headquarters. Information, views, pamphlets, petitions, and copies of submissions presented to the Secretariat are circulated by indigenous organizations to others in the room, and occasionally to the press. Tables at the back of the meeting room contain pamphlets for distribution to delegates. By the end of the first of two weeks, newspaper articles begin to appear, based on interventions made earlier. Press releases and telephone interviews have by this time already begun to work their magic.

Occasionally meetings concerned with developing human rights standards or institutions become, outside the main meeting room, focal points for information and censure. This usually relates to developments unfolding in the indigenous world, events that have already garnered some notice. Such an event reached an indigenous caucus meeting at the U.N.

headquarters in Geneva on February 15, 2000. Four days earlier, the Colombian army fired tear gas on a group of U'we protesters who had set up roadblocks on a road used by Occidental Petroleum in the remote rainforest that they claimed as ancestral land. The U'we are a small people, with only five thousand members, but their alliance with lawyers, human rights organizations, and environmental groups in Colombia and the United States had begun to raise the profile of their conflict with Occidental and the government of Colombia. As part of their protest strategy they had threatened to commit mass suicide if a proposed exploratory well was drilled on land they considered sacred. The threat harkens back to an event during Spanish colonization in the seventeenth century in which scores of U'we walked off the top of a 1,400-foot precipice (Chang 2000). Some might see this as idle posturing, an empty threat of the ultimate publicity stunt, with little connection to the act committed by some of the U'we's ancestors. But if indeed this was a serious expression of their desperation, the early morning raid of February 11 pushed the U'we closer to such an act and in the process resulted in the deaths of four infants who drowned as the protesters fled across a river. Probably because of the remoteness of the event, this information took four days to reach the indigenous caucus meeting, but once there it spread quickly. The same afternoon a declaration of protest was drafted in Spanish, hastily translated into English to reach a wider base of support, and presented to indigenous delegates for signature. A press conference was then called by the Latin American delegation to denounce the actions of the Colombian government. Emerging as it did from a meeting already under way at the United Nations, the information presented to the press had the imprimatur of truth and significance.

Media attention is not an end in itself; and the effects of this kind of organized protest that actually make a difference in people's lives are rarely immediate. But a critical mass of such notice is sometimes enough to bring reluctant governments to the table, and very occasionally—often enough at any rate to make the effort more than worthwhile—a contract will be canceled, a project shelved, or an agreement with states and industry undertaken that improves conditions in indigenous communities and raises the stature of the leaders who brought it into effect.

In the politics of shame, international organizations have become the most important conduits of information filtered to the public via the press. The judgments of international panels of experts add to (or take away from, depending on the conclusions) the credibility of a grievance or cause. It is not just the interested parties, usually an indigenous organization in a relationship of conflict with a state or corporation, vying for public approval in a contest of popular support, but an independent evaluation of the merits of each story. The James Bay Crees, for example, were one of ten plaintiffs in the 1992 hearings of the International Water Tribunal (IWT) in Amsterdam, the Netherlands, convened to consider the worst violations of water rights from around the world. The Cree delegation to the hearings did not attend passively but used the opportunity of their presence in Amsterdam to bring their case directly to the public. They flew a large canoe to Amsterdam—or, rather, a hybrid canoe/ kayak, which they called an *odeyak* (from the Cree word *uut* and Inuit *qayak*), as a symbol of the Cree and Inuit peoples affected by hydroelectric development in northern Québec—and paddled it through the canals of Amsterdam, speaking to the curious crowds and giving interviews to the press. They thus raised the profile of their case even before their testimony before the IWT was heard.

Such lobbying, of course, rarely goes unopposed. Jacques Finet, vice-president of Hydro-Québec, for example, accused the Crees of using their concerns about the environment as a way of gaining control over the resources of the North so that they could act, not as environmental stewards, but as profiteers, no different from the enterprises that extracted resources: "The Cree's environmentalism is just a façade. . . . It wouldn't be six months before you would see bulldozers in the area if it was their country and they had control over natural resources" (*Gazette* 1992). Counterlobbying of this kind usually invokes imagined threats to national prosperity: a lack of jobs, insufficient energy resources, and loss of export revenue.

This might be one reason why indigenous lobbying is more effective when exported. In western Europe especially (perhaps with the exception of the Nordic countries, home to the Samis), few of the concerns usually invoked as consequences of indigenous claims can have much effect. The people and land in question are simply too far away to be seen as a threat to jobs and prosperity.[18]

It is, of course, difficult to determine if the press attention briefly given to the Crees in Europe had any influence on the outcome of the IWT hearings. In its ruling, however, the jury expressed surprise at the inconsistency between Canada's reputation as a country that respects human rights and its insensitivity to the rights of the Crees. It also called on Hydro-Québec to find alternatives to large dams in its energy policy, including a reduction of wasteful consumption (Niezen 1998: 119). Cree delegates considered this a breakthrough in their campaign to stop the second phase of hydroelectric development in northern Québec: "The jury's ruling was a great victory for our people. The ruling was unambiguous and clear: the International Water Tribunal determined that the first phase of the James Bay mega-project was imposed on the Crees, and that the devastating impacts on our health and the environment were never taken into account" (Grand Council 1992: 9). There can be little doubt that an accumulating mass of such publicity had a part in New York Governor Mario Cuomo's decision in 1992 to drop contracts for the purchase of electric power from Québec. And there is similarly a likely connection between such loss of contracts in New England (potentially amounting to some 10 percent of Hydro-Québec sales) and the 1994 decision by Québec Premier Jacques Parizeau to shelve a proposed multi-billion-dollar hydroelectric project on the Great Whale River (Niezen 1998: 120).[19]

Despite such occasional success, the politics of shame has several unfortunate side effects. One of these derives from a condition in which indigenous formulations of tradition and nationhood require some degree of public approval. It is not enough that peoples and communities are destroyed, removed from the land, politically marginalized, unemployed in an unfamiliar formal economy, exposed to addictions, and educated in a way that convinces many individuals of their innate inferiority. To satisfy the public that can help them—the audiences most concerned with human rights and the environment—they must also be noble, strong, spiritually wise, and, above all, environmentally discreet. The reality of destroyed communities, however, is rarely consistent with the expectations placed upon them. There can be little nobility, wisdom, or environmental friendliness where addictions are rampant, economic desires are unfulfilled, and political frustration pushes regularly against the barriers preventing violence.[20]

This is an example of a phenomenon that has broad implications for the indigenous peoples' movement. Indigenous nationalism is shaped more significantly by the demands of consumer export than are other forms of group identity. This is so because indigenous peoples represent "a way of life" that is disappearing and embody features that are increasingly absent from the lives of those being carried along by the main current of modernity.[21]

Indigenous nationalism thus usually shapes itself around those core values that resonate most strongly with the nonindigenous public. And there is some comfort to be taken in this. Surely there can be little harm in an identity based largely on environmental wisdom. The harm comes more from public disapproval of necessary things, like legal knowledge and resource extraction. An artificial boundary is sometimes erected around indigenous communities that limits their options and inhibits their prosperity.

A second drawback of the need for public support is its tendency to weaken with use. "Compassion fatigue" is the term sometimes used to describe the reaction of the public in democratic countries against too many issues thrown at them for too long. Sympathy has a tendency to focus on the most immediate crises, the human rights catastrophes with the highest body count, the greatest evidence of horror and mass suffering. The human rights abuses that leave only trails of torment but little or no blood are difficult to bring to public notice. One of the secondary evils of genocide is that it disproportionately draws upon a finite reserve of public compassion, reducing lesser causes to the level of the "ordinary," the tacitly accepted.

Even those states that strive toward pluralism and cultural tolerance find it difficult to go much beyond the accommodation of recreational diversity, the celebration of differences through such things as sporting events, arts, and festivals. The subtext of state-sponsored celebrations of difference is usually a variation of the idea that, despite a variety of human appearances, languages, and cultures, all citizens are in one important sense the same: all are subject to the same law, the same constitution, the same rights, loyalty to the same state. In the histories of many states, blood has been shed in liberation struggles to establish and safeguard higher standards of such diversity within equality.

Indigenous peoples are problematic for many states because they stand outside the accepted protocols of cultural difference. The rights that have accrued to indigenous peoples do not correspond to those of peoples who are culturally distinct but constitutionally equal.

The pursuit of self-determination is the focal point of indigenous peoples' participation in human rights meetings and processes, but it means something different for each representative of the various internationally active indigenous peoples—or rather, the hopes and aspirations attached to it vary from one people or organization to the next. For many, the importance of self-determination is that it represents control of land, resources, and livelihood. For others, it provides an opportunity to redress systemic injustice in state judicial systems. For still others, it represents above all new opportunities to express culture and language without the expectation that these will be systematically maligned, suppressed, and extinguished by state-sponsored programs. The emphasis placed on such aspirations may vary, but all would probably agree that each of these things is an important dimension of indigenous self-determination.

The point at which indigenous self-determination has become entangled in the development of human rights standards is where its implications in international law come to the fore, implications that associate self-determination with a right, under conditions of extreme and systematic human rights violations, of secession from a nation-state. To some extent, state concerns over indigenous peoples' status as "peoples" have not been allayed by the fact that indigenous self-determination is often couched in nationalist terms. In their development of an identity that fits within the framework of international organizations, and that at the same time provides collective sources of esteem, indigenous leaders have made ready use of the symbols and structures of nation-states. At the same time, it is still possible to see that the social realities behind such symbols are usually not consistent with independent statehood and that some states, moreover, are using their concerns over indigenous nationalism as a means of obstructing the development of human rights standards specific to indigenous peoples. The human rights agenda, which has in recent decades come to include indigenous peoples, has built into it a form of age-old contest between states pressing for uniform political control and cultural domination and minority peoples with their own claims of sovereignty, attachment to territory, and cultural integrity.

The claims (and exercise) of self-determination by the James Bay Crees tell us something about the relationship between self-determining indigenous peoples and states. The James Bay Crees, politically represented by the Grand Council of the Crees, have a highly developed system of regional autonomy functioning within a multicultural state. Yet the government of Canada was long opposed to recognition of indigenous peoples' rights of self-determination as "peoples" in international law. By presenting a strong argument for the rights of aboriginal peoples living within the province of Québec to decide for themselves their territorial and political affiliation in the event of Québec's secession, presenting their arguments in international forums, the Canadian courts, and to the public, the Crees, Inuits, Naskapi, and other aboriginal groups in Québec could well have influenced the outcome of the 1995 referendum on Québec independence and contributed to the subsequent declining fortunes of the province's separatist agenda. In this case, arguments for indigenous self-determination have meant, not the division of a nation-state, but concrete support for its unity.

The new politics of resistance connects indigenous leaders with national and international laws that provide legitimacy for local expressions of self-determination through written laws and formal procedures. The worlds of Montesquieu and Maine do not just quietly come together through this phenomenon; they collide with a force that produces uncomfortable juxtapositions and fragments of incoherence. Each step toward the use of written laws as an expression of indigenous self-determination is understandable in itself: it makes sense that, confronted by the mechanisms of state domination, indigenous leaders would try to reconstitute their sovereignty in terms easily interpreted by state officials, and it is equally understandable that reconstituting the values of oral societies in the form of written legal codes might carry more authority with states and international organizations than the mere assertion of oral traditions, often inaccessible to bureaucracies. Indigenous laws in this sense carry a message that is otherwise difficult to get across: "We are a sovereign people. We have always governed ourselves, and here is the evidence that we continue to do so. The laws that you make as a state presume to control us, to take away our land, to diminish who we are as a people, but these laws were not made by us. We have our own laws, made by the will of our people. You have made a promise that we should be able to govern ourselves. International law tells us that we should be allowed to govern ourselves. And here is the result of our governance." Such reasoning goes some way toward explaining the reluctance of states and international organizations to go further in their recognition of indigenous rights of self-determination. The main disincentive to recognition of indigenous rights of self-governance is not so much the Swiss cheese effect of empty, ungovernable spaces in the states' constitutional frameworks as the loss of control over territory and natural resources that would result from it.

At the same time, as a strategy of cultural preservation—or at the very least of protection against change that is rapid, far-reaching, and potentially socially dislocating—inherent-jurisdiction lawmaking is a more dubious strategy. While ostensibly derived from practices and values that predate the imposition of colonial sovereignty, it requires the development of institutions, technologies, and procedures that are quintessentially modern. Of course it can be argued that indigenous societies have long histories of adaptation, of innovating in their use of the tools and institutions of other societies to advance their ability to pursue forest-based or pastoral subsistence. It remains to be seen, however, to what extent indigenous peoples' uses of formal laws and procedures furthers their stated goal of preserving their cultural distinctiveness or contributes to their assimilation, perhaps not within states, but within a global pattern of cultural and institutional similarity.

The new politics of resistance also connects indigenous societies, more than ever before, with the "outside" world, with international networks consisting of other indigenous organizations, nonindigenous support groups, and more passively sympathetic audiences. On the face of it, this has tremendous advantages over "ordinary resistance." Although local acts of noncooperation, mendacity, and sabotage can exert upon states a cumulative burden of administrative inconvenience and even regional gridlock, they do not have the same implications for state power as the coordinated activities of indigenous peoples organizations engaged in the "politics of shame." New strategies of and resources for information gathering and dissemination make it more often problematic for state governments, especially liberal democracies, to appear callous and indifferent to the welfare of indigenous communities. It is a well-recognized principle of liberal states, though by no means always followed, that no minority group can be visibly neglected or victimized by the state without in some way compromising the rights of all citizens, especially the members of other minorities. There is thus a connection between the geographical and political isolation of indigenous societies. If their misery were encountered daily by others, above all by nonindigenous citizens of the state, such visibility would translate readily into greater political will to respond. The technology of travel and communication is to some extent having the effect of bringing conditions in isolated communities to the attention of a wider public, presented mainly through the lenses of activist lobbying and journalism. This requires a cultural presentation of self, a reflection upon what is important to communicate about a society unknown (it is usually assumed) to a mutually unknown audience. This encounter of strangers is predicated upon assumptions of vaguely similar values: environmental preservation, appreciation of "different" cultures, and rejection of poverty, misery, and illegitimate death.

Indigenous peoples are unlike other ethnic minorities in the extent to which they must rely upon such presentations of collective self to achieve a desired degree of political influence, to have an impact on decision making in industry, state governments, and international organizations. Indigenous identity is thus not a simple reflection of timeless values and practices; it is based in large measure on a compendium of cultural facts and artifacts intended for consumption within a dominant national society and an international audience. Indigenous lobbying is inseparable from the cultural and spiritual trends within its audiences, trends that seek some form of perfection or ancestral source of wisdom from the native, aboriginal, or indigenous "others." From the point of view of indigenous lobbyists, this is as much a source of constraint as influence. The realities of collective suffering in their communities intrude upon their presentation of a cultural ideal, and the expectations of those from a dominant culture seeking indigenous wisdom as a corrective to their own lives intrude upon the abilities of indigenous peoples to adapt, to develop their economies, and to move beyond compelling cultural images as the source of their entry into global society.

6 Indigenism, Ethnicity, and the State

The human world is not just a cultural patchwork but also a political one. Tremendous numbers of men and women owe their allegiance not just, and sometimes not principally, to the state but also, or above all, to an entirely different "nation," one that is often oppressed, maligned, castigated, and sometimes threatened with extinction, for no other reason than the mere fact of existing simultaneously with one or more nation-states.

This community-oriented dimension of human identity and membership, and the monistic tendencies of actual or aspiring nation-states to swallow it up or react to it with violence, has given human rights a global relevance. The Commission on Human Rights must contend with a position rife with ambiguity and conflicting responsibilities in which it is required to protect the citizens of states from the worst abuses of states, while functioning within an organizational complex largely controlled by states. The only way it has been able to accomplish anything on behalf of minorities and indigenous peoples is by working with a plethora of agencies outside the system. Nongovernmental organizations (NGOs) have become the most important components of an international civil society, a form of opposition to the centralizing tendencies of both states and international organizations. The Working Group on Indigenous Populations is the clearest expression of such pluralism, with its unique openness to participation by individuals and organizations in which the accreditation requirements usually imposed on nonstate participants are suspended and a voluntary fund covers the expenses of those who could not otherwise afford to travel to international meetings.

To the cynical, the real effect of this nonstate presence is exiguous, the main purpose of such pluralism being simply to allow those with the deepest grievances with states to "blow off steam" and satisfy themselves that they have embarrassed their governments by bringing their stories to the United Nations. But there is much more to indigenous participation in international organizations than such a safety-valve function. The issue of self-determination has moved the human rights of indigenous peoples to an unexpected level of contentiousness and potential for change.

The fulfillment of the self-determination goals of indigenous peoples would constitute a completion of the process of decolonization through mechanisms that would not (or not necessarily) involve the creation of new nation-states. Self-determination is premised above all on autonomy within states through constitutional reform and the implementation of treaties and agreements between indigenous and state governments.

What does this mean for international politics? International organizations today are evincing a shift toward an anti-imperialist pluralism starkly different from the international order supported by the League of Nations. The League was interested in global stability through humane domination of state minorities and benevolent, or at least not starkly oppressive, colonialism. The Holocaust shattered the illusion that such a political orientation was in the best interests of the world's dominant powers. The rise of nationalism in what became known as the "Third

World" presented the obvious solution of nation-statehood. This was the outcome desired by the European-educated elite of the colonies and was the least costly option for the imperial powers. Until recently, the statist orientation of the U.N. system has gone more or less unchallenged. From India's independence to the systematic decolonization of the 1960s, self-determination in international politics was couched in terms of autonomous statehood.

Since then, the demand of indigenous peoples for self-determination has raised the profile of nongovernmental influence in the U.N. system. With the stakes dramatically higher, the safety-valve function of international meetings has shifted toward power sharing. Because existing international mechanisms do not support the kind of ongoing arbitration of competing interests envisaged by claims of indigenous self-determination, it has become accepted that a Permanent Forum on Indigenous Issues (not "Peoples," reflecting the continued resistance by some states to self-determination for entities other than states) will be the next stage in the reform of the U.N. system to accommodate the expectations of indigenous peoples.

For indigenous leaders the most important issue is not whether their people will be led wisely or foolishly or will themselves promote liberty or small-scale tyranny. Such matters are hardly ever discussed. What is important to them is whether their people will be given the opportunity to determine their own cultural, political, and economic destiny or will continue to be ruled by outside powers. In the view of Mick Dodson (1998), Aboriginal and Torres Strait Islander Social Justice Commissioner, indigenous peoples are engaged in "a global struggle . . . between the world's Indigenous peoples and the world's colonial governments" (64). The prevalent logic and appeal of the indigenous peoples' movement is a form of anticolonialism. The quest for international recognition of the rights of indigenous peoples to self-determination is driven by the illegitimacy of rule by an alien power, regardless of the extent to which such rule is benevolent, efficient, and stable. It is illegitimate because it is imposed upon those with unextinguished rights to self-determination and under these circumstances cannot ever be fully consistent with the expectations and identities of the colonized.

While the basic ideas and sentiments of the indigenous peoples' movement may be the same as those that accompanied the retrenchment of European imperialism in the mid-twentieth century, the political solutions being pursued today are quite different. "Negotiated peace," resulting in special accommodations within nation-states, is the preferred outcome of the indigenous exercise of self-determination.

Besides aiming, at least partially, to reverse the displacements that occurred through European expansion, indigenous anticolonialism is seeking to address the inequities and imbalances arising from the decolonization efforts of the more recent past, manifested in "Third World" nation-states. The indigenous peoples' movement is in this sense pursuing a process of decolonization once removed. The development goals of newly independent states have proven to be at odds with the subsistence viability and cultural survival of those living in frontier environments. Decolonization led almost inexorably to the inflammation of old hatreds. Wealth, what little there was of it, was not distributed equally among ethnic groups, creating desperate "have-nots" within have-not nations. This hatred also derives from the simple fact that state borders cut across ethnic regions, dividing peoples and lineages, turning what was once a seasonal movement or migration, or simple contact between families, into acts of defiance against states.

The indigenous peoples' movement began in the hemispheres with histories of successful imperialism in northern Europe, the Americas, and the South Pacific and then extended to the recently decolonized hemispheres of Asia and Africa. The intellectual and strategic dissonances of this process were outweighed by what indigenous leaders felt to be their common experience of state colonization.

We are now in a position to see decolonization through the extension of statehood to the colonized as the first step in a more complex process. Statehood does not necessarily meet the needs or expectations, or even the rights, of self-determination for all "peoples." States, whether brought into being from successful transposition of colonial populations or from decolonization, do not always, or even often, meet the needs of their national minorities. States are not the proper guardians of the politics, culture, and economies of indigenous peoples for the same reason that states are not always the purveyors of unbiased justice toward them: they are too much interested in the outcomes of contests.

Whatever we may think of arguments that indigenous self-determination is the thin end of the wedge leading inexorably to global secessions, the dialogue and institutional reform that have already taken place in the U.N. system point to an internationally sanctioned pluralism in which peoples are defining their own identities in ways that make sense to them (ideally within the limits of human rights norms), with laws and values that are, as Montesquieu would say, "appropriate to the people for whom they are made."

At the same time, however, the global cultural revolution that constitutes the indigenous peoples' movement does not find itself perfectly mirrored in the human rights standard-setting process. It is true that every U.N. entity now recognizes indigenous peoples as a distinct category of human population in need of urgent intervention and support. But there is dissonance between the way this support has been expressed by the United Nations and the expectations of indigenous representatives. Eliminating the "scourge of racism," easing the suffering of the sick and hungry, and restoring dignity and security to the victims of war are noble purposes, but they do not address the claims of indigenous peoples to self-determination. The desultory progress being made in human rights standard setting, above all the stalemate obstructing approval of the Draft United Nations Declaration on the Rights of Indigenous Peoples, is attributable to concerns that anything more than "equality," anything more ambitious than pursuit of an end to discrimination and its consequent suffering, is a counterproductive invitation to contests over power and a multiplication of the woes of strident ethnonationalism.[1]

WHITHER THE NATION-STATE?

Uncertainty about the future of nation-states and expectations of their imminent decline are as old as nation-states themselves. The political ideology in which the interests of unity and self-determination of a people were seen to be realizable only through statehood was, to the more liberal nineteenth-century observers, unlikely to last much beyond the dismantling of multinational empires. Nationalism was, in Isaiah Berlin's

(1998) colorful words, "a pathological inflammation of wounded national consciousness" (587) that would soon abate.

Today a process not of healing but of competition from global institutions is most commonly invoked as the force behind the withering of nation-states. Jean-Marie Guéhenno (1995) argues, for example, that nation-states are being bypassed at many levels "by transnational games that are far more powerful than are the states themselves" (3). States, as territorial communities commanding national allegiances, are fading under the influence of mobile, temporary interest groups. Arjun Appadurai (1996) arrives at the same conclusion: the hyphen between "nation" and "state" is weakening; the state is no longer able to command the allegiance and sentiment of its citizens. The language of rights and entitlement is being used by what he calls "culturalisms" or "large-scale identities" to capture statehood or pieces of state power. At the same time, disembodied, nonterritorial allegiances are coming to the fore, superseding the functions of nation-states. "Nation-states, as units in a complex interactive system, are not very likely to be the long-term arbiters of the relationship between globality and modernity," and "the very epoch of the nation-state is near its end" (19). One outcome is an inevitable uncertainty that, depending on one's view of the nation-state, is fraught with possibilities for liberation or peril.

Indigenism is a transnational phenomenon, and as such it represents a process some might see as corrosive of nation-state authority and stability. In fact, indigenous organizations are a form of transnational solidarity invading the institutional space of states from two directions, both internationally and locally. If we accept the idea that the information age contributes to the erosion of national legal and political systems, the interest groups so fervently communicating with one another are not discussing and supporting exclusively international interests; transnational activism at the same time challenges states by legitimizing and logistically supporting local claims of self-determination.

Indigenism is thus one example of global processes acting as a counterweight to the hegemonic strategies of states. But whether this is contributing to the withering away of nation-states *as a global process* is another issue altogether. The real question is whether the exercise of *col-*

lective rights (which indigenous peoples and organizations uniformly aspire to) is corrosive of nation-state unity. Is it weakening for states to make the constitutional compromises necessary to include peoples who do not wish to be governed except (or at least as much as possible) by themselves, who possess and exercise distinct rights to natural resources and government programs, who are different and not equal? We can pose this question in a form nearly as old as political thought itself: Is state hegemony a source of stability, and, conversely, is state-sponsored pluralism (in this case both intra- and suprastate) a source of fragility?

Indigenous peoples are seen by some (especially state and international officials) as being inherently irredentist, pursuing claims of autonomy that can only inflame intrastate quarrels, adding the potential for escalating indigenous zero-sum affairs to the current scourge of ethnic violence. There is some truth to the view that indigenous societies are eminently qualified to take up arms in regional struggles: they are politically suppressed, sometimes subject to state-sponsored massacres, building up backlogs of hatred, attached to and knowledgeable of their given territories, and ripe for claims of autonomy. But is there truth to the view that an inflammation of this situation would be an outcome of recognizing their rights?

The activation of hatred results more from the failure to secure human rights than from their recognition and implementation; it results more from isolation and the sense of having one's back against the wall than from international connections or the sense of common experience and shared resources with others. Within nation-states, the paradox that openness and pluralism create unity is confirmed with a consistency that makes the frequency of intolerance and ethnic violence confounding and frustrating.

If ethnological research began in the nineteenth century with the assumption that meaningful cultural differences had to be recorded before their inevitable obliteration, the indigenous peoples' movement shows us that the tendency toward cultural convergence and homogeneity, far from being realized as once imagined, has in unexpected ways changed course. The international movement of indigenous peoples is perhaps the clearest example of the ability of formerly (and still largely) oral societies to use administrative and legal procedures in strategies of resistance and survival. It is therefore not entirely accurate to say that nationalism is in decline; what we are witnessing is the nation-state being forced into competition with a proliferation of rival nationalisms, not just those of inconvenient and sometimes violently irredentist ethnic minorities. If the nation-state is in decline, it is in part because nationalism is on the rise, in ever-smaller territorial units.

INDIGENOUS NATIONALISM

Not least of the ironies inherent in the recent emergence of indigenism is the fact that some of those people most in harm's way during the age of nation building are now self-identifying and shaping their communities as nationalists.[2] There is strong resistance among indigenous leaders to the terms "minority" and "ethnic group" applied to indigenous peoples, but these leaders make prominent use of the symbols of nationhood and from a broad view share some of the basic premises of ethnic and state nationalism. Some of these are the felt need to belong to a group with common territory, traditions, laws, language, spirituality, and social institutions; a shared sense of oppression acquired through cumulative historical experiences of rejection or obstruction of group cohesion and survival by a dominant, alien political community; and the conviction that the nature and purpose of the family, tribe, or regional bloc can only be realized in the nation (whether it is so called is secondary), that the individual is not, and cannot be, the essential unit in which human nature is realized but must be subordinated to the actualization and will of the nation. There are even hints of strident claims of superiority in indigenous nationalist discourse, expressed in the notion that not all nations are created equal but that some possess transcendent truths, higher goals, a superior adaptation to nature, an answer to the cold empiricism of science and the rapacity of industry, a message that is ignored to humanity's peril. The indigenous nation, not the nation-state, embodies all that is most consistent with human survival and is the first to be endangered by human destructiveness.

It could well be that many or most of the ingredients in indigenous nationalism embody strong elements of truth; but this does not eliminate the features indigenism shares with other forms of nationalism. The intellectual history of nation-states reveals that some of our most cherished, "timeless" values may be far more recent than was once widely supposed, and the same can be said about many of the values associated with indigenism. The social and political category "indigenous peoples" has achieved an extraordinary currency in, by the standards of political history, the blink of an eye; and, like state-sponsored nationalism, it now somehow seems as though it has always been part of the world we live in.

One reason for this could be that those to whom the concept "indigenous" appeals are usually able to visibly demonstrate features of cultural continuity. Hunting technologies, myths, clothing, house construction, and language—such things are concrete embodiments of cultural maturity, associated with the phrase "from time immemorial." The same sense of permanence easily transposes onto the global category "indigenous," acting to conceal the fact that the term and the international movement associated with it are of very recent origin.

An idea used in support of indigenous nationalism is that conditions once seen as "primitive" were actually a consequence of colonial domination—that indigenous societies possessed the tools for participation in a global political order much sooner than is assumed but that this possibility was largely unrealized because of state ambitions expressed in policies of removal and assimilation. Thus we have the description by Working Group Chairperson Erica-Irene Daes of indigenous participation at the United Nations as "belated nation-building."

Indigenous peoples are now perhaps more interesting for the things they have come to share with nation-states than for the things that set them apart. They and nation-states are, first, often welded together in histories of conquest, colonialism, and nation building (with indigenous societies usually the conquered, colonized, and excluded). The formative events used to define indigenist primordialism were usually outcomes of the formation of nation-states. The many, sometimes ingenious, patient, and perverse, efforts to assimilate "savages" into nation-states, principally through policies of residential (or boarding school) education and urban relocation, have contributed more than anything to the resurgence of indigenous identities and claims to collective justice. In so creating the histories of oppression that help to sharpen the boundaries of indigenous communities, the individualism of nation-states has indirectly contributed to the vogue of cultural survival.

Nation-states and indigenous communities have also now come to share the same international institutional space, albeit on an unequal footing. "What is novel about modern nationalism," Duara (1958) tells us, "is the world system of nation-states. This system, which has become globalized in the last hundred years or so, sanctions the nation-state as the only legitimate expression of sovereignty" (8). Indigenous peoples appear set on eroding the uniqueness of this quality. Whether or not the permanent forum is given a mandate with a significant scope or influence, the fact remains that indigenous peoples have become a presence within the world system of nation-states, voicing their own claims of sovereignty while attempting to limit the inroads of the state into their affairs and their territories.

If we equalized our cultural sympathies by abandoning all nationalism (its continued vitality is revealed by the way this stretches the imagination), if nation-states and powerful ethnic peoples could and should also disappear quietly into that good night, what would be the result? For one thing, there would be no stable source of human identity and attachment; and humans—not all individuals but humans as collectivities—have become irrevocably attached to their identities. Both nation-states and many smaller self-consciously "traditional" societies are recent phenomena—despite their claims of timelessness—yet they seem to answer to a deep, universal need for belonging. Traditionalism is a response to the vicissitudes of modernity, an anchorage and protection against a fractured self.

ARE INDIGENOUS PEOPLES SECESSIONISTS?

What is the difference between the primary attachments of ethnonationalism and those of small-scale indigenous nationalism?

Concerns over the consequences of indigenous self-determination for the integrity of states center almost exclusively on the risk of indigenous secession. Juan Léon, spokesman for the Defensoría Maya, pointed out to me the connection between states' concerns about secession and their resistance to indigenous self-determination: "States don't want to recognize that we are peoples, indigenous peoples, and not just groups, or ethnic groups, or populations. . . . We have explained that we are not going to divide the states, to create isolation in the state. But they still argue that if they recognize the terminology we use, we would try in the future to create secessions all over the world." To what extent are such concerns justified?

During the past several decades, an increasing number of ethnic minorities have vigorously pursued independent statehood, and a greater number of nation-states than ever before have become divided along ethnic boundaries. A tried and true recipe for statehood involves, first, acquiring recognition as a distinct people with rights of self-determination, then finding a territory to claim and winning control. Currently, some forty-four countries are experiencing some form of ethnonationalist conflict. The unraveling of states from within through the separatist actions of ethnic minorities has become a more common source of violent conflict and constitutional downfall than aggression between states. As McGarry and O'Leary (1993) point out, "[S]ince the collapse of the communist empires of Ethiopia, Yugoslavia and the Soviet Union secession has become a growth-industry, the in-vogue method of ethnic conflict resolution" (11).

Indigenism, another form of primordialist claim of distinctiveness tied to assertions of self-determination, is commonly placed in the same category as ethnicity or ethnonationalism. Indigenous peoples, however, do not as a rule aspire toward independent statehood. Even though some indigenous nations have developed effective regional governments, such as the Sami Parliaments and the Grand Council of the Crees, they have not used their control over local administrations to develop the institutions of autonomous statehood. Indigenous peoples are in this sense false *irredentas:* that is, they do evince many features of nationalism but do not as a rule aspire to independent statehood, even though this is a concern mistakenly (or strategically) invoked in response to their claims to self-determination. Although international law provides for secession as an option in situations in which states are violating a people's basic human rights and fundamental freedoms, the rhetoric of self-determination, self-government, autonomy, and ownership of the land is not aimed at carving out pieces of existing states to establish breakaway indigenous peoples' republics.[3] Indigenism can thus be distinguished from ethno-nationalism by the consistent reluctance of indigenous peoples, at least up to the present, to invoke secession and independent statehood as desired political goals.

There are, as I see it, three interconnected reasons for this. First, independent statehood by indigenous peoples would absolve former host states of treaty and other trust obligations, which are often more far-reaching, at least in principle, than the federalism and power-sharing arrangements occasionally used to accommodate ethnic minorities. One common element in the historical backgrounds of indigenous peoples is the development of relations based upon trust. This is often overlooked, even by indigenous peoples themselves, because the states' violations of that trust through illegal acquisition of lands, failure to provide essential services, interference in political autonomy, and extinguishments of indigenous peoples' rights becomes far more prominent in historical records and collective experiences. The trust relationship between indigenous peoples and states, however, is an almost inevitable outcome of the colonial situation and the state's drive toward nation building. Once the state rejected the options of war and genocide as a means of occupying the land, it had to come to some form of accommodation with the original inhabitants. Treaties were a common way of reaching this accommodation, although a trust relationship could develop through less formalized policy actions. The Assembly of First Nations (1995), in a discussion paper on treaties in Canada, provides an understanding of the indigenous peoples' view of their treaty relationships with governments: "[T]he treaty is a sacred covenant between two sovereign nations. The treaties held out a promise that we would receive the Crown's protection. The elders are saying that we need to maintain the awareness of our treaties and educate the younger generation. . . . All of our treaties have a common thread. All represent a Crown commitment to recognize and protect our Nations. In all cases we have sought to ensure our people's livelihood" (1). In many cases, the benefits of treaties, even when major obligations are fulfilled by states, are minimal and inappropriate, but in others they are one of the few sources of commitment from states to provide resources, services, and protection of lands. Secession would require indigenous peoples to forfeit that part of their identity founded upon distinct rights. If indigenous peoples were to claim independent statehood, this would absolve state governments of their legal responsibilities toward the original occupants of the land. Obviously, in conditions of gross violations of human rights, the obligations incurred by states are all but meaningless. But hope dissuades drastic measures. Even the existence of unfulfilled promises can be a disincentive to secessionist ambitions.

Second, the mere fact that the international movement of indigenous peoples is an *international* movement is a disincentive to strident secessionism. Unlike the ethnic groups that we have come to recognize as powerful social forces willing in all too many times and places to spill blood for their proper place in the community of nations, indigenous peoples already belong to an international community with a body of shared knowledge, rules of behavior, and strategic goals. Indigenous peoples do not need statehood to possess international status and the protections of in-group membership. These already exist in their participation in international meetings, though not in as exalted a form as the U.N. General Assembly.

Finally, most indigenous societies are too small, their resources too meager, to acquire membership in an international community any other way. They would be unable to establish economically, politically, and militarily viable states, even if the leadership and population were so inclined. There is an immense difference between the informal, consensus-oriented local leadership of most indigenous communities and the legislative and bureaucratic infrastructure necessary for the functioning of a viable state. This is not to say that indigenous societies are inherently averse to the use and control of bureaucracies but rather that local administrations tend to be circumscribed in their control of power or, in conditions of less restricted local autonomy, to be oriented more toward securing "traditional" political identity than the trappings of statehood.

Hypothetically, states could still lose territory through the exercise of self-determination by indigenous peoples if the latter met the criteria for secession (significant, ongoing human rights abuses) and then successfully attached themselves to an adjoining state. This exercise of the right to choose would result in a form of secession without statehood. The obvious drawback of such a strategy would be its great potential for escalating tensions between states. The advantage, from the indigenous peoples' point of view, would be its potential for prodding the host state into reforming its policies and practices or, if all else failed, finding a genuinely kinder and gentler state with which to amalgamate. The Crees, for example, in the event of Québec secession (no longer the imminent possibility it was just a few years ago), could invoke this strategy to retain or regain their affiliation with Canada in preference to an independent Québec state. This was precisely the scenario that seemed to worry federalists, who were not ignorant of the potentially dangerous consequences of strong support from the Canadian government of the native peoples of Québec. Their concern appeared to be that without broadly inclusive constitutional planning, native groups could find themselves in open conflict with the Québec government and might request Canada's intervention in the potential aftermath of the province's secession.

From a global perspective, it remains extremely doubtful that the exercise of self-determination by indigenous peoples would lead to a rapidly spreading fire of transnational secessions and territorial realignments, if only for the simple reason that it would be extremely difficult in most cases to find a new host state willing to take the risks inherent in annexation, or a state in which constitutional and social conditions would promise to be much improved. Yet this remains at least a formal possibility inherent in the process of securing international recognition for the self-determination of indigenous peoples.

Relationships between states and indigenous peoples *within states,* however, are the most likely place where indigenous self-determination will be exercised. The possible choices of ways to put their rights to self-determination into practice range along a spectrum from political assimi-lation within states to refusal of cooperation with state governments (what some might call de facto secession within states).

Indigenous self-determination thus has the potential to affect govern-ment control of lands and resources without engaging in any overt and politically risky declarations of independent statehood. Indigenous dele-gates to U.N. meetings have intuited a concern by many states over the implications of indigenous self-determination to state control of land and resources, even in the absence of any risk of secession. John Henriksen (2000), Human Rights Coordinator of the Sami Council, for example, has observed that "governments often oppose an international recognition of indigenous peoples' right of self-determination more due to their fear of losing control over indigenous lands and resources than their fear of losing some of their general power" (136). This seems to be widely rec-ognized in the international community without being an overt focus of contention.

INDIGENOUS LIBERATION AND CIVIL SOCIETY

Even if indigenous peoples do not commonly pursue autonomy along the path marked out by secessionist, often violent, ethnonationalists, what are the implications of their pursuit of autonomy within states? Will increasingly powerful indigenous governments uphold human rights themselves or pursue local versions of oppressive state ambitions? Will a reinvigorated international identity provide an ideological grounding for indigenist insurgency?

The starting point for uncovering the consequences of the international movement of indigenous peoples for indigenous peoples themselves can be found in the movement's resistance to the hegemony of nation-states. Clearly the movement is founded on a premise of critique, nonviolent, restless opposition to monopolies of power and profit. It thus fits Gellner's (1994) initial criteria of civil society: "that set of diverse non-governmental institutions which is strong enough to counterbalance the state and, while not preventing the state from fulfilling its role of keeper of the peace and arbitrator between major interests, can nevertheless prevent it from dominating and atomizing the rest of society" (5). Gellner's definition, however, is completed by distinguishing civil society from another form of society, equally resistant to state monopolization or rule from an oppressive center: the self-administering, partly or wholly autonomous societies existing (or that once existed—Gellner erroneously assumes their disappearance) on the peripheries of states. Such "segmentary communities"—so called because of a structure usually based on lineages rather than formal institutions—provide individuals with inescapable identities and ascribed roles. They avoid centralized tyranny by absorbing individuals into social subunits and for this reason do not resemble civil society. Unlike civil society, segmentary communities fail to confer upon individuals the freedom to choose and redefine personal identity.

Gellner's approach to this contrast between "ancient and modern liberty" falls into error when he assumes that the historical transition away from segmentary communities and ascribed identities toward modern individualism and state-controlled socialization has already come to its conclusion. By positing a complete, or nearly complete, bureaucratically and technologically driven process of social convergence, Gellner fails to consider the suffering and perils of transition. His contrast between segmentary resistance and civil society overstates the incompatibility of social forms and overlooks the ways that ancient and modern liberty have combined forces. NGOs subscribing to universal human rights are applying themselves to the defense of societies that have defined, or redefined, themselves as "traditional," placing positive value on ascribed identities and politics founded in kinship and clientism. So-called ancient and modern forms of liberty are confused in this process; they interpenetrate and reinforce one another.

Whatever nostalgia might still be felt by cultural romantics for the kind of society with well-worn, cradle-to-grave pathways for its members, this is not the form of society encouraged, or perhaps even envisaged, by the prophet-jurists of human rights. Ascribed identities are an anathema to human rights liberalism.

The indigenous peoples' movement thus finds itself caught between seemingly incompatible forms of society. It seeks to protect the values and institutions of individual-absorbing societies within a global movement that affirms individual rights and liberties. Once the basis of membership in indigenous communities or organizations shifts from ascribed to chosen identities, the controls and constraints that define indigenous or "segmentary" societies, and that give them permanence and power, are dispensed with.

Indigenous peoples could thus easily become voluntary traditional subunits, virtually devoid of real power over individuals. Wider freedoms and choices sanctioned by international human rights, backed up by the growth of formal economies, restrict the ability of kinship-based societies to control their members. Indigenism might thus become (if it isn't already) a form of subscribed orthodoxy, much like a tolerant religion, with clear values and traditions but little control over apostasy.

No society, however, is fully comfortable with porous boundaries or fluid, voluntary membership; and in the absence of cohesion once brought about by clans, tribes, and village politics, we are witnessing the advent of small-scale nationalism, combining the symbols and powers of indigenous societies with those of nation-states. Where the obligations of kinship and tribal membership no longer control the behavior of individuals or the boundaries of social membership, nationalism provides a new form of identity, with the strong advantage of being distinct from, and often opposed to, the nationalism of dominant states.

The most dangerous moment for any national entity is at the time of its emancipation. Vindication through the transfer of power is usually accompanied by new opportunities for the expression of pent-up frustration and hostility. There are always warps in the national fabric, always those who are not true believers, who may once have been loyal to outside powers, who profess to a different religion from that upheld by the nation, or who can be identified as alien-apostate-would-be-spoilers in myriad other ways. Emancipation quickens both national coherence and imagined forces of disloyalty. Pride is readily accompanied by a desire to root out and destroy those who represent the rejections and affronts of the past. If ever there was a collision of wills over the value of national identification, this is the time when the losers stand to lose even more.

Sometimes this takes the form of expulsions and torch-lit reprisals; or it may be less dramatic, more easily justifiable, perhaps little more than a denial of political expression or obstacles to any public service occupation. Micronationalism does not automatically put an end to the oppression of minority groups, but can extend the reach of intolerance.

The promotion of rights and freedoms among small-scale peoples is not a guarantee that all cultural distinctions and political differences will be accommodated. The affirmation of the identities of national minorities can still produce those who say they do not and cannot belong, who do not see themselves as part of either the minority nation or the nation-state, who feel, rightly or wrongly, different and excluded. This means that ever-smaller social and political units can find a basis for identity based upon collective suffering. This presents us with a new kind of political challenge that runs in the opposite direction to the creation of global political movements: a collective self-actualization based upon minor nationalist differences, the rejection of emerging national minorities by ever-smaller political units, and the notion that pluralism and political compromise can never reach a people's innermost being.

If the indigenous peoples' movement consisted only of self-sustaining micronationalist communities, we might indeed expect to see frequent instances of militancy, terrorism, and unbridled suppression of internal dissent. But given the levels of frustration faced by indigenous peoples and the (complementary) strength of redefined indigenous identities, the most compelling problem is not the occurrence of indigenist revolts such as those that occurred in Wounded Knee, South Dakota; Oka, Québec; and Chiapas, Mexico; or the involvement of indigenous leaders like Rigoberta Menchú in Guatemala's ten-year civil war; or the hostage crisis, riots, and failed coup attempt of July 2000 in Fiji, led by traditionalist leader George Speight—the interesting question is not why such events occur but why they occur so infrequently. Why, given the growing numbers of peoples identifying themselves as indigenous, and given the callousness and hostility with which they are commonly treated by states, are there not more, many more, examples worldwide of indigenist terrorism and insurgency?

Part of the explanation for this can be found in the fact that, as the weakest and most isolated of the world's nationalist entities, indigenous peoples rely more heavily than other "minorities" upon public sympathy within nation-states and the lobbying efforts of international NGOs with their own ties to public fund-raising and support. One of the consequences of this is a "looping effect" in which broad public expectations, interests, and spiritual needs have an influence on indigenous national identity. Those features of indigenous folklore, practice, and society most likely to resonate positively with the consumers of activism then find their way into reconstructed identities.[4]

Indigenous identity is based largely on the historic failure of states in attempting to impose order and direction on social transition. Everyone who saw tribal or kin-based societies with simple technologies squared off against states with growing technological powers knew, or thought they knew, what was best for those seen to be impaired and doomed by their differences. Philanthropic hubris led to the notion that if only some individuals could be liberated from the thralldom and superstition of their origins they might in turn stand as a model for others to follow. Absolutism was built into humanitarian effort. The notion that a people was impoverished and suffering led easily to the conclusion that they were improvident and wanting in the attributes of the hardworking and prosperous. The goal of assistance led almost inevitably to that of "improvement"—usually in the image of a dominant society. Perceived failings become object lessons of reform. The self-satisfied superiority of the benevolent translated effortlessly into their intolerance of the underprivileged. The major contradictions of liberal assimilationism were its reliance on imposed liberty, choices made available by constraint, and self-sufficiency promoted through the elimination of autonomy.

So in various ways, indigenous identity—being and becoming indigenous, Indian, native, or aboriginal, expressed in thousands of particular tribal names—has been refracted through the lens of a dominant society, either through direct assimilation efforts or through the necessity of securing the approval and political support from a broad public. Under these circumstances aggressive political violence is counterproductive, leading readily to a tarnished image, loss of public support, and loss of capital in the "politics of shame." The "standoff" under the public gaze and in the shadow of vastly superior military power has become the most common expression of violence sanctioned, within strict limits of time and bloodshed, by a critical mass of public spectators. Once this path is voluntarily chosen, there are doors that begin to close to the expression of grievance, including the doors of international forums.[5] It is widely recognized by participants in human rights standard setting for indigenous peoples that their efforts provide a global source of restraint.

Indigenism is neither unambiguously a manifestation of civil society—at least not in the sense associated with the assertion of individual liberty—nor unambiguously a form of repressive society. It is a political hybrid that pursues pluralism within state systems while absorbing individuals in the embrace of ascribed identities, informal networks of obligation and patronage, and cultural orthodoxy. It is a countervailing force of criticism and agitation, acting against the centralizing tendencies of states and international agencies, that asserts its own variations of social totalism. It is, unlike evangelical faith, pluralistic in the sense that it depends upon and struggles for the toleration of multiple cultures, religions, and social orders; but it does so to protect particular social subunits and local institutions that exercise greater control over individuals than do states. Indigenism demands freedom from the state in order to exercise the freedom of societies to absorb individuals in circumscribed forms of community membership, not to provide individuals with the choices of life they might prefer. It consists of small-scale closed societies seeking openness and pluralism from nation-states and international orders.

Yet indigenism strives to keep state governments honest, to honor their obligations, to act meaningfully as trustees. Liberal states in particular suffer an erosion of credibility in their efforts to liberalize or "uplift" indigenous societies. Repelled, perhaps, by the collective nature of indigenous societies, by the fact that such societies represent the very antithesis of individual liberty and choice, liberal reformers have often exercised a form of political hypocrisy in which the values of freedom and pluralism are pursued using the repressive powers of the state. It is this oft-repeated history of social catastrophe above all that makes the collective rights of indigenous peoples difficult to ignore.

In this chapter I have inquired into the implications of an emerging global form of identity based upon original occupation of territories and on shared experiences of assimilation policy, loss of sovereignty, and loss of subsistence. Are the values and aspirations of indigenous peoples antithetical to the interests, above all the political integrity, of nation-states? Is this yet another piece of evidence that the world is breaking apart?

Answers to such questions have so far tended to come from political quarters rather than arising from more dispassionate reflection; and in these political answers the self-determination claims of indigenous peoples have sometimes been portrayed as a dangerous innovation with the potential to fragment nation-states. The similarities between indigenous identity and ethnonationalism seem too close for comfort; secession from nation-states appears as an inevitable outcome of indigenous claims of self-determination.

It is perhaps true that this perception has been unintentionally encouraged by indigenous leaders themselves, who have ambitiously cultivated the argument and outward appearance that they are members of indigenous nations, that their people are more than just "minorities," more than just "cultures," that they possess legitimate claims to being distinct "peoples," nations within nation-states. To some extent this argument is proven by the mere fact that it is being made. We are certainly more inclined to see indigenous peoples as "nations" by virtue of the fact that their representatives are presenting their arguments in international forums and organizing themselves internationally in the pursuit of legal recognition. Whether or not we feel that the invocation of nationalism by indigenous leaders is strategically sound, the fact remains that indigenous peoples also share many of the essential traits of other national entities: attachment to homelands, distinct cultures, and languages, histories of oppression by dominant societies, and rekindling of identity.

I have to a certain extent taken the essential features of indigenous nationalist identity as a given and have gone from there to consider the implications of this identity for nation-states. Recognizing and acting upon the distinct rights of indigenous peoples does not pose a significant threat to the stability or territorial integrity of nation-states. Indigenous peoples are not likely to contribute in a significant way to the world's burden of strident secessionism. The reasons for this lie in what makes indigenous peoples distinct. More than ethnic groups, they have distinct relationships with states, based on state obligations of trusteeship. They are connected to other like-minded and similarly constituted groups through national and international networks, making irredentism sanctionable by a global indigenous community. And their identities are based in large measure on forms of subsistence that are at odds with the economic and institutional requirements of statehood.

At the same time, there is nothing about indigenous nationalism that makes it inherently more virtuous, peaceable, or rights abiding than other foundations for group identity. Renewed indigenous identity emerging out of oppression, marginalization, and wounded pride can have the same tendencies toward exclusivism, intolerance, discrimination, and misguided zeal as in any society under similar circumstances. This leads to a more difficult problem: Do reinvigorated indigenous societies pose the danger of a new form of tyranny that combines the social restrictions of segmentary society with the state's powers of domination? Or can they to some degree meet the high expectations placed on them, represent higher standards of environmental sustainability and stewardship, successfully combine consensus politics and democracy, and uphold the human rights standards that they are pursuing as a source of protection, redress, and self-determination?

7 Conclusion

In a sense, states have always been at a disadvantage when it comes to earning and keeping the loyalty of their citizens. They are usually too large to offer the kind of comfort and moral security often provided by small communities, and at the same time they are incapable, without developing expansionist ambitions, of providing a universal vision of moral order.

The international movement of indigenous peoples attempts to simultaneously provide its members with three levels of moral certitude and social empowerment. It affirms above all local claims of difference, using such concepts as treaty rights, regional autonomy, and self-determination. The struggle for cultural and political affirmation, taking place largely through and within bureaucratic organizations, aims to restore and reinforce ways of life based upon personal ties of kinship, friendship, and obligation. For many individuals and societies, the tarnished mirror of the recent past cannot reveal the essence of their being, at least not without an additional effort of self-awareness, a return to one's roots, a reconstruction of the self by invoking an earlier, perhaps traumatic, but truth-revealing state of existence. The concept of "indigenous peoples" is in part a tool for clarification of identity through a global assertion of the values of community.

On a second level, indigenous peoples often use the language and symbols of nation-states, not, I have argued, to assert claims of independent statehood, but to clarify for everyone, above all their own citizens, their continuing claims of self-determination, based on the political integrity and autonomy of ancestors that preceded the formation or imposition of nation-states in and around their ancestral territories.

Third, they have embraced the universal vision of human rights as a way of protecting and developing their other sources of identity and power. The consensus-oriented system of human rights law and procedure holds out the promise of a regime of social justice that transcends the barriers of class, gender, race, income, and nationality. Indigenous peoples' organizations appear, from their uses of international law, to subscribe to human rights for their effectiveness in resisting the abuses of states, but there is also in human rights law a source of moral appeal shared with that large part of humanity that seeks the certainties of a transcendent universal ethic, that finds a system of truths so convincing, powerful, and liberating that it must be shared with others, ideally to the point where it is held by *all* of humanity.

Worldwide, the search for global moral certainty has contributed to the growing energy put into efforts to extend the limits of tolerance within nation-states, to redress gender and racial bias, to resist the centralizing tendencies of states by challenging them to accommodate the interests of distinct ethnic minorities. Among the strongest of such challenges comes from those who feel that as indigenous peoples, as the original occupants of territories later claimed by colonial powers and nation-states, they have distinct rights of citizenship and self-determination. Unlike other forms of antidiscrimination, the indigenous peoples' movement does not strive principally for minority protection or higher standards of equality but seeks to reinforce the primary loyalties within their communities, above all to entrench those loyalties in distinct rights of self-determination. More than most other efforts to extend the reach of tolerance, certainly more than those oriented exclusively toward gender or racial equality, the claims of indigenous peoples would pluralize the correspondence between the nation and the state.

In pursuing its goals of antidiscrimination and self-determination, the indigenous peoples' movement makes use of ideas that facilitate identity formation, ideas developed largely by nonindigenous sympathizers. Colonial domination has sometimes been characterized as a source of oppressive ideas about the colonized, a feature that calls for liberation from imposed identities as much as from power. Images of subject populations possessing a host of stereotypical qualities has become part of an accepted canon of cultural ideas, insidiously received as self-images, from which the colonized draw as a source of self-assessment, self-knowledge, and identity. The indigenous peoples' movement, however, does not often combat imposed identities as sources of oppression but, on the contrary, finds many of its powers of liberation in the ideas of dominant societies. The term "indigenous peoples" has itself become a marker of global identity, associated with mainly positive ideas about cultural wisdom and integrity and with politically significant claims to self-determination. Liberation from the various forms of oppression imposed upon indigenous peoples could not become a political objective until the idea of indigenous peoples had itself gained currency. This occurred through developments in international law, which first saw indigenous peoples as those impoverished, "backward" minority populations most in need of a guiding hand toward "citizenship," or at least more complete participation in national economies and cultures. The idea then shifted, through the increasing participation of indigenous representatives themselves, to a greater emphasis placed on cultural integrity and rights of self-determination that transcend the interests and even the sovereignty of nation-states.

As a global category of human population with a loose definition (or definitions), "indigenous peoples" has come to include an extremely diverse array of societies, including those with attachments to hunting and gathering, shifting agriculture, and pastoral nomadism. Some have been greatly influenced by Christianity, Islam, or Buddhism and so are on the peripheries of so-called high cultures. Others reject such religions or combine them with "syncretist" attachments to traditions of spirit worship and shamanism. They vary almost as widely as human differentiation will allow in terms of subsistence method, spirituality, marriage patterns, and political organization. That which has united them is above all a category and a process in international law that recognizes their distinctive position of marginality in their relationships with nation-states.

The people of such diverse regions and cultures did not unite under the rubric "indigenous peoples" simply because the concept was available and the technology of communication made it possible to do so; the globalization of this identity was energized by an idea, or set of ideas, about rights and recognition that has come to inhere in the notion of what it is to be or belong to an indigenous people. Indigenous peoples do not just assert the now-familiar arguments associated with multiculturalism: the need for recognition and affirmation of distinct identities and cultures, the right to equal treatment of all citizens of the state regardless of gender, race, religion, sexual orientation, or ethnic affiliation. Recognition of difference for indigenous peoples includes rights that go beyond notions of differences with equality. Indigenous claims are not only multicultural but also multiconstitutional. The indigenous peoples' movement is founded on a struggle for inherent rights of social membership and identity, for the authority to (re)make the rules that govern conduct, for recognition not only of distinct identity and culture but also of distinct rights. The assertion by indigenous peoples of their rights of self-determination is thus their main point of defense against the assimilation goals of nation-states. Such a strategy is seen by its proponents to hold out an alternative to state political domination and state-centered cultural homogenization. In a sense, indigenous peoples hope to resist assimilation into nation-states by promoting assimilation into themselves.

State resistance to indigenous self-determination as "peoples" in international law has centered upon the possibility that this might bring about a surge of indigenous secessions from nation-states. The specter of indigenous nations within nation-states is one thing, but, it is sometimes asserted, the world community cannot under any circumstances create conditions that would encourage indigenous nations to strive for inde-

pendent nation-statehood. Surprisingly, such concerns, while still apparently influencing the policy direction of the United Nations, have lost
some of their potency. The number of nation-states that recognize indigenous rights of self-determination has progressively increased. There is,
it seems, nothing in the values of liberal democracy inherently at odds
with the notion of self-governing indigenous peoples, and there is de-
creased resistance to power sharing with them, especially when developed through constructive arrangements with nation-states.

One issue that continues to trouble some liberal human rights theorists, however, is the extent to which recognition of indigenous rights to
self-determination might strengthen illiberal governments. If indigenous
peoples' collective rights are recognized, they, or illiberal states following the same principles, can easily use these rights as a tool of repression,
justified on the grounds of relativism and the need to secure rights of distinct cultures over the rights of individuals.

Human rights collectivism is thus a challenge to both human rights
liberals and indigenous peoples. The assertion of collective rights readily lends support to the aggrandizing and hegemonic tendencies of illiberal states, states that sometimes control the destinies of those claiming
status as indigenous peoples. If collective rights are paramount for self-
determining "peoples," who is to say what collective body best expresses
and carries forward the right to culture or the right to development?
What use are individual rights, such states might ask, when a nation as a
whole is undeveloped and its people undernourished? The welfare of individuals lies in the strength of the state. If any wish to oppose the culture, religion, or prosperity of the state, then individual rights become
forfeit; citizens of the state cannot wish for both development and the
freedom to stand in its way. Of course, if states claim to be the legitimate
vehicles of collective rights, not only individuals but also minority cultures, including indigenous peoples, can be cast in the light of enemies,
spoilers, rogues, and rebels.

Thus, if indigenous claims to self-determination are to avoid play-
ing into the hands of despotic governments, they must have individual
rights built into them. If a minority people is to claim rights of self-
determination under international law, it must commit itself to self-

govern in accordance with human rights standards. This means that indigenous peoples are seeking protection from a system of values and rights that strives, or is likely to strive at some point in the future, to alter or eliminate some of the social practices that are important to the collective identities of some indigenous societies. Human rights do not offer protection of cultural practices that themselves violate individual human rights. Full compliance with human rights norms is in principle inconsistent with some of the cherished features of some indigenous societies: the authority of elders (which can stand in the way of representative democracy), the duty of children (especially as it applies to labor and the "cruelty" that can be found in some rites of passage), and the subservience of women (expressed above all in marriage duties and exclusion from politics). Human rights are at the same time duties. Protection against the state-sponsored eradication of culture and imposition of values can bring with it another form of culture-changing universalism.

Like other creeds, liberalism, including the liberal approach to human rights, has its inherent tensions and inconsistencies. It has faltered in particular when tolerance reaches the limits imposed by intolerant others. Beyond these limits, tolerance sometimes fades into weakness or even complicity with intolerance. Vigorous self-assertion, however, very quickly makes liberalism resemble other impositions of cultural homogenization. Liberalism struggles to find a position somewhere between self-effacing toleration of illiberal cultures and resemblance of them through too-strident evangelism.

This adds both credibility and risk to indigenous peoples' assertion of their rights of self-determination. Making states the exclusive agent responsible for meeting human rights obligations is an invitation to greater state interference in distinct societies. Human rights, applied from above through unequal power relations, thus becomes yet another assimilationist tool, part of the project to make all citizens equal not only in rights but also in the basic ingredients of identity and culture. The self-determination goals of distinct societies offer a way out of state hegemony but leave open the question of how individual rights can be accommodated within assertions of collective values and powers. This becomes a more tangible problem as indigenous societies, in the transitions brought about by technology, bureaucracy, and law, take on new organizational structures and acquire new powers through their interactions and formal arrangements with states and international organizations. Activating the self-determination of indigenous peoples without a baseline of individual rights could in some circumstances become an innovative form of oppression within liberation.

This seems to be far from the minds of indigenous people themselves, for whom the construction of state identities and powers has often created conditions of marginalization and suffering. Indigenous identities are largely built on the foundations of victimization and grievance, invoked through both collective memory and daily experience. Tracing these identities to their sources, we find that those who call themselves indigenous peoples are at the same time those most commonly the targets of untrammeled ethnic and racial hatred, dispossessed of lands and livelihood through coercion, impoverished by exclusion from formal economies, and deprived, by virtue of their "distinct" status, of the rights and benefits of citizenship within states. Their suffering and the collective identities that derive from it come largely from a tendency on the part of states and corporations to remove them from their lands and resources, making it impossible for them to practice their own subsistence methods and other dimensions of culture, and then to deny them new economic opportunities by invoking, directly or indirectly, their attachment to "traditional" practices.

Indigenous identity, sometimes used to designate the distinctiveness of indigenous societies in the constitutional and moral orders of nation-states, carries significant authority and some degree of power, especially when legally articulated. It is largely an outcome of unintentional cultural and political collaboration. The concept "indigenous peoples," developed principally within Western traditions of scholarship and legal reform, has nurtured the revival of "traditional" identities. It has transcended its symbolic use by acquiring legal authority. It is the focus of widening struggles by increasing numbers of "peoples" for recognition, legitimacy, and validation. It has been taken control of by its living subjects—reverse-engineered, rearticulated, and put to use as a tool of liberation.

Notes

CHAPTER I

1. Alison Brysk (2000) discusses the transnational Indian rights movement of Latin America as a product of globalization, in which "the pace, forms, and weight of politics across borders have increased," together with the "presence, use, and salience of information both in national and local struggles and as a newly significant arena of international relations" (12). Indian rights campaigns, she argues, fare better in internationally structured situations, in which a range of international alliances and appeals are pursued (23).

2. The main arguments in favor of a recent appearance of nationalism can be found in Benedict Anderson's *Imagined Communities* (1991), Ernest Gellner's *Nations and Nationalism* (1983), and E. J. Hobsbawm's *Nations and Nationalism since 1780* (1990). John Hall (1993) expresses a common denominator of these nationalism-in-modernity positions: "The crude logistics of most societies in history—bereft of effective mass communication and cheap transport—meant that

most human beings were stuck in highly particularized segments, quite unable
to share a sense of destiny with people they had no chance of meeting" (3).

3.   There have long been terms of abuse used to designate people outside the
orbit of civilization. The practice is in fact older than civilization itself, as those
who have lived among people who despise their neighbors usually come to realize. For the Greeks, it was the *inhumani* who lived in the frozen wastes to the
north, the land of exile, who embodied, as the term suggests, the absence of
human attributes. The Romans coined the term "barbarian" and handed it on to
postmedieval Europeans, who then made good use of it in the development of
colonial empires. Then there are the words that began with neutral intentions but
acquired derogatory impact more from pejorative attitudes than from any inherent meaning. "Savage," derived from the Latin *silvaticus,* which means "forest
dweller," acquired its sting as it became associated with all that was untamed,
wild, and brutal, but anthropologists used it with equanimity well into the twentieth century. Similarly, "primitive" was an almost obligatory ingredient in the
title of any reputable ethnographic monograph prior to World War II. It plum-
meted from fashion with the changing attitudes of decolonization and Third
World development programs.

    The term "indigenous" or "indigenous peoples" is quite different from these
now improper antecedents. Its ownership, for one thing, is changing hands.
Where once it was used as a technical term by international organizations to designate the original and culturally distinct occupants of state or colonial territory, it
is now being used by its designees to refer to themselves. It has acquired a "we."

4.   Another use of the term can be found in Ward Churchill's (1996: 509–46)
discussion of North American "indigenism," which draws parallels with Latin
American *indigenismo.* This is close to the articulation of a global indigenous identity but is more closely tied to national than international political concerns and
influences. Similarly Ramos (1998) constructs a definition of indigenism grounded
in Indian participation in the national "indigenist project" of Brazil. Her study offers useful detail on Brazil's legal forms of oppression and the emerging strategies of indigenous resistance.

5.   I have not discovered how this estimate was made or where it was first published, but the three hundred million figure is widely circulated and accepted in
the international legal literature. It possibly began with a statement by former
U.N. Secretary General Boutros Boutros-Ghali (1994) at the inauguration of the
International Decade of the World's Indigenous Peoples. According to World-
watch Institute, there are globally four thousand to five thousand indigenous societies, in total comprising something between 190 and 635 million individuals
(cited in Baer 2000: 223). The tremendous range between the high and low population figures suggests that three hundred million is merely a convenient estimate
and that more precision is confounded by both the paucity and irregularities of

national census information and the problem of defining "indigenous peoples" with the kind of consistency that would lend itself to statistical analysis.

6. Frederick Barth, in his introduction to *Ethnic Groups and Boundaries* (1969), contrasts his approach with such a simplistic view of geographical and social isolation.

7. Jean-Loup Amselle (1999), for example, discusses the revival of African tribal identities as a product of colonial imaginings and the resurgence of post-colonial "regionalism," which *"bouleverse totalement la vision que l'on peut avoir des sociétés africaines précoloniales"* [completely overturns the picture one might have of precolonial African societies] (43).

8. Expressions of this approach to culture in the human rights literature can be found in Wilson (1997: 9) and Preis (1996).

9. A typology of the actions and accommodations of ethnic groups that is use-ful to some degree but not always consistent with the untidiness of their case studies is provided by John McGarry and Brendan O'Leary (1993).

10. Richard Handler, in *Nationalism and the Politics of Culture in Quebec* (1988), provides a discussion of the origins of Québec secessionism in nationalist cultural objectification, and René Lévesque, in *An Option for Quebec* (1968), provides a de-finitive platform for it.

11. The undiminished insistence of the Parti Québecois on secession from Can-ada was confirmed by Louise Beaudoin, Québec's Minister of International Rela-tions, in a January 2001 interview in *Le Monde*: *"[I]l est plus urgent, plus nécessaire que jamais de trouver cette voie vers la souveraineté"* [It is more urgent, more neces-sary than ever before, to find this path toward sovereignty] (*Le Monde* 2001: 4).

12. Oddly enough, the clearest evidence of indigenous networking can be found on the Internet. During the 1997–98 academic year, the Web site NativeWeb (http://www.nativeweb.org/stats/) recorded 2,591,274 hits (Brysk 2000: 15), and at the time of this writing, a Web search using the advanced search engine Google resulted in approximately 1,320,000 entries for the keyword "indigenous" and 204,000 for "indigenous peoples." While not all of these sites are directly con-cerned with indigenous issues, the heavy volume of material on the Internet is ev-idence of the international nature of indigenous lobbying and interorganizational cooperation. If, as Benedict Anderson argues in *Imagined Communities* (1991), print as commodity was vital to the development of national consciousness from the sixteenth century onwards, the development of information technology has similar implications for the rise of international consciousness among those mar-ginal to nation-states. At the same time, however, those who cannot afford the technology of communication and do not have the knowledge to use it are today the most powerless and marginal sector of global society.

13. This finds its clearest expression in his *Discourse on the Origin of Inequality* (Rousseau [1755] 1987). Rousseau is most comfortable with an unelaborated so-

ciety, in which the fear of vengeance takes the place of formal (and corruptible) laws. "[A] middle position between the indolence of our primitive state and the petulant activity of our egocentrism, must have been the happiest and most durable epoch. . . . [A]ll the subsequent progress has been in appearance so many steps toward the perfection of the individual, and in fact toward the decay of the species" (65). Rousseau also expresses admiration for rustic politics in *The Social Contract* ([1762] 1968): "When we see among the happiest people in the world bands of peasants regulating the affairs of state under an oak tree, and always acting wisely, can we help feeling a certain contempt for the refinements of other nations, which employ so much skill and mystery to make themselves at once illustrious and wretched?" (149).

14.   The feud is a more structured form of multigenerational suffering, with almost formulaic calls to action between similar social units—extended families, clans, or tribal segments. The suffering of genocidal events, by contrast, revives itself with great uncertainty. It offers the experience of illegitimate victimization rather than the exercise of honor through a blood payment or exculpatory homicide; and it provides a reminder of vulnerability before powerful political foes and military forces rather than the reassurance of a known enemy-counterpart.

15.   The term "people" is another, more exclusively legal, source of controversy; I discuss it in chapter 5.

16.   This complexity and the variety of contexts in which indigenous identity can apply are discussed by Howitt, Connell, and Hirsch (1996). Kingsbury (1998) elaborates a legal approach to indigenous peoples that takes as its starting point the problems encountered in the context of the South Asian mainland (see note 18 below).

17.   This is also implicit in the definition of "indigenous peoples" provided by Article 1 of the ILO Convention (No. 169) Concerning Indigenous and Tribal Peoples in Independent Countries (1989): "[P]eoples in independent countries . . . are regarded as indigenous on account of their descent from the populations which inhabited the country, or a geographical region to which the country belongs, at the time of conquest or colonisation or the establishment of present state boundaries and who, irrespective of their legal status, retain some or all of their own social, economic, cultural and political institutions." The retention of their own institutions would be irrelevant if indigenous communities were not dominated by outside powers.

18.   Benedict Kingsbury (1998) anticipates such difficulties in the positivist definition of indigenous peoples: "[I]t is impossible at present to formulate a single globally viable definition that is workable and not grossly under- or over-inclusive. Any strict definition is likely to incorporate justifications and referents that make sense in some societies but not in others. It will tend to reduce the fluid-

ity and dynamism of social life to distorted and rather static formal categories" (414). Kingsbury argues that abstract, formal definitions need to be supplemented by a "constructivist approach" that is not sharply defined by universally applicable criteria but rather embodies "a continuous process in which claims and practices in numerous specific cases are abstracted in the wider institutions of international society, then made specific again at the moment of application in the political, legal and social processes of particular cases and societies" (415). This is, in fact, close to the approach already taken by the Human Rights Committee in its consideration of cases submitted by those who claim the status of "indigenous peoples." See, for example, note 19 below.

19.   The term *baster* refers to progeny born out of wedlock (equivalent to its English cognate "bastard"), the descendants of such unions (sometimes called "half-castes"), and the "minority" that calls itself the Rehoboth Basters (Gordon and Douglas 2000: 271n).

20.   The Rehoboth claims were considered by the Human Rights Committee under the 1966 Optional Protocol to the International Covenant on Civil and Political Rights (*J. G. A. Diergaardt et al. v. Namibia*). The committee found, among other things, that the link of the Rehoboth community to their "expropriated" lands dated back some 125 years and was thus not associated with the rise of a distinctive culture. Expressed in very different ways, there is some measure of consistency between the views of the Human Rights Committee and the spontaneous reaction of the indigenous community with respect to the claims of the Rehoboth Baster community.

21.   Collective self-identification is the source of indigenous identity and the definition of indigenous peoples with which this book is principally concerned. Indigenous peoples are not only those who say they are indigenous but also those who are accepted by a global network of nations and communities with similar claims and sources of recognition.

22.   Some of the background to my field research in these two regions is discussed in the preface to this book. In my use of original research material I have been guided by the need to protect the identities of some individuals and have, in some instances, used pseudonyms. The sources of interview material are identified by name only when they are government officials or other public figures representing constituencies.

CHAPTER 2

1.   This section is a revised version of material that appears in Ronald Niezen, "Recognizing Indigenism: Canadian Unity and the International Movement of Indigenous Peoples," *Comparative Studies in Society and History* 42, no. 1 (2000):

119–48. Copyright 2000 by *Comparative Studies in Society and History.* Adapted with permission.

2.   "L'Assemblée, tout en reconnaissant le droit fondamental des minorités à être protégées par la Société des Nations contre toute oppression, insiste sur le devoir qui incombe aux personnes appartenant aux minorités de race, de religion ou de langue de coopérer en citoyens loyaux avec la nation à laquelle ils appartiennent maintenant."

3.   "De donner à une petite nation l'occasion d'être au moins entendue."

4.   The development of legal definitions and political policies specifically directed toward original peoples with distinct cultures and intact subsistence economies was also a problem for postcolonial states. In 1951, the Indian government's Commissioner for Scheduled Castes and Scheduled Tribes solicited reports from regional offices concerning the *adivasis* or "original inhabitants." In response, the Vindhya Pradesh office submitted a report describing the *adivasis* as those with "dark skin and flat noses, [exhibiting a] preference for fruits, roots, and animal flesh, rather than food grains, the use of bark and leaves of trees as clothes on ceremonial occasions, nomadism, witch-doctoring, and the worship of ghosts and spirits" (cited in ILO 1953: 14). In other words, they constituted the very antithesis of a progressive and civilized human society.

5.   One might easily imagine that support of the goals of the international agency is probably the most readily violated criterion, but it has in fact only once been invoked to reject an application for recognition to a U.N. body. Human Life International, an antiabortion group, had its application for consultative status in the Economic and Social Council rejected because of its hostility to an entire realm of U.N. endeavor (Willetts 1996: 4).

6.   The efficiency of the British postal service in the nineteenth century, for example, is pivotal to the plot of Wilkie Collins's serialized mystery *The Woman in White* ([1861] 1985). Modern readers might be surprised at the fact that characters in this novel take for granted that the letters they post in the morning will usually be delivered to almost anywhere in England on the same day. Similarly, the telegraph can be seen as the invention with the greatest implications for international communication. Philanthropic and scientific societies may have had their charters firmly grounded in Victorian values, but they would not have developed international orientations without improvements to the technologies of travel and communication.

7.   These figures, assembled by the Union of International Associations, came to my attention through Seary (1996: 16) and Florini (2000: 9).

8.   It could be argued that the relaxation of oppression and repression is more important for liberation movements than the inspirational experience of suffering. A cornerstone of Tocqueville's ([1856] 1955) analysis of the French Revolution, for example, is the observation that conditions among the serfs improved

well before the dismantling of the aristocracy. "It was precisely in those parts of France where there had been most improvement that popular discontent ran highest. This may seem illogical—but history is full of such paradoxes. For it is not always when things are going from bad to worse that revolutions break out. . . . [T]he social order overthrown by a revolution is almost always better than the one immediately preceding it, and experience teaches us that, generally speaking, the most perilous moment for a bad government is one when it seeks to mend its ways" (176–77). As a nonviolent alternative to revolution or rebellion, the efforts to secure places for indigenous peoples in international organizations have probably similarly benefited from the relaxation of state oppression, however incomplete it remains.

CHAPTER 3

1.   Five years later I was taken to the island by Bernie's cousin and shown the remains of a "nest" in a thicket where Bernie had gathered spruce boughs around himself as a layer of insulation. Some of the wet clothing he had removed to prevent or delay hypothermia was still hanging on nearby bushes.

2.   These interviews were conducted by Nelson Settee and translated from the Cree by Darwin Paupanekis.

3.   When I asked a Cross Lake elder what it meant to be healthy, he used the Cree word *minowin*, which, in its literal sense, is close to the English expression "well-being." For the elder, though, *minowin* has a wider meaning: "being side by side with the land," as he put it. Health, in other words, is closely connected to the Cree way of life based on hunting, fishing, and gathering, and, by extension, the well-being of the land itself is part of what health means for the people who sustain themselves from it. In this sense, our understanding of social suffering can be connected to the fate of a river.

4.   A healing fund was established with the Canadian government's 1998 Statement of Reconciliation (Canada 1998), but Cross Lake's Pimicikamak Health Services has not yet been able to access this fund to start healing programs.

5.   When the Jenpeg dam was constructed some nine miles upstream from Cross Lake, twenty-three thousand acres of cleared and uncleared forests were inundated. Even today, submerged trees sometimes float to the surface and eventually accumulate along hundreds of miles of shoreline in the lakes upstream from the generating station. This can make boat travel treacherous. Once the propeller of a boat I was on with five others struck a barely submerged stump (or "spider" as people in Cross Lake call them, after their arachnidlike roots), sending everyone sprawling. As the boat steadied, we laughed with relief at the near accident. No one had fallen overboard. The propeller was cracked but still got us

home. Since then I have noticed that almost every boat in the waters near Cross Lake carried a spare propeller tied to the gunwale. Boat collisions with debris are common enough to make this a necessary precaution. In winter, travel on the river downstream from the dam is made hazardous by water fluctuations. The controlled releases that occur at times of peak energy demand cause water to rise dramatically over a period of hours, producing areas of slush, and sometimes even open water, on snowmobile routes. In the spring, when energy demand tapers, water levels drop several feet below the ice surface, causing weakened "hanging ice," a perilous, invisible trap to even experienced Cree hunters. The number of deaths that have occurred under these circumstances is undocumented. I once went through the death record with someone who knew the circumstances surrounding all the drownings and deaths from hypothermia since 1976 and we arrived at a figure of eighteen, but only one case was pursued over the years it took for the courts to find Manitoba Hydro liable.

6.   When flooding occurs in a new impoundment, inert mercury contained in rock and soil methylizes and enters the food chain. The highest mercury levels occur in the first four years after flooding and probably steadily return to normal after that; but a 1996 study found that northern pike in the Cross Lake area still contained higher than acceptable mercury levels. Meanwhile, mercury testing of the Cree population had not been done since 1984, when hair samples were taken and letters sent to those whose mercury levels were high.

7.   Prior to missionary contact, the dead were usually wrapped in birch bark and placed on tree scaffolds. Burial along shorelines seems to have been a post-Christian practice for about a century before village centralization and the creation of village cemeteries. Shoreline remains are usually dated between 50 and 150 years old.

8.   Cross Lake has six known burial sites that have been either eroded or inundated by the hydroelectric project. Two sites have been stabilized by a Manitoba Hydro mitigation program, the bones on the shore having been returned from the archaeological consultants who removed them, to be ceremonially reburied *in situ*.

9.   This argument was first developed in, and this paragraph is reprinted from, Ronald Niezen, "'With the Health of a River Goes the Health of a People,'" *Native Americas Journal*, Summer (2000). Copyright 2000 by Akwe:kon Press.

10.   The procedures set in place by the government of Canada for the ratification of the Comprehensive Agreements had the effect of dividing each of the NFA communities into two camps, those for and those against the agreements. This came about largely because in each community the ratification process was based upon referenda in which per capita payments, usually of $1,000, were promised as an immediate outcome of NFA "settlement"—contingent upon approval of the agreement. Factionalization went further in Norway House than

anywhere else. In this community, a July 29, 1997, referendum, in which the new implementation agreement was defeated by five votes (referred to some jubilant opponents of the agreement as a symbol of divine grace, the "hand of God"), was followed a few days later by an announcement on local radio that the first vote did not reflect strong support for the agreement and that a second "confirmation vote" would be held a few months later. It was through this second referendum, with a lowered threshold for approval, that Norway House's implementation agreement was "approved." At the same time, it created a community of "dissidents" whose story was communicated on Cross Lake's local access television and radio, adding substance to concerns about the state's new strategy of NFA implementation.

11. To add flavor to this event, some later reported that Chief Robinson "burned" the draft agreement in a garbage pail, but interviews (including several with Chief Robinson), written accounts of the event, and common sense (he would not likely have started a fire in a crowded building) suggest otherwise. The different account is noteworthy, however, because it does more than just liven up the story; it symbolically represents an irrevocable rejection of the document. It reveals private fear and hope: a discarded document can later be retrieved, while a burned one cannot.

12. Benedict Kingsbury, in his essay "The Applicability of the International Legal Concept of 'Indigenous Peoples' in Asia" (1999), summarizes some of the differing positions taken by governments in Asia in debates about the concept of "indigenous peoples," noting that, for various reasons, the governments of China, India, Bangladesh, Burma, and Indonesia are most strongly opposed to its application to peoples within their territories.

13. Kingsbury (1998) paraphrases an argument presented by the representative of India to the 1991 meeting of the Working Group on Indigenous Populations to the effect that "most of the tribes in India share ethnic, racial and linguistic characteristics with other people in the country, and that three to four hundred million people there are distinct in some way from other categories of people in India" (435).

14. This argument is contained, for example, in comments sent by the People's Republic of China to a 1995 working group of the U.N. Commission on Human Rights:

The Chinese Government believes that the question of indigenous peoples is the product of European countries' recent pursuit of colonial policies in other parts of the world. Because of these policies, many indigenous peoples were dispossessed of their ancestral homes and lands, brutally oppressed, exploited and murdered, and in some cases even deliberately exterminated. To this day, many indigenous peoples still suffer from discrimination and diminished status. . . . As in the majority of Asian countries, the various nationalities in China have all lived for aeons on Chinese territory. Although there is no indigenous peoples' question in China, the Chinese government and people have every sympathy with indigenous peoples' historical woes and historical plight. (cited in Kingsbury 1998: 417–18)

15.   The denial of indigenous identity by rival indigenous groups can also take place through national laws. A proposal to amend the Arts and Crafts Act of 1990, prohibiting misrepresentation in the marketing of Native arts and crafts products in the United States, for example, would allow federally registered tribes and individuals and their crafts organizations to bring charges against "counterfeiters," who could potentially include "Indians of the Americas" outside the United States (including Canada) and Puerto Rican people with an indigenous heritage. At the same time, federal legal protections for "registered" Indians cannot be used by those claiming indigenous identity within the United States who do not have a "registered" status (George Guilmet, personal communication, November 2000).

16.   The progressive acceptance of the concept of "indigenous peoples" in Africa is also finding its way into regional human rights organizations and the drafting of "soft law" (human rights legislation with no supervisory mechanism). Thus the African Commission on Human and Peoples' Rights has recently formed a Working Group on Indigenous Populations, the main objective of which is to "elaborate principles for an African approach to indigenous peoples which might result in the elaboration of an optional protocol to the African Charter on Human and Peoples' Rights" (United Nations 2001: 3).

17.   The T'boli struggle to retain their subsistence base in the face of unscrupulous forest developers and the state in the Philippines (Hyndman and Duhaylungsod 1996) suggests parallels with the manner of land alienation in Australia and North America. As in the case of the creation of some treaties in the Americas and elsewhere, T'boli land was at one point appropriated through fraudulent agreements, orally misrepresented and "signed" with thumbprints. The main difference between the Southeast Asian context and today's liberal states is the manner in which the state weighs in on the resource disputes that follow from such usurpation. Whereas in liberal states indigenous peoples are often subjected to legal mechanisms, in the Philippines the T'boli have been subjected to forced removal, killings, even military artillery bombardment (on the pretext that ranchers who have title to the land had offered it as a target range).

18.   The idea that many societies in the hinterlands were left out of the decolonization-into-nation-state process receives independent confirmation from Benedict Anderson's schema for the creation of minorities in Southeast Asia in *The Spectre of Comparisons* (1998). Anderson argues that colonial relationships involved development of privileged minorities, those he refers to as "coalition-worthy indigenous minorities," whose size and ability to advance political and

economic agendas placed them in advantaged positions in national coalition politics. Other minorities, however, were not quite so adept or well situated in the colony-to-independence transitions. These Anderson describes in terms strikingly reminiscent of narratives of indigenous victimization: "In most cases their wish is simply to be left alone, or to make quiet, slow adaptations to the outside world. But this outside world—not merely the nation-state, but more importantly the great engines of planetary power—will not leave them be" (329–30). Anderson's assessment of their predicament, almost contemporaneous with the reach of the indigenous peoples' movement in Asia (the essay on which his material is based was first published in 1987), is that these groups will have little choice but to engage in postcolonial ethnic politics, in ways similar to those claiming an American Indian or Native American identity but in a more perilous environment. Anderson did not anticipate that the extension of such native or "indigenous" identity to Asia, with actual ties to the Americas and elsewhere, was a literal possibility.

An introductory essay to a volume by Howitt, Connell, and Hirsch (1996) makes a similar point by highlighting "neo-colonial continuities" in the handling of resource competition, with indigenous peoples in both the nation-states of Southeast Asia and states in the Pacific region usually considered (to varying degrees) more liberal: Australia, New Zealand, New Caledonia, and New Guinea.

19. The preceding summary of indigenous views from the "decolonized" world is based largely on the proceedings of a seminar entitled "Multiculturalism in Africa: Peaceful and Constructive Group Accommodation in Situations Involving Minorities and Indigenous Peoples," held in Arusha, Tanzania, on May 13–15, 2000 (United Nations 2000e), and the proceedings of a similar meeting the following year in Kidal, Mali (United Nations 2001).

20. In the Gao region, this style of Islamic reform was active in several dozen Songhay villages. Reformers placed emphasis on scriptural ideals and were uncompromising and confrontational with their rival villagers who maintained their support of village clerics and Sufi brotherhoods. In so doing, they developed a form of regional governance that increased the autonomy of villages within, and sometimes exceeding, the limitations imposed by the Malian government (Niezen 1990, 1991).

21. Edgar Pisani, in his capacity as a mediator in Mali's state/nomad conflict, in a 1992 interview on TV5-Europe, even went so far as to refer to the centralizing tendencies of Mali as "almost Jacobin" (Maïga 1997: 12).

22. A cow selling for 150,000 francs CFA in predrought times sold for 5,000 to 7,000 francs during the drought. Part of the drop in price was caused by trade restrictions imposed by the Nigerian government.

23. The term *Anasara*, used throughout much of the African Sahel, is derived

from "Nazarene," or "Christian," as a way of designating those of visibly European (or North American) origin.

24.   Some nomads, knowing that donors equated "development" with "settlement," constructed what appeared to be "permanent" camps on the eve of food distributions, solely for the purpose of satisfying aid administrations (Maïga 1997: 175).

25.   "Nos ancêtres les Gauloises étaient blonds" (Jansen 1979: 51).

26.   For example, in February 1993 an Arab trader from Gao was abducted and later found strangled in a well. He had apparently supported a faction, the Front Islamique Arabe pour la Libération de l'Azawad, seen by his killers as an enemy group (Amnesty International 1994: 207).

27.   Since the violence of the mid-1990s the relationship between security forces and nomads on the Malian frontier has stabilized and peace efforts have resumed. The U.N. Commission on Human Rights selected Kidal, Mali, as the site for the Second Workshop on Multiculturalism in Africa (United Nations 2001), which also served as an informal venue for talks between government and Tuareg leaders. It remains to be seen whether these renewed efforts will lead to more lasting peace and a more widely accepted regime of Tuareg regional autonomy.

28.   It is, of course, possible for states to minimize the dislocating effects of formal education. Some of the Samis I met in Finland had their own stories of boarding school experience from the 1950s, but since then lessons have been drawn. Today there is daily transport to school from remote villages, even from a distance of one hundred kilometers, so that students can continue to live at home; Sami has been made an optional language of instruction, resulting in a situation in which municipal schools funded by the state now have the effect of reestablishing Sami identity in families where parents have lost their connection to the language; and distance learning via the Internet is being introduced as a way to further maintain students' place within family and community (Martin Scheinin, personal communication, July 2001). The James Bay Crees provide an example of a semiautonomous school board implementing similar measures of local schooling and language preservation (Niezen 1998: ch. 5).

CHAPTER 4

1.   William Theodore de Barry (1998) makes an important contribution to this debate with a historically sensitive consideration of Confucianism in the light of universal human rights norms. He argues that proponents of communitarian values from China (and, we may assume, from other Asian governments as well as African governments picking up on their views) are actually defending statism —that is to say, defending the right of the state to act on behalf of all citizens,

often in an authoritarian way that impinges upon individual freedoms. "What is missing in the argument," de Barry writes, "is any consideration of the community as a form of infrastructure that might mediate between individuals and the state, and perform the function of a civil society in protecting the interests of either the individual or people in groups (rather than en masse)" (92).

2.   It has long been accepted by indigenous representatives to U.N. meetings that human rights protection also means commitment and responsibility in upholding human rights. Principle 7 of the Declaration of Principles of Indigenous Rights, adopted in 1984 by the Fourth General Assembly of the World Council of Indigenous Peoples, for example, states that "the institutions of indigenous peoples and their decisions, like those of states, must be in conformity with internationally accepted human rights both collective and individual." If this were taken further, however, a legal purist would object to the notion of minority responsibility for human rights because (1) an individual is a victim of human rights abuses; and (2) even if that violation results from the action of a minority community, the state bears ultimate responsibility for any violations that occur in its territory. States thus have the interconnected obligations, sometimes approached in a contradictory manner, to introduce measures to bring an end to human rights violations (including those resulting from acts committed by minorities) and to simultaneously respect minority rights.

3.   The colonial affiliations that did exist have not yet been adequately described. Clifford Geertz (1990), for example, takes Evans-Pritchard to task for a Kiplingesque lapse in one of his obscure writings, while overlooking at least one easier target—the ethnography in the service of the colonies made explicit by S. F. Nadel.

4.   The argument that Article 5 of the Universal Declaration could be interpreted to include self-inflicted pain is, in fact, dubious because the wording, "No one shall be *subjected to* torture [emphasis added]," strongly implies victimization by the more powerful.

5.   This is an issue taken up by Abdullahi Ahmed An-Na'im (1992), who argues that the development of techniques for internal cultural discourse and cross-cultural dialogue is the preferred method of overcoming human rights ethnocentricity. It is thus possible to recognize the need for societies to interpret and apply human rights standards in their own way, to avoid dictating to noncompliant societies (or societies whose interpretation of human rights standards differs significantly from that of most others), and to maintain the legitimacy of universal moral standards. The internal struggles for power and cultural influence within societies provide the best practical opportunities for universalism; it is by taking sides, not confrontationally evangelizing, that universal standards have the best chance of being constructively disseminated. This leaves partially unanswered the question of how one arrives at a starting point for intra- and intercul-

tural dialogue; where does the moral vision come from that is to be strategically inserted into the internal struggles for cultural supremacy? Presumably An-Na'im's approach still forces us to rely on existing human rights instruments, however vague, incomplete, and unrepresentative of all human cultures they might be.

6.   Erve Chambers (1985) informs us that "[t]he idea of a *practicing anthropology* emerged during the 1970s as a way of identifying anthropologists who were employed outside academic settings" (16).

7.   Scheper-Hughes (1987) takes a position against "anthropological blindness, in the guise of an inappropriate ethical relativism," concerning "violations of power relations between adults and children in sexual behavior" (19), but the ultimate causes of infanticide, selective neglect, and child battery are to be found not so much in demented individuals or pathological cultures as in "structural inequalities in the world economic order [which create] an imbalance in resources and in the relationships between fertility and childhood mortality" (24). The assumption here is that suffering and neglect occur among the impoverished and powerless and thus that responsibility must lie elsewhere, in unequal power relations and global economic imbalance. The ethical responsibility of social actors, and hence relativism, seem to shift with power. The implication is that the more a society is politically and economically self-determining or dominant over others, the more it becomes possible to find abuses of power that supplant cultural explanations for such things as violence toward and neglect of children.

8.   A summary of human rights violations committed by the oil industry in Ecuador, written by the Center for Economic and Social Rights (1999), for example, is rightly critical of the exploration and drilling activities of the Texaco-Gulf consortium in the Oriente, the tropical rain forest at the headwaters of the Amazon. "Overall," the center reports, "more than 30 billion gallons of toxic wastes and crude oil have been discharged into the land and waterways of the Oriente since 1972" (132), all of which is having an extremely deleterious effect on the indigenous population of the Amazon. The Center for Economic and Social Rights observes that "eight different nations, each with a total population of between 100,000 and 250,000 people, inhabit the Oriente. The Quichua and Shuar account for the majority, with the rest divided among the Huaorani, the Secoya, the Siona, the Shiwiar, the Cofan, and the Achuar. These peoples have distinct cultures and traditions that are inextricably bound to the rain forest in which they have lived for thousands of years. Their economic and spiritual existence revolves around sustainable management of rain forest resources" (133). The very nature of the ecological concerns, covering vast areas of rain forest, appears to stand in the way of a sustained examination of the human victims of human rights violations.

9.   Montesquieu's youthful work *The Persian Letters* ([1721] 1964), which he first published anonymously but for which later in life he became famous, in-

cludes some of the same arguments that appear in *The Spirit of the Laws*, but with less firm sociological grounding. It is based upon a premise—an exchange of letters between Usbek, a Persian nobleman on a voyage to Paris, and his friends and members of his household in the Orient—that allowed Montesquieu great latitude in his choice of topics and their factual underpinnings. Usbek's observations of the Parisian nobility's social customs (above all marriage arrangements and sexual intrigues), filtered through his own Eastern assumptions, underscored a fundamental confrontation of values. Neither the Persian nor the French way of life was shown to be inherently superior or inferior; rather, each had to be understood on its own terms. Systems of belief and social arrangements impinge in various ways on individual freedom and at times appear absurd to outside observers (such as the alien Usbek), but they seem to make sense, or even to be of tremendous importance, to members of each society.

10.   Giambattista Vico ([1744] 1968), a few years earlier, expressed a strikingly similar view: "Vulgar traditions must have had public grounds of truth, by virtue of which they came into being and were preserved by entire peoples over long periods of time" (64). Gottfried Herder was perhaps an even more influential relativist—or, as some might prefer, pluralist—critic of the mainstream of Enlightenment ideas. The emphasis in Herder's writing was on patriotism and love of country (as expressed, for example, in the idea that poetry is a form of expression tied intimately and in unique ways with the nation through the bonds of language, thoughts, needs, and feelings) rather than the range of human cultural differences, but on this basis his writing has with time acquired a more modern flavor. On this subject, Isaiah Berlin's *Three Critics of the Enlightenment* (2000), is a useful introduction and is gaining currency as a masterpiece of intellectual history.

11.   In his indirect contrast of Montesquieu and Rousseau, Maine ([1861] 1977) gives Montesquieu credit for suspending judgment on the early conditions of man. Rousseau, he finds, "bitterly and broadly condemns the present for its unlikeness to the ideal past; while . . . [Montesquieu], assuming the present to be as necessary as the past, does not affect to disregard or censure it." (52). Montesquieu, Maine tells us, "pays little or no regard to the inherited qualities of the race, those qualities which each generation receives from its predecessors and transmits but slightly altered to the generation which follows it" (69).

12.   The contest between indigenous claims of self-determination and human rights individualism was played out in a 1984 decision by the Human Rights Committee in a case involving aboriginal land rights and cultural rights in northern Alberta (*Bernard Ominayak v. Canada*). In his original submission to the Human Rights Committee, Chief Bernard Ominayak of the Lubicon Lake Band argued that his community's rights of self-determination (under Article 1, paragraphs 1 to 3 of the International Covenant on Civil and Political Rights) were violated when the Canadian government allowed the provincial government of

Alberta to expropriate the ancestral territory of the Lubicon Lake Crees for the benefit of private corporate interests, mostly in the form of leases for oil and gas exploration and timber cutting. The committee, however, did not accept the complaint as it stood. It pointed out that it was allowed to hear only individual complaints and then reasoned that an individual could not claim a right of self-determination and therefore could not argue that this right had been violated. The committee found, however, that many of the issues surrounding the negative consequences for the Lubicon Crees of oil and gas extraction and timber cutting fell within the purview of Article 27 of the International Covenant on Civil and Political Rights ("In those States in which ethnic, religious or linguistic minorities exist, persons [i.e. individuals] belonging to such minorities shall not be denied the right, in community with the other members of their group, to enjoy their own culture, to profess and practise their own religion, or to use their own language"). The committee concluded that the government of Canada had failed to rectify the historical inequities that continued to threaten the way of life and culture of the Lubicon Lake Band. (Although the decision may be seen as going against the government of Canada, the committee also found that the mechanisms for resolving the complaint of the Lubicon Indians were already in place at the time of the decision.)

13.   Among such protections are Article 27 of the Universal Declaration, which recognizes "the right to freely participate in the cultural life of the community," and Article 15 of the International Covenant on Economic, Social and Cultural Rights, which recognizes the right of all "to take part in cultural life" while requiring states to take those steps "necessary for the conservation, the development and the diffusion of science and culture."

14.   Donnelly's (1989) rejection of relativism in human rights law focuses largely on its use as a justification for the abuses of states, such as Malawi President Hastings Kamuzu Banda's use of "traditional courts" to deal with political opponents outside the regular legal system. Such state abuses are often accomplished, he points out, through the sacrifice of local customs. He points out that, "in fact, authentic traditional cultural practices and values can be an important check on abuses of arbitrary power" (121). But to Donnelly universalism means just that, and by virtue of his individualist interpretation of human rights, traditional societies cannot legitimately claim the protections of collective rights.

CHAPTER 5

1.   Some material in this chapter (and elsewhere in the book) consists of informal statements made by delegates in plenary sessions of international meetings. In some instances I recorded and transcribed these statements, in others I wrote

them verbatim into my notes during the meeting. In both instances I have adjusted the spoken version of these statements to eliminate repetitions and minor grammatical errors. They should be taken as fragments of dialogue, not as formal policy statements emerging from governments or indigenous peoples' organizations.

2.   This section is a revised version of material that has appeared previously in Ronald Niezen, "Recognizing Indigenism: Canadian Unity and the International Movement of Indigenous Peoples," *Comparative Studies in Society and History* 42, no. 1 (2000): 119–48. Copyright 2000 by *Comparative Studies in Society and History.* Adapted with permission.

3.   A figure that, together with the scope of the project, has subsequently expanded to roughly $24 billion.

4.   The James Bay Cree population has since grown to approximately thirteen thousand.

5.   Evelyn Peters (1989) provides a useful summary of the James Bay and Northern Québec Agreement of 1975. Various aspects of the implementation and impact of the James Bay Agreement are discussed in Feit (1985), Niezen (1993, 1998), Salisbury (1986), Vincent and Bowers (1988), and Wertman (1983).

6.   Other organizations that have achieved such status include the Aboriginal and Torres Strait Islander Commission, the Four Directions Council, the Indigenous World Association, The INNU Council of Nitassinan (INNU Nation), the International Indian Treaty Council, the Indian Law Resource Center, the International Organization of Indigenous Resource Development, the International Working Group for Indigenous Affairs, the Inuit Circumpolar Conference, the Métis National Council, the National Aboriginal and Islander Legal Services Secretariat, the National Indian Youth Council, the New South Wales Aboriginal Land Council, the Sami Council, Treaty Four, and the World Council of Indigenous Peoples.

7.   The number was seventy-eight in March 1996 (Corbett 1996: 1)—the latest figure I have available—but has subsequently been growing.

8.   Gruyère cheese, in fact, does not have significant holes. He is likely referring to Emmenthal.

9.   The "statesmen" I am referring to are both men and women. There is no gender-neutral word for those who take a leading part in the affairs of a body politic without necessarily being politicians.

10.   The Organization of American States (OAS) currently faces the same controversy in the process of drafting a proposed American Declaration on the Rights of Indigenous Peoples. The working document for a January 2001 meeting on the proposed declaration consistently situates the words "peoples"/"populations" in square brackets, indicating that consensus had not been reached. The notion of equality, by contrast, expressed as antiracism and antidiscrimination, is not controversial, as in the draft Article 4 of the preamble: "Reiterating the re-

sponsibility incumbent upon all states to combat racism and all forms of discrimination with a view to eliminating them" (OAS 2001b). Equality and antidiscrimination, applied in particular to indigenous peoples, continue to be less controversial for state governments than the distinct rights of "peoples."

11.   Contests over reindeer-herding rights and resources in northern Finland
have also found their way into cultural expression, with non-Sami Lapps taking
on, for example, some aspects of Sami costume, but without accurately imitating
regional and lineage-designating designs. An administrator in the Sami Parliament in Inari pointed out to me that a brochure published by the European Union
depicted so-called Samis wearing such inauthentic costume. According to her,
the reason the Lapps engage in such imitation is to become indistinguishable (at
least to political outsiders) from Samis and therefore to strengthen their claims to
the same rights and benefits that accrue to those recognized as "indigenous."

12.   Although the scope of parliamentary initiatives is limited to cultural issues,
the Samis of Finland have acted upon concerns over lands and resources by sub-
mitting several complaints to the Human Rights Committee under the Optional
Protocol to the International Covenant on Civil and Political Rights (ICCPR), arguing that unwanted resource extraction makes them victims of violations by
Finland of Article 27 of the ICCPR (in particular the right "in community with the
other members of their group, to enjoy their own culture"). A 1990 submission by
the Samis (*O. Sara et al. v. Finland*) points to the importance of old-growth forests
for the production of several species of lichen (necessary, in turn, for the reindeer's winter diet) and as a buffer zone that limits transport of industrial pollution from Russia. Although the Human Rights Committee did not decide in their
favor, the principle was laid down in the 1992 decision on a submission by Ilmari
Länsman that extractive "measures whose impact amount to a denial of the right
will not be compatible with the obligations under article 27" (*I. Länsman et al. v.
Finland*). In other words, environmental destruction beyond the limits in which
reindeer herding can continue as a culturally significant activity would constitute a violation of the Samis' rights under the Optional Protocol of the ICCPR.

13.   Another recent target of Pimicikamak Cree Nation lawmaking was the Indian Act (the legal nemesis, in earlier form, of Deskaheh in his Geneva campaign
of the 1920s). The people of Cross Lake revised the application of the act to their
community with two laws, the Citizenship Law and the Election Law, passed in
tandem on July 1, 1999. The effect of the Indian Act on Cross Lake had already
been modified with the establishment of the Okimawin Trust and the elected
board of trustees that administers it by making available a consolidated revenue
fund outside the control of the Department of Indian Affairs; but the new laws
that give control of citizenship and election procedures to the community go
much further, in effect nullifying federal jurisdiction over these key aspects of
band administration. The Election Law, however, does not have the punitive qual-

ities of the Hydro Payment Law because Canada's Indian Act allows for elections to be conducted in accordance with federally approved "traditional" methods.

14.   The Pimicikamak Cree Nation responded by filing a lawsuit seeking $100 million from Manitoba Hydro for its unfulfilled Northern Flood Agreement obligations. It remains to be seen whether this legal strategy will be actively pursued and, if so, whether it will diminish Cross Lake's commitment to inherent-jurisdiction lawmaking.

15.   The location of families on traplines, for example, was sometimes recorded with the use of sharpened sticks placed in well-frequented locations, pointed in the direction of a camp, with the length of the sticks indicating the camp's approximate distance. This is an example of what the Crees saw as a way of recording an oral law, since the decision to locate a family in a particular area would have meant that others should not hunt there without permission.

16.   For example, *Sparrow v. R.* (1990) establishes a flexible standard of aboriginal rights, acknowledging their adaptation over time. *Van der Peet v. R.* (1996) holds that the courts must take into account both the significance of the land to aboriginal peoples and their distinctive cultures and social organizations. Most significantly, *Delgamuukw v. British Columbia* (1997) adapts the laws of evidence to allow oral testimony and oral traditions and elaborates a test of aboriginal title, which includes reference to "pre-existing systems of aboriginal law" (cited in Imai 1998: 232).

17.   The significance of electronic media in Cross Lake goes even further. With public approval of a proposed law a constitutionally necessary aspect of lawmaking, the dissemination of information also has a directly legislative function. Television is, in a sense, the means by which the entire community is able to function, for the duration of general meetings on proposed laws, as a legislative assembly. This role of the media encourages a view that goes beyond Tocqueville's ([1840] 2000: 182–89) optimistic view of the press as the only guarantor of the freedom and safety of citizens; in Cross Lake the media function as an open channel through which the citizens define themselves. Local-access television serves to create not only an imagined community, setting the boundaries of identity, but also a more tangible polity, setting the boundaries and opportunities of the nation's laws themselves.

18.   The cultural imaginings and longings of the European New Age movement appear strongest in Germany, possibly because its colonial entanglements with living, breathing, rights-seeking aboriginal people are not as immediate as those of many other European nations. The *Gastarbeiter* are closer to home as targets of intolerance.

19.   Similarly, the Arun III Hydroelectric Project in Nepal came under the scrutiny of the World Bank's Inspection Panel, largely through the lobbying activities of residents in harm's way of the project, who created the Arun Concerned Group.

The World Bank can experience loss of legitimacy and the projects they sponsor can even lose profitability if they are the cause of social conflict, litigation, and embarrassing media coverage. Projects are assessed by the Inspection Panel according to the criteria of the policies and procedures of the World Bank itself, without direct reference to human rights treaties. The Inspection Panel, after investigating the impact of the Arun III project on the ethnic groups in the area to be impacted by the project (whether or not they were labeled "indigenous"), recommended strict social-impact monitoring, environmental impact assessments, and informed public participation in the project. Given the extent of measures required to prevent the project's interference with vulnerable populations, the president of the Bank decided not to proceed with the project and recommended that the World Bank support the government of Nepal in seeking an alternative energy strategy. This decision was taken even though discontinuation of the project was not a recommendation of the Inspection Panel (Scheinin 2000: 186−90).

20.   Martin Scheinin (2000) emphasizes the need for a judicial approach to cultural rights in which even modern forms of economic activity, such as running casinos, should require protection as aboriginal rights if they provide an economic foundation for self-government and hence the preservation of an indigenous culture. He argues that "the ultimate outcome of affording protection only to economic activities that were practiced 'at the time of contact' will, in many cases, be the extinction of the culture" (197−98). A variety of economic opportunities is called for, especially in "pathological" situations in which cultures have already been largely destroyed.

21.   State judiciaries have also promulgated conceptualizations of indigenous cultures that stress their core value as being stagnantly "distinctive." In Canada this is exemplified by a "species-by-species" approach to hunting and fishing rights emerging from Supreme Court rulings. In *Van der Peet v. R.* (1996), for example, the Musqueam Indians' right to participate in British Columbia's salmon fishery was predicated upon their ability to demonstrate that the activity was for them "an element of a practice, custom or tradition integral to [their] distinctive culture" (para. 46). Rights, in other words, must be subject to tests of cultural authenticity, based largely upon ethnohistorical accounts of aboriginal societies at the time of European assertion of sovereignty. Such a "frozen-in-time" approach to subsistence rights does not take into account the need of all societies to use new technologies, or harvest new species, in adaptation to economic, social, and cultural challenges. The Court's requirement of authenticity overlooks the basic kinds of adaptations societies engage in during such events as migration or the introduction of revolutionary technologies. The motivations behind judicial stereotyping are clearly different from the romantic impulses of the New Age movement or the environmental lobby, although some trace of cultural romanticism in the judiciary cannot be altogether ruled out. It is clearer that "distinctive"

cultural rights are less of a burden on the state than general political rights; cultural rights break indigenous claims of sovereignty into manageable pieces. The alternative—recognizing aboriginal political rights—would, as Michael Asch (2000) points out, "produce a fundamental challenge to Canada's claim to have secured legitimate sovereignty in the absence of treaties or adhesions in which Aboriginal peoples voluntarily surrendered their sovereignty, jurisdiction, and underlying title. Such assumptions would raise serious questions about the jurisdictional arrangements between First Nations and various levels of Canadian government" (135). The antiquated approach to culture on the part of the judiciary is more an outcome of the containment of political claims than a longing for a better world, at least not a world in which indigenous cultures are the repositories of the political rights of peoples.

In one respect, however, the "frozen-in-time" judicial conceptualization of culture has a similar effect to that of popular romanticism. Both impose definitions and expectations of culture that in some ways limit the manner in which indigenous societies can present themselves. They both curtail the range of choices to be drawn upon in making adaptations to rapidly changing circumstances. Whether or not an indigenous society chooses to assert its sovereignty, it is called upon by many, from a variety of sources, to diminish it.

CHAPTER 6

1.   This is the kind of political dilemma to which Isaiah Berlin's words about tolerance in the epigraph to this book apply most clearly. There is little chance that the expectations of indigenous peoples will be fully met by states and international organizations. States' and indigenous peoples' political points of view will probably always be starkly different, failing to meet on basic premises, and at times diametrically opposed, yet they must somehow coexist and build a foundation of tolerance.

Michael Ignatieff, in *The Warrior's Honor* (1997), builds on Berlin's approach with observations from an impressive number of the world's war zones. The modern basis of entrenched identities, which Ignatieff (following Freud) aptly refers to as "the narcissism of minor differences," is associated with a pathological form of empowerment that "consolidates the hold of the group on the individual and that locks individuals in victimhood" (60). Social peace (for Ignatieff as for his late mentor Berlin) begins with affirming the possibility of empathy among strangers, despite the incompatibility of their worldviews or supreme values; with reducing the importance of intractable differences; and with placing value on listening, on acknowledging that what others have to say, especially about themselves, can be meaningful and important. At the same time, all who profess to liberal pluralism must contend with the fact that commitment to tolerance is not widely enough shared and is often accepted only superficially as a kind of benign imperialism by groups with latent, strident identities.

2.   Disagreement about the usefulness of the terms "nation" and "nationalism" as applied to indigenous peoples is found not only among state governments with significant interests at stake but also among scholars writing about indigenous societies. Fleras and Elliott, in *The Nations Within* (1996), provide an extended (if, at times, indirect) argument for both the use of the term and the wide-ranging policy reforms that would follow from it. "Those struggling to have their sovereignty reinstated go beyond the vocabulary of race, class, or ethnicity to adopt the vocabulary of nationhood. . . . [A]boriginal groups have moved beyond the narrow view of themselves as a minority" (xi). Alcida Ramos (1998), writing about indigenous-state politics in Brazil, expresses more skepticism: "If the concept of nation is slippery in its Western application, it becomes utterly opaque when used to designate non-Western political units" (186). She concludes from this observation that "nation, conceptually troublesome and politically explosive as it is . . . seems to do more harm than good. . . . Overflowing with meaning, the concept of nation ends up emptying itself out, especially when it becomes a political metaphor, as indigenous nations is" (194). Metaphor or not, the reality of indigenous politics of resistance is that self-determination, expressed through "nationhood" or equal status with nation-states as "peoples," is being pursued with great determination.

3.   Indigenous representatives at U.N. meetings have occasionally cited the 1970 Declaration of Principles of International Law Concerning Friendly Relations and Cooperation among States in Accordance with the Charter of the United Nations in support of their claim to rights of self-determination on a par with those of other peoples, including the right, under certain circumstances, to secede from states. The declaration explicitly addresses the principle of equal rights and self-determination of peoples in the following terms: "Nothing in the foregoing paragraphs shall be construed as authorizing or encouraging any action which would dismember or impair, totally or in part, the territorial integrity or political unity of sovereign and independent States *conducting themselves in compliance with the principle of equal rights and self-determination of peoples* as described above and thus possessed of a government respecting the whole people belonging to the territory without distinction as to race, creed or colour [emphasis added]".

The Commission on Human Rights, faced with an apparently intractable controversy over indigenous peoples' claims of self-determination, solicited an explanation of the secessionist implications of indigenous self-determination from Working Group chairperson Erica-Irene Daes (1993), who obliged with the following observation:

Once an independent State has been established and recognized, its constituent people must try to express their aspirations through the national political system, and not through the creation of new States. This requirement continues *unless the national political system becomes so exclusive and non-democratic that it no longer can be said to be "representing the whole people."* At that point, and if all international and diplomatic measures fail to protect the peoples concerned from the State, they may be justified in creating a new State for their safety and security. . . . Continued government representivity and accountability is [sic] therefore a condition for enduring enjoyment of the right of self-determination and for continued application of the territorial integrity and national unity principles [emphasis added]. (5)

This explanation must have provided little comfort to those governments that continued to resist indigenous claims of self-determination, mainly because so many indigenous peoples appear to fall into the category of the unprotected and unrepresented—in other words, of those who meet the legal criteria for legitimately pursuing independent statehood.

4.   The *tamanawas* dances of the Northwest Coast, for example, a nineteenth-century ethnographic "catch-all" category with a common denominator of repugnance that included the winter ceremonials of the Tsimshian-speaking groups incorporating "dog-eating" rites and the initiation ceremonies of the central-coast Kwakwaka'wakw and Nuxalk involving ritual cannibalism (including possessed novices' taking bites from the arms and legs of spectators and human corpses), were legislated against by the government of Canada in 1884–85, despite the fact that missionaries and Indian agents had already been largely successful in modifying the ceremonies in such ways that they would arouse less moral condemnation (Niezen 2000b: 136–37; Cole and Chaikin 1990: 19). The offending practices had altered, largely of their own accord, making the legislation suppressing them oppressively redundant. Another example can be found in the response of the Tupi (of present-day Brazil) to Portuguese injunctions against the practice of ceremonially killing and eating their enemies. Although the Portuguese enforced a rule that captives should be killed on the battlefield or, better yet, sold as slaves to the colonial authorities, the Tupi chose instead to practice attenuated forms of killing and cannibalism (such as breaking the skulls of already dead enemies) that retained the ceremonial aspect of warfare in ways acceptable to the Portuguese (Carneiro da Cunha 1992: 293).

5.   It remains to be seen whether the recent movement toward regional autonomy in Chiapas, Mexico, will have the effect of further legitimating regional, low-intensity armed struggle as an indigenous strategy of resistance elsewhere in Latin America.

References

Alfonso Martínez, Miguel. 1999. "Study on Treaties, Agreements and Other Constructive Arrangements between States and Indigenous Populations." Commission on Human Rights. U.N. doc. E/CN.4/Sub.2/1999/20.

American Anthropological Association. 1947. "Statement on Human Rights." *American Anthropologist* 49: 539–43.

American Friends of PCN. 2000. "Unplug from Manitoba Hydro: Today There Are Better Alternatives." http://www.unplugmanitobahydro.com.

Ames, Herbert. 1923. *Letter to Right Hon. W. L. Mackenzie King.* Ottawa, Canada, December 28. League of Nations doc. no. 11/33556. Geneva.

Amnesty International. 1991. *Amnesty International Report, 1991.* London: Amnesty International Publications.

———. 1994. *Amnesty International Report, 1994.* London: Amnesty International Publications.

Amselle, Jean-Loup. 1999. "Ethnies et espaces: Pour une anthropologie topologique." In *Au coeur de l'ethnie: Ethnie, tribalisme et état en Afrique,* edited by Jean-Loup Amselle and Elikia M'Bokolo. Paris: La Découvert.

Anaya, James. 1996. *Indigenous Peoples in International Law*. Oxford, England: Oxford University Press.

Anderson, Benedict. 1991. *Imagined Communities*. London: Verso.

———. 1998. *The Spectre of Comparisons: Nationalism, Southeast Asia and the World*. London: Verso.

An-Na'im, Abdullahi Ahmed. 1992. "Toward a Cross-Cultural Approach to Defining International Standards of Human Rights: The Meaning of Cruel, Inhuman, or Degrading Treatment or Punishment." In *Human Rights in Cross-Cultural Perspectives: A Quest for Consensus*, edited by Abdullahi Ahmed An-Na'im. Philadelphia: University of Pennsylvania Press.

Annas, Catherine L. 1999. "Irreversible Error: The Power and Prejudice of Female Genital Mutilation." In *Health and Human Rights*, edited by Jonathan Mann, Sofia Gruskin, Michael Grodin, and George Annas. New York: Routledge.

Appadurai, Arjun. 1996. *Modernity at Large: Cultural Dimensions of Globalization*. Minneapolis: University of Minnesota Press.

Asad, Talal. 1997. "On Torture, or Cruel, Inhuman and Degrading Treatment." In *Human Rights, Culture and Context: Anthropological Perspectives*, edited by Richard A. Wilson. London: Pluto.

Asch, Michael. 2000. "The Judicial Conceptualization of Culture After *Delgamuukw* and *Van der Peet*." *Review of Constitutional Studies* 5: 119–37.

Assembly of First Nations. 1995. "Treaties." Assembly of First Nations Discussion Paper. Unpublished document.

Baer, Lars-Anders. 2000. "The Right of Self-Determination and the Case of the Sami." In *Operationalizing the Right of Indigenous Peoples to Self-Determination*, edited by Pekka Aikio and Martin Scheinin. Turku, Finland: Institute for Human Rights, Åbo Akademi University.

Ballantyne, Edith. 1977. "Foreword." In *Report of the International NGO Conference on Discrimination against Indigenous Populations in the Americas*. Geneva: United Nations, September 20–23.

Baqué, Philippe. 1995. "Nouvel enlisement des espoirs de paix dans le conflit touareg au Mali." *Le Monde Diplomatique*, April, 30–31.

Barnes, R. H., Andrew Gray, and Benedict Kingsbury, eds. 1995. *Indigenous Peoples of Asia*. Publication no. 48. Ann Arbor, Mich.: Association for Asian Studies.

Barry, William Theodore de. 1998. *Asian Values and Human Rights: A Confucian Communitarian Perspective*. Cambridge, Mass.: Harvard University Press.

Barth, Fredrik, ed. 1969. *Ethnic Groups and Boundaries: The Social Organization of Culture Difference*. Boston: Little, Brown.

Berlin, Isaiah. 1998. *The Proper Study of Mankind: An Anthology of Essays*. Edited by Henry Hardy and Roger Hausheer. New York: Farrar, Straus & Giroux.

———. 2000. *Three Critics of the Enlightenment: Vico, Hamann, Herder*. Edited by Henry Hardy. Princeton, N.J.: Princeton University Press.

Blake, Michael. 2000. "Rights for People, Not for Cultures." *Civilization*, August/September, 50–53.

Bosum, Abel. 1994. "The Human Rights of Indigenous Peoples at the United Nations." Statement to the Workshop on Indigenous Peoples' Rights, John F. Kennedy Library, Dorchester, Mass., December 10.

Bourassa, Robert. 1985. *Power from the North.* Scarborough: Prentice-Hall Canada.

Brownlie, Ian. 1988. "The Rights of Peoples in Modern International Law." In *The Rights of Peoples,* edited by James Crawford. Oxford, England: Clarendon.

Brysk, Alison. 2000. *From Tribal Village to Global Village: Indian Rights and International Relations in Latin America.* Stanford, Calif.: Stanford University Press.

Burgos-Debray, Elizabeth, ed. 1984. *I, Rigoberta Menchú: An Indian Woman in Guatemala.* Translated by Ann Wright. London: Verso.

Canada. 1923. *Statement Respecting the Six Nations Appeal to the League of Nations.* League of Nations doc. no. 11/34286/28075. Geneva.

———. 1981. *Indian Acts and Amendments, 1868–1950.* 2d ed. Ottawa: Department of Indian and Northern Affairs.

———. 1987. "Evolution of Standards Concerning Indigenous Populations." Unpublished statement to the U.N. Working Group on Indigenous Populations, 5th session, Geneva.

———. 1996a. "Articles 3, 31 & 34." Statement presented at the 53rd session of the Working Group on the U.N. Draft Declaration on the Rights of Indigenous Peoples. Geneva, October 31.

———. 1996b. "Evidence, Standing Committee on Aboriginal Affairs and Northern Development. Meeting No. 21." House of Commons, 35th Parliament, 1st session.

———. 1997. *Gathering Strength: Canada's Aboriginal Action Plan.* Ottawa: Department of Indian Affairs and Northern Development. Also available at http://www.inac.gc.ca.

———. 1998. *Statement of Reconciliation: Learning from the Past.* Ottawa: Department of Indian Affairs and Northern Development.

Carneiro da Cunha, Manuela. 1992. "Custom Is Not a Thing, It Is a Path: Reflections on the Brazilian Indian Case." In *Human Rights in Cross-Cultural Perspectives: A Quest for Consensus,* edited by Abdullahi Ahmed An-Na'im. Philadelphia: University of Pennsylvania Press.

Center for Economic and Social Rights. 1999. "Rights Violations in the Ecuadorian Amazon: The Human Consequences of Oil Development." In *Health and Human Rights,* edited by Jonathan Mann, Sofia Gruskin, Michael Grodin, and George Annas. New York: Routledge.

Chambers, Erve. 1985. *Applied Anthropology: A Practical Guide.* Prospect Heights, Ill.: Waveland.

Chang, Chris. 2000. "A Leap of Faith." *Audubon* 102(1): 14.

Chiefs of Ontario. 1996. "First Nations International Court of Justice, Order Made April 9." Available at http://www.bloorstreet.com/fn/decision1.htm.

Churchill, Ward. 1996. *From a Native Son: Selected Essays on Indigenism, 1985–1995*. Boston: South End.

Cole, Douglas, and Ira Chaikin. 1990. *An Iron Hand upon the People: The Law against the Potlatch on the Northwest Coast*. Seattle: University of Washington Press.

Collier, George. 1994. *Basta! Land and the Zapatista Rebellion in Chiapas*. Oakland, Calif.: Institute for Food and Development Policy.

Collins, Wilkie. [1861] 1985. *The Woman in White*. 2d ed. New York: New American Library.

Coon-Come, Matthew. 1994. "The Status and Rights of the James Bay Crees in the Context of Secession from Canada." Paper presented at the Center for Strategic and International Studies, Washington, D.C., September 19.

Corbett, Helen. 1996. "A History of the U.N. Draft Declaration on Indigenous Peoples." Unpublished report.

Daes, Erica-Irene. 1993. "Explanatory Note Concerning the Draft Declaration of the Rights of Indigenous Peoples." Commission on Human Rights. U.N. doc. E/CN.4/Sub.2/1993/26/Add. 1.

Decraene, Philippe. 1980. *Le Mali*. Paris: Presses Universitaires de France.

Desjarlais, Robert, Leon Eisenberg, Byron Good, and Arthur Kleinman. 1995. *World Mental Health: Problems and Priorities in Low-Income Countries*. Oxford, England: Oxford University Press.

Deskaheh, Levi General. 1922. *To the Government of Her Majesty the Queen of the Netherlands*. League of Nations doc. no. 11/29185/28075. Geneva.

———. 1923. *The Red Man's Appeal to Justice*. League of Nations doc. no. 11/30035/28075. Geneva.

Dodson, Mick. 1998. "Linking International Standards with Contemporary Concerns of Aboriginal and Torres Strait Islander Peoples." In *Indigenous Peoples, the United Nations, and Human Rights*, edited by Sarah Pritchard. London: Zed/Federation.

Donnelly, Jack. 1989. *Universal Human Rights in Theory and Practice*. Ithaca, N.Y.: Cornell University Press.

Douglas, Mary. 1966. *Purity and Danger: An Analysis of Concepts of Pollution and Taboo*. London: Routledge.

Duara, Prasenjit. 1995. *Rescuing History from the Nation: Questioning Narratives of Modern China*. Chicago: University of Chicago Press.

Entman, Robert. 1989. *Democracy without Citizens: Media and the Decay of American Politics*. New York: Oxford University Press.

Falk, Richard. 1988. "The Rights of Peoples (in Particular Indigenous Peoples)." In *The Rights of Peoples*, edited by James Crawford. Oxford, England: Clarendon.

Feit, Harvey. 1985. "Legitimacy and Autonomy in James Bay Cree Responses to Hydro-Electric Development." In *Indigenous People and the Nation-State: Fourth World Politics in Canada, Australia and Norway,* edited by Noel Dyck. St. John's: St. John's Institute of Social and Economic Research, Memorial University of Newfoundland.

First Nations International Court of Justice. 1996. "The First Nations of Turtle Island and Her Majesty the Queen in Right of Canada (Transcripts of Proceedings)." Vol. 1. Toronto, File no. F.N. 001/95. Unpublished document.

Fleras, Augie, and Jean Leonard Elliott. 1996. *The Nations Within: Aboriginal-State Relations in Canada, the United States, and New Zealand.* Toronto: Oxford University Press.

Florini, Ann. 2000. "What the World Needs Now?" In *The Third Force: The Rise of Transnational Civil Society,* edited by Ann Florini. Washington, D.C.: Carnegie Endowment for International Peace.

Gazette (Montreal). 1992. "Cree Itching to Take Charge of James Bay Project: Hydro." February 13, A6.

Geertz, Clifford. 1990. *Works and Lives: The Anthropologist as Author.* Stanford, Calif.: Stanford University Press.

Gellner, Ernest. 1983. *Nations and Nationalism.* Oxford, England: Basil Blackwell.

———. 1992. *Postmodernism, Reason and Religion.* New York: Routledge.

———. 1994. *Conditions of Liberty: Civil Society and Its Rivals.* New York: Penguin.

Gillespie, Colin. 1999. "Speaking Notes for a Public Hearing on Hydro Development and Aboriginal Peoples in Northern Manitoba." Unpublished document. June 22.

Globe and Mail (Toronto). 1994. "Crees Will Have No Friends, PQ Negotiator Warns." October 19, A1–A2.

Gordon, Robert, and Stuart Sholto Douglas. 2000. *The Bushman Myth: The Making of a Namibian Underclass.* 2d ed. Boulder, Colo.: Westview.

Grand Council of the Crees. 1985. *Submission to the Commission on Human Rights, Sub-Commission on the Prevention of Discrimination and Protection of Minorities.* Working Group on Indigenous Populations, Fourth Session. Geneva.

———. 1988. "The Grand Council of the Crees of Quebec at the United Nations: Report from the Head of Delegation." April 7.

———. 1992. *1991–1992 Annual Report.* Nemaska, Québec: Grand Council of the Crees.

———. 1996. *Sovereign Injustice: Forcible Inclusion of the James Bay Cree and Cree Territory into a Sovereign Quebec.* Nemaska, Québec: Grand Council of the Crees.

Griaule, Marcel. 1977. *Conversations with Ogotemmeli: An Introduction to Dogon Religious Ideas.* Oxford, England: Oxford University Press.

Guéhenno, Jean-Marie. 1995. *The End of the Nation-State.* Translated by Victoria Elliott. Minneapolis: University of Minnesota Press.

Guglielmo, Rachel. 1997. "'Three Nations Warring in the Bosom of a Single State': An Exploration of Identity and Self-Determination in Quebec." *Fletcher Forum of World Affairs* 21(1): 197–223.

Habermas, Jürgen. 1994. "Struggles for Recognition in the Democratic Constitutional State." In Charles Taylor, *Multiculturalism*, edited by Amy Gutmann. Princeton, N.J.: Princeton University Press.

Hall, John A. 1993. "Nationalisms: Classified and Explained." *Daedalus* 122(3): 1–28.

Handler, Richard. 1988. *Nationalism and the Politics of Culture in Quebec.* Madison: University of Wisconsin Press.

Harvey, Neil. 1998. *The Chiapas Rebellion: The Struggle for Land and Democracy.* Durham, N.C.: Duke University Press.

Held, David. 1995. *Democracy and the Global Order: From the Modern State to Cosmopolitan Governance.* Stanford, Calif.: Stanford University Press.

Henriksen, John B. 2000. "The Right of Self-Determination: Indigenous Peoples versus States." In *Operationalizing the Right of Indigenous Peoples to Self-Determination,* edited by Pekka Aikio and Martin Scheinin. Turku, Finland: Institute for Human Rights, Åbo Akademi University.

Hiskett, Mervyn. 1984. *The Development of Islam in West Africa.* London: Longman.

Hobsbawm, E. J. 1990. *Nations and Nationalism since 1780.* Cambridge, England: Cambridge University Press.

Howitt, Richard, John Connell, and Philip Hirsch, eds. 1996. *Resources, Nations and Indigenous Peoples: Case Studies from Australasia, Melanesia and Southeast Asia.* Oxford, England: Oxford University Press.

Hyndman, David, and Levita Duhaylungsod. 1996. "Reclaiming T'boli Land: An Ancestral Domain Claim in the Southern Philippines." In *Resources, Nations and Indigenous Peoples: Case Studies from Australasia, Melanesia and Southeast Asia,* edited by Richard Howitt, John Connell, and Philip Hirsch. Oxford, England: Oxford University Press.

Ignatieff, Michael. 1997. *The Warrior's Honor: Ethnic War and the Modern Conscience.* New York: Henry Holt.

Imai, Shin, ed. 1998. *The 1999 Annotated Indian Act and Aboriginal Constitutional Provisions.* Toronto: Carswell Thomson.

Inoguchi, Takashi, Edward Newman, and John Keane, eds. 1998. *The Changing Nature of Democracy.* Tokyo: United Nations University Press.

International Indian Treaty Council. 1977. "The Geneva Conference." *Treaty Council News* 1(7): 1–35.

International Labour Organization. 1953. *Indigenous Peoples: Living and Working Conditions of Aboriginal Populations in Independent Countries.* Studies and Reports, No. 35. Geneva: International Labour Office.

Jansen, G. H. 1979. *Militant Islam*. New York: Harper & Row.

Kaba, Lasine. 1974. *The Wahhabiyya: Islamic Reform and Politics in French West Africa*. Evanston, Ill.: Northwestern University Press.

Katz, Elihu. 1998. "Mass Media and Participatory Democracy." In *The Changing Nature of Democracy*, edited by Takashi Inoguchi, Edward Newman, and John Keane. Tokyo: United Nations University Press.

Kingsbury, Benedict. 1998. "'Indigenous Peoples' in International Law: A Constructivist Approach to the Asian Controversy." *American Journal of International Law* 92: 414–57.

———. 1999. "The Applicability of the International Legal Concept of 'Indigenous Peoples' in Asia." In *The East Asian Challenge for Human Rights*, edited by Joanne Bauer and Daniel A. Bell. Cambridge, England: Cambridge University Press.

———. 2000. "Reconstructing Self-Determination: A Relational Approach." In *Operationalizing the Right of Indigenous Peoples to Self-Determination*, edited by Pekka Aikio and Martin Scheinin. Turku, Finland: Institute for Human Rights, Åbo Akademi University.

Kundera, Milan. 1996. *Slowness*. Translated by Linda Asher. New York: Harper-Collins.

Kymlicka, Will. 1995. *Multicultural Citizenship*. Oxford, England: Oxford University Press.

League of Nations. 1924. *La tribu indienne des Six Nations; petitions diverses*. Doc. nos. 11/33687 and 11/33556. Geneva.

———. 1929. "The Anti Slavery and Aborigines Protection Society." Geneva. League of Nations doc. no. 31276–31276.

Le Monde. 2001. "Louise Beaudoin, ministre des relations internationales du Québec: Après la démission de Lucien Bouchard, il faut conserver l'objectif de la souveraineté." January 14–15.

Leslie, John, and Ron Haguire, eds. 1978. *The Historical Development of the Indian Act*. 2d ed. Ottawa, Canada: Treaties and Historical Research Centre, Department of Indian and Northern Affairs.

Lévesque, René. 1968. *An Option for Québec*. Toronto: McClelland & Stewart.

Lusignan, Guy de. 1969. *French-Speaking Africa since Independence*. New York: Frederick A. Praeger.

Lynge, Aqqaluk. 2001. "From Environmental Protection to Sustainable Development: An Inuit Perspective: Remarks on the Occasion of the Tenth Anniversary of Arctic Environmental Cooperation." Paper presented at the annual meeting of the Arctic Council, Rovaniemi, Finland, June 12.

Maïga, Mohamed Tiessa-Farma. 1997. *Le Mali: De la sécheresse à la rebellion nomade*. Paris: L'Harmattan.

Maine, Henry. [1861] 1977. *Ancient Law*. New York: Dutton.

Martínez Cobo, José R. 1987. "Study of the Problem of Discrimination against Indigenous Populations." Vol. 5. U.N. doc. E/CN.4/Sub.2/1986/7/Add.4.

Matthiessen, Peter. 1983. *In the Spirit of Crazy Horse*. New York: Viking.

Maybury-Lewis, David. 1997. *Indigenous Peoples, Ethnic Groups, and the State.* Needham Heights, Mass.: Allyn & Bacon.

McGarry, John, and Brendan O'Leary, eds. 1993. *The Politics of Ethnic Conflict Regulation*. New York: Routledge.

Minde, Henry. 1996. "The Making of an International Movement of Indigenous Peoples." *Scandinavian Journal of History* 21: 221–45.

Montesquieu, Charles-Louis de Secondat. [1721] 1964. *The Persian Letters*. Translated by George Healy. Indianapolis: Hackett.

———. [1748] 1989. *The Spirit of the Laws*. Translated and edited by Anne Cohler, Basia Miller, and Harold Stone. Cambridge, England: Cambridge University Press.

Morocco. 1985. *Statement before the United Nations Working Group on Indigenous Populations*. U.N. doc. no. E/CN.4/Sub.2/AC.4/1985/WP.1/Add.1.

Moses, Ted. 1993. "International Year of the World's Indigenous Peoples; Statement by Chief Ted Moses on Behalf of the North American Region." Statement presented at the World Conference on Human Rights, Vienna, June 14–25.

———. 1994. "Introductory Statement." Statement presented at the Meeting on the U.N. Draft Declaration on the Rights of Indigenous Peoples, Raoul Wallenberg Institute of Human Rights and Humanitarian Law, Lund, Sweden, June 19.

———. 1996. "Customary Law and National/International Law." Statement presented at the International Encounter of Amerindian Communities, Paris, June 19–21.

———. 1997. "Statement by the Grand Council of the Crees, Agenda Item 7: International Decade of the World's Indigenous Peoples." Working Group on Indigenous Populations, fifteenth session, July 28–August 1.

———. 2000. "The Right of Self-Determination and Its Significance to the Survival of Indigenous Peoples." In *Operationalizing the Right of Indigenous Peoples to Self-Determination*, edited by Pekka Aikio and Martin Scheinin. Turku, Finland: Institute for Human Rights, Åbo Akademi University.

Myntti, Kristian. 2000. "The Right of Indigenous Peoples to Self-Determination and Effective Participation." In *Operationalizing the Right of Indigenous Peoples to Self-Determination*, edited by Pekka Aikio and Martin Scheinin. Turku, Finland: Institute for Human Rights, Åbo Akademi University.

Nettheim, Garth. 1988. "'Peoples' and 'Populations': Indigenous Peoples and the Rights of Peoples." In *The Rights of Peoples*, edited by James Crawford. Oxford, England: Clarendon.

Niezen, Ronald. 1990. "The 'Community of Helpers of the Sunna': Islamic Reform among the Songhay of Gao (Mali)." *Africa* 60: 399–424.
———. 1991. "Hot Literacy in Cold Societies: A Comparative Study of the Sacred Value of Writing." *Comparative Studies in Society and History* 33: 225–54.
———. 1993. "Power and Dignity: The Social Consequences of Hydro-Electric Development for the James Bay Cree." *Canadian Review of Sociology and Anthropology* 30: 510–29.
———. 1998. *Defending the Land: Sovereignty and Forest Life in James Bay Cree Society.* Needham Heights, Mass.: Allyn & Bacon.
———. 2000a. "Recognizing Indigenism: Canadian Unity and the International Movement of Indigenous Peoples." *Comparative Studies in Society and History* 42(1): 119–48.
———. 2000b. *Spirit Wars: Native North American Religions in the Age of Nation Building.* Berkeley: University of California Press.
———. 2000c. "With the Health of a River Goes the Health of a People." *Native Americas Journal,* Summer.
Nomura, Giichi. 1994. "Giichi Nomura: Executive Director, Ainu Association of Hokkaido (Northeast Asia)." In *Voices of Indigenous Peoples: Native People Address the United Nations,* edited by Alexander Ewen. Santa Fe, N.M.: Clear Light.
Northern Flood Committee. 1993. "The Northern Flood Agreement: History of Negotiation and Implementation, and Recommendations for Improvement. Prepared for the Royal Commission on Aboriginal Peoples." Unpublished report.
Organization of American States. 2001a. "OAS Considers Draft American Declaration on Indigenous Rights." Press release, April 2.
———. 2001b. *Working Document Comparing the Proposed American Declaration on the Rights of Indigenous Peoples (Approved by the IACHR in March 1997) and the Proposals Made by States and Indigenous Representatives at OAS Meetings in 1999. Committee on Judirical (sic) and Political Affairs.* GT/DADIN/doc.9/01, January 12, 2001.
Ottlik, George, ed. N.d. *Annuaire de la Société des Nations, 1920–1927.* Geneva: Librairie Payot & Cie.
Pagden, Anthony. 1995. *Lords of All the World: Ideologies of Empire in Spain, Britain and France c. 1500–c. 1800.* New Haven, Conn.: Yale University Press.
Pan American Health Organization. 1997. *Health of Indigenous Peoples: XL Meeting, Washington, D.C., July 8, 1997.* Doc. no. CD40/14.
Parkipuny, Moringe. N.d. "The Indigenous Peoples Rights Question in Africa." Statement before the U.N. Working Group on Indigenous Populations.
Perry, Richard J. 1996. *From Time Immemorial: Indigenous Peoples and State Systems.* Austin: University of Texas Press.

Peters, Evelyn. 1989. "Federal and Provincial Responsibilities for the Cree, Naskapi and Inuit under the James Bay and Northern Québec and Northeastern Québec Agreements." In *Aboriginal People and Government Responsibility: Exploring Federal and Provincial Roles,* edited by David Hawkes. Ottawa, Canada: Carleton University Press.

Pimicikamak Cree Nation. 1998. "NFA Working Paper: A New Relationship—Standards and Structures." Unpublished document.

———. 2000. "Our Nation." http://www.Pimicikamak.ca.

Pratt, Mary Louise. 1986. "Fieldwork in Common Places." In *Writing Culture: The Poetics and Politics of Ethnography,* edited by James Clifford and George E. Marcus. Berkeley: University of California Press.

Preis, Ann-Belinda. 1996. "Human Rights as Cultural Practice: An Anthropological Critique." *Human Rights Quarterly* 18: 286–315.

Ramos, Alcida Rita. 1998. *Indigenism: Ethnic Politics in Brazil.* Madison: University of Wisconsin Press.

Raymundo, Francisco. 1997. "Justicia en el Area Ixil." *Chuj Wallijo'q; Informacion Mensual de la Defensoría Maya* 1(1):4–6. Also available at http://www.derechos.net/ngo/defemaya/feb97.txt.

Robinson, Mary. 2000. "Opening Statement by Mary Robinson, United Nations High Commissioner for Human Rights, to the Open-Ended Working Group on the Permanent Forum for Indigenous People." Unpublished document. Geneva, February 14.

Rostkowski, Joelle. 1995. "Deskaheh's Shadow: Indians on the International Scene." *Native American Studies* 9(2): 1–4.

Rousseau, Jean-Jacques. [1755] 1987. *The Basic Political Writings.* Translated by Donald Cress. Indianapolis: Hackett.

———. [1762] 1968. *The Social Contract.* Translated by Maurice Cranston. New York: Penguin.

Saint-Exupéry, Antoine de. 1939. *Wind, Sand and Stars.* Translated by Lewis Galantière. New York: Reynal & Hitchcock.

Salisbury, Richard. 1986. *A Homeland for the Cree: Regional Development in James Bay 1971–1981.* Montreal: McGill-Queen's University Press.

Scheinin, Martin. 2000. "The Right to Enjoy a Distinct Culture: Indigenous and Competing Uses of Land." In *The Jurisprudence of Human Rights Law: A Comparative Interpretive Approach,* edited by Theodore Orlin, Allan Rosas, and Martin Scheinin. Turku, Finland: Institute for Human Rights, Åbo Akademi University.

Scheper-Hughes, Nancy. 1992. *Death without Weeping: The Violence of Everyday Life in Brazil.* Berkeley: University of California Press.

Scheper-Hughes, Nancy, ed. 1987. *Child Survival.* Dordrecht, the Netherlands: D. Reidel.

Scott, James C. 1985. *Weapons of the Weak: Everyday Forms of Peasant Resistance.* New Haven, Conn.: Yale University Press.

Seary, Bill. 1996. "The Early History: From the Congress of Vienna to the San Francisco Conference." In *"The Conscience of the World": The Influence of Non-Governmental Organizations in the U.N. System,* edited by Peter Willetts. Washington, D.C.: Brookings Institution.

Speed, Shanon, and Jane Collier. 2000. "Limiting Indigenous Autonomy in Chiapas, Mexico: The State Government's Use of Human Rights." *Human Rights Quarterly* 22: 877–905.

Stoll, David. 1999. *Rigoberta Menchú and the Story of All Poor Guatemalans.* Boulder, Colo.: Westview.

Swepston, Lee. 1990. "The Adoption of the Indigenous and Tribal Peoples Convention, 1989 (No. 169)." *Law and Anthropology* 5: 221–35.

Tail, Eli J. 2000. "Address to the Government and Indigenous Representatives at the Working Group on the Permanent Forum for Indigenous Peoples." Unpublished document. Geneva, February 22.

Tambiah, Stanley. 1996. *Leveling Crowds: Ethnonationalist Conflicts and Collective Violence in South Asia.* Berkeley: University of California Press.

Taylor, Charles. 1994. *Multiculturalism.* Edited by Amy Gutmann. Princeton, N.J.: Princeton University Press.

Tennant, Chris. 1994. "Indigenous Peoples, International Institutions, and the International Legal Literature from 1945–1993." *Human Rights Quarterly* 16: 1–57.

Tetuwan Oyate. 2000. "Pine Ridge Takeover: Statement of the Tetuwan Oyate, Teton Sioux Nation Treaty Council." Unpublished document. Geneva, January 25.

Thomas, Keith. 1983. *Man and the Natural World: Changing Attitudes in England 1500–1800.* Oxford, England: Oxford University Press.

Thompson, Andrew. 1923. *Report by Col. Andrew T. Thompson, Commissioner to Investigate and Enquire into the Affairs of the Six Nations Indians.* Ottawa, Canada: F. A. Acland.

Tocqueville, Alexis de. [1840] 2000. *Democracy in America.* Edited by Harvey Mansfield and translated by Delba Winthrop. Chicago: University of Chicago Press.

———. [1856] 1955. *The Old Regime and the French Revolution.* Translated by Stuart Gilbert. New York: Doubleday.

United Nations. 1977. *Report of the International NGO Conference on Discrimination against Indigenous Populations in the Americas—1977.* Special NGO Committee on Human Rights (Geneva), Sub-Committee on Racism, Racial Discrimination, Apartheid and Decolonization.

———. 1981. *International NGO Conference on Indigenous Peoples and the Land.* Geneva: Women's International League for Peace and Freedom.

————. 1999. *Draft Report of the Open-Ended Inter-Sessional Ad Hoc Working Group on a Permanent Forum for Indigenous People.* Commission on Human Rights. Geneva.

————. 2000a. *Document Presented by the Delegation of Spain for the Permanent Forum.* Commission on Human Rights. UN doc. no. E/CN.4/AC.47/2000/ CPR.5.

————. 2000b. *Indigenous Issues: Resolution to the Economic and Social Council.* U.N. doc. no. Commission on Human Rights. E/CN.4/2000/L.68. April 18.

————. 2000c. *International Decade of the World's Indigenous People, 1995–2004; Draft List of Organizations.* Office of the U.N. High Commission for Human Rights. February 2000.

————. 2000d. *Notes of the Meeting of the Commission on Human Rights: Indigenous Issues. 56th Session, April 13.*

————. 2000e. *Report on the Seminar on "Multiculturalism in Africa: Peaceful and Constructive Group Accommodation in Situations Involving Minorities and Indigenous People." Arusha, United Republic of Tanzania, May 13–15, 2000.* Office of the U.N. High Commission for Human Rights.

————. 2001. *Report on the Second Workshop on Multiculturalism in Africa: Peaceful and Constructive Group Accommodation in Situations Involving Minorities and Indigenous People. Kidal, Mali, January 8–13, 2001.* Commission on Human Rights. U.N. doc. no. E/CN.4/Sub.2/AC.5/2001/3.

Vico, Giambattista. [1744] 1968. *The New Science of Giambattista Vico.* Translated by Thomas Bergin and Max Fisch. Ithaca, N.Y.: Cornell University Press.

Vincent, Sylvie, and Garry Bowers, eds. 1988. *James Bay and Northern Québec: Ten Years After.* Montreal: Recherches Amérindienne au Québec.

Warren, Kay. 1998. *Indigenous Movements and Their Critics: Pan-Maya Activism in Guatemala.* Princeton, N.J.: Princeton University Press.

Wertman, Paul. 1983. "Planning and Development after the James Bay Agreement." *Canadian Journal of Native Studies* 3: 277–88.

Willetts, Peter, ed. 1996. *"The Conscience of the World": The Influence of Non-Governmental Organizations in the U.N. System.* Washington, D.C.: Brookings Institution.

Wilson, Richard A., ed. 1997. *Human Rights, Culture and Context: Anthropological Perspectives.* London: Pluto.

Winnipeg Free Press. 1998. "Cross Lake Band Plans to Stiff Manitoba Hydro." October 29, A-3.

York, Geoffrey, and Loreen Pindera. 1991. *People of the Pines.* Boston: Little, Brown.

LEGAL REFERENCES

International Instruments

UNITED NATIONS

Charter of the United Nations. June 26, 1945, 59 Stat. 1031, T.S. 993, 3 Bevans 1153, entered into force Oct. 24, 1945.

Declaration of Principles of Indigenous Rights. Adopted by the Fourth General Assembly of the World Council of Indigenous Peoples, Panama, September 1984, U.N. doc. E/CN.4/Sub.2/1985/22, Annex 3 (1985).

Declaration of Principles of International Law Concerning Friendly Relations and Cooperation among States in Accordance with the Charter of the United Nations. General Assembly Resolution 2625, October 24, 1970.

Declaration on the Granting of Independence to Colonial Countries and Peoples. General Assembly Resolution 1514 (XV), December 14, 1960.

Draft United Nations Declaration on the Rights of Indigenous Peoples, as Agreed upon by the Members of the Working Group on Indigenous Populations at its Eleventh Session. Adopted by the Subcommission on Prevention of Discrimination and Protection of Minorities by its resolution 1994/45, August 26, 1994.

International Covenant on Civil and Political Rights. December 16, 1966, 999 U.N.T.S. 171.

International Covenant on Economic, Social and Cultural Rights. December 16, 1966, 993 U.N.T.S. 3.

International Labour Organization Convention (No. 107) Concerning the Protection and Integration of Indigenous and Other Tribal and Semi-Tribal Populations in Independent Countries. June 26, 1957, 328 U.N.T.S. 247.

International Labour Organization Convention (No. 169) Concerning Indigenous and Tribal Peoples in Independent Countries. June 27, 1989.

International Labour Organization Legislative Ordinance No. 52 Conferring upon the Residents the Power to Compel Natives to Perform Work in Connection with Plantations and Other Undertakings Carried on for Profit. November 7, 1924. [League of Nations (1929) doc. 31276–31276.]

International Labour Organization Recommendation (No. 104) Concerning the Protection of Indigenous and Other Tribal and Semi-Tribal Populations in Independent Countries. International Labour Conference, June 26, 1957 [*International Labour Conventions and Recommendations, 1919–1991*, at 636, 1992.]

Optional Protocol to the International Covenant on Civil and Political Rights. December 16, 1966, 999 U.N.T.S. 302.

Universal Declaration of Human Rights. General Assembly Resolution 217 A(III), December 10, 1948.

Vienna Declaration and Programme of Action. World Conference on Human Rights, Vienna, June 25, 1993, U.N. doc. A/CONF.157/23 (1993).

National Statutes and Agreements

CANADA

Comprehensive Implementation Agreement, Split Lake. An Agreement among Her Majesty the Queen in Right of Canada, Her Majesty the Queen in Right of the Province of Manitoba, the Split Lake Cree First Nation, and the Manitoba Hydro-Electric Board, April 24, 1992. http://www.hydro.mb .ca/mitigation/sla/spl_pre.htm. Accessed February 20, 2002.

Constitution Act. Enacted as Schedule B to the Canada Act 1982, (U.K.) 1982, c.11, April 17, 1982.

Indian Act. R.S. 1985, c. I-5. (See also Canada 1981 and Imai 1998.)

James Bay and Northern Quebec Settlement Act. 1976–1977, c. 32, 14 July, 1977. [Published in: *James Bay and Northern Québec Agreement and Complementary Agreements.* Québec: Les Publications du Québec, 1991.]

Northern Flood Agreement. An Agreement among Her Majesty the Queen in Right of Manitoba, The Manitoba Hydro-Electric Board, the Northern Flood Committee, and Her Majesty the Queen in Right of Canada. December 16, 1977. http://www.hydro.mb.ca/mitigation/nfa/t_of_c.htm. Accessed February 20, 2002.

Nunavut Land Claims Agreement Act. An Act Respecting an Agreement between the Inuit of the Nunavut Settlement Area and Her Majesty the Queen in Right of Canada, c.29, June 10, 1993.

Treaty 5 between Her Majesty the Queen and the Salteaux and Swampy Cree Tribes of Indians. 1875.

REPUBLIC OF MALI

Accord de Tamanrasset. 1991.

Pact National. 1992.

UNITED STATES

Federal Prohibition of Female Genital Mutilation Act of 1995. 104th Congress, 1st Session, S. 1030, July 13, 1995.

Cases

CANADA
Delgamuukw v. British Columbia. [1997] 3 S.C.R. 1010.
Sparrow v. R [1990] 1 S.C.R. 1075.
Van der Peet v. R. [1996] 2 S.C.R. 507.

HUMAN RIGHTS COMMITTEE
Bernard Ominayak and the Lubicon Lake Band v. Canada. 1990. U.N. doc.
    CCPR/C/38/D/167/1984.
I. Länsman et al. v. Finland. 1994. U.N. doc. CCPR/C/52/D/511/1992.
J. G. A. Diergaardt et al. v. Namibia. 2000. U.N. doc. CCPR/C/69/D/760/1997.
O. Sara et al. v. Finland. 1994. U.N. doc. CCPR/C/50/D/431/1990.

Index

263

Griaule, Marcel, 103
"Group of 77," 138
Guéhenno, Jean-Marie, 198

Habermas, Jürgen, 135
Hadza, 74–75
Haldimand Treaty of 1784 (Britain), 33
Hall, John, 223n2
Handler, Richard, 153, 225n10
Hawaii, indigenous representatives of, 169
Health: Cree definition of, 64, 229n3; and female genital mutilation, 112–13; mental, 61–63, 173; WHO Consultation on the Health of Indigenous Peoples, xii, 132, 163–64
Held, David, 41
Hendriksen, John, 207
Herder, Gottfried, 237n10
Herero, 74
Herskovits, Melville, 104
Himbe, 74
Hinduism, 17
Hirsch, Philip, 226n16
historical particularism, 102
Hitler, Adolf, 41, 108
Hobsbawm, E. J., 223n2
Hoctevilla, 158
Holocaust, 8, 15, 55, 108, 194
Hopi, 158
Hottentots, 54
Howitt, Richard, 226n16
Huaorani, 236n8
Human Life International, 228n5
human rights, 4, 12, 18–19, 24, 26–28, 30, 40–42, 48–52, 56–57, 93, 95–98, 100, 105, 107–8, 110, 113–14, 116–17, 120–21, 126–28, 133, 137–38, 143–45, 148, 158, 161–62, 179, 181–82, 186–88, 193–94, 199, 216, 219, 235nn2,4,5, 237n12; abuses, 8, 111, 187, 204, 206; and civil rights, 99; collective, 128, 133–39; and indigenous peoples, xiv, 56, 110–11, 114–17; individual, 113, 120, 128, 131, 145; and medical ethics, 113; movement, 37, 104–5, 116; standards, xii, xiv, 95, 143, 147, 149, 160–62, 183, 188, 197, 212, 214, 220. See also specific human rights organizations
Human Rights Committee (U.N.), 227n20, 237n12, 240n11
hunting and gathering, 5, 11, 57–58, 65–66, 77, 86–87, 241n15
Hutu, 183
hydroelectric development, xiv–xv, 58, 65–69, 90, 149–50, 178, 181–82, 185–86

Hydro Payment Law, 173–74, 181, 241n13
Hydro-Québec, 149–50, 185–86

Ignatieff, Michael, 243n1
I. Länsman et al. v. Finland (1994), 240n12
imperialism, 130–31, 196
India, 8, 17, 20, 31, 41, 73, 116, 163, 195, 231n11,12
Indian Act (Canada, 1876), 31–33, 99, 175, 241n13
Indian agents, 31, 245n4
Indian Law Resource Center, 239n6
Indian status, 176
indigenism, 2–11, 13, 17, 26, 52, 69, 117–18, 136, 142, 152, 198, 200–201, 203–4, 209, 212
indigenismo, 224n4
indigenous peoples, 2, 4–5, 7, 13–14, 29–30, 37–38, 47–49, 70, 86–87, 93, 98–99, 114–18, 121, 125, 127, 130, 138–40, 143–46, 149, 155–56, 162–63, 179, 183, 186, 209, 213, 224n3; identity, xi–xii, xiv–xvi, 9–13, 18–26, 46, 51, 57, 59–60, 65, 76–77, 86–93, 180, 187, 191, 202, 211, 221, 225n7, 227n21; international movement of, xi, xv, 4, 9, 15–16, 18, 22, 23–24, 26, 30, 56, 69–72, 75–76, 95, 126, 142, 152, 170, 187–88, 194, 196–97, 199, 207–9, 217–18, 225n12; leaders, 3–4, 13, 23–24, 41–42, 142–43, 146–47, 151–52, 157–60, 166–68, 188–89, 195–96, 200–202, 205, 216, 218, 221; nationalism, 166, 173, 177, 186–87, 200–202, 214; rights of, xiv, 17–18, 25, 31, 39–40, 60, 97–98, 111, 132–33, 140, 146, 150, 154–57, 179–80, 188, 195, 199, 205, 218, 240n11, 242n20,21; romanticism of, 11, 13, 78, 159, 180. See also assimilation; education; self-determination; states
Indigenous World Association, 239n6
indirect rule, 131
individualism, 27, 120, 141, 144; and human rights, 126, 145; and nation-states, 202
Indonesia, 231n12
industrialization, 17, 127
information technology, and indigenous politics, xiii, xvi, 2, 6, 9, 13, 175, 178, 191, 198, 225n12, 241n17
inherent jurisdiction lawmaking, 27–28, 148, 170–79, 190
inheritance, systems of, 126
INNU Council of Nitassinan (INNU Nation), 239n6
interethnic violence, 84
International Bill of Human Rights, 40–41, 97, 104, 132–33, 143

Text:	10/14 Palatino
Display:	Snell Roundhand Script, Bauer Bodoni
Compositor:	G&S Typesetters, Inc.
Printer:	Maple-Vail Manufacturing Group